Shaking the Tree

ALSO BY MERI NANA-AMA DANQUAH

*Willow Weep for Me: A Black Woman's Journey
Through Depression*

*Becoming American: Personal Essays by
First Generation Immigrant Women* (editor)

Shaking the Tree

A Collection of
New Fiction and Memoir
by Black Women

EDITED BY
Meri Nana-Ama Danquah

W. W. Norton & Company
New York • London

Manufacturing by Courier Companies
Book design by Brooke Koven
Production manager: Julia Druskin

Library of Congress Cataloging-in-Publication Data

Shaking the tree : a collection of new fiction and memoir by Black women /
edited by Meri Nana-Ama Danquah.
          p. cm.
Includes bibliographical references.
     ISBN 0-393-05067-X
     1. American prose literature—African American authors. 2. American
prose literature—Women authors. 3. American prose literature—21st century.
4. African American women—Biography. 5. African American women—
Fiction. 6. African Americans—Biography. 7. African Americans—Fiction.
I. Danquah, Meri Nana-Ama.
     PS647.A35S53 2003
818'.6080809287'08996073—dc21

                                                            2003001411

     W. W. Norton & Company, Inc., 500 Fifth Avenue, New York, N.Y. 10110
                        www.wwnorton.com

W. W. Norton & Company Ltd., Castle House, 75/76 Wells Street, London W1T 3QT

1 2 3 4 5 6 7 8 9 0

For my daughter, Korama A. Danquah,
and for all our daughters,
whose voices shall be louder, stronger, braver

Contents

The Incoming Wave: An Introduction   *xiii*

asha bandele   "Home"
                          From *The Prisoner's Wife*   *5*

Lorene Cary   From *Black Ice*   *13*

Veronica Chambers   From *Mama's Girl*   *23*

Meri Nana-Ama Danquah   From *Willow Weep for Me: A Black
                          Woman's Journey Through Depression*   *32*

Edwidge Danticat   "Children of the Sea"
                          From *Krik? Krak!*   *43*

Debra J. Dickerson   "Beginning Again"
                          From *An American Story*   *60*

Carolyn Ferrell   "Wonderful Teen"
                          From *Don't Erase Me*   *72*

Dana Johnson   "Markers"
                          From *Break Any Woman Down*   *85*

Lisa Jones   "It's Racier in the Bahamas"
                          From *Bulletproof Diva: Tales of
                          Race, Sex, and Hair*   *102*

Helen Elaine Lee   From *The Serpent's Gift*   *111*

Catherine E. McKinley   "July 1978"
                               From *The Book of Sarahs:*
                               A Family in Parts   *122*

Itabari Njeri   "What's Love Got to Do with It?"
                               From *Every Good-bye Ain't Gone*   *131*

ZZ Packer   "The Stranger"   *152*

Phyllis Alesia Perry   "April 1974—Johnson Creek"
                               From *Stigmata*   *162*

Patricia Powell   From *The Pagoda*   *175*

Nelly Rosario   "Leila, 1998"
                               From *Song of the Water Saints*   *187*

Danzy Senna   "The Body of Luce Rivera"
                               From *Caucasia*   *197*

Martha Southgate   "The Wall of Pain"
                               From *The Fall of Rome*   *206*

Natasha Tarpley   From *Girl in the Mirror:*
                               Three Generations of Black Women
                               in Motion   *218*

Lisa Teasley   "Nepenthe"
                               From *Glow in the Dark*   *230*

Rebecca Walker   "Larchmont"
                               From *Black, White, and Jewish:*
                               Autobiography of a Shifting Self   *238*

Yolanda Young   "On Our Way to Beautiful"
From *On Our Way to Beautiful*   *252*

Shay Youngblood   "Lover"
From *Black Girl in Paris*   *263*

Contributors   *283*
Acknowledgments   *289*
Credits   *291*

The Incoming Wave:
An Introduction

I didn't know of or read any Black writers, let alone Black women writers, until I was in college. I have, many times, read this statement—or some variation of it—in interviews of Black writers. And each time, without fail, I am shocked beyond words because I can't begin to imagine what my youth would have been like without the influence and inspiration of Black women writers and the stories they share.

My introduction to the world of literature came at an early age through an experience that was so moving, I knew right away that it was not simply a world, but *the* world, in which I wanted to live and work.

It must have been around 1974 or 1975. I was about eight or nine years old, spending the day, as I so often did, at my Uncle Paul's house in Washington, D.C. While there, I was introduced to a woman by the name of Maya Angelou. She was tall, elegant, and had a commanding presence that, being so young, I found extremely intimidating. "Well, hello," she said, as she pulled me into an embrace. "You may call me Auntie Maya."

Her voice was so rhythmic and intoxicating, so filled with warmth, that the intimidation I had initially felt melted away, and I developed an immediate attachment to her. I spent the next hour or so shadowing her as she mingled and chatted with friends, just so I could hear her speak. She must have noticed me following her and taken a liking to me as well, because later that afternoon, with my uncle's permission, she invited me to ride along with her to Annapolis, Maryland.

Time has stolen away most of the details of that day. I remember sitting in the backseat of the car, staring silently and listening intently. There was so much to take in. Back then, the only thing I knew about Maya Angelou was that she was a family friend. I had no idea why people kept doing double takes when they looked into our car, why they would wave, roll down their windows and shout things like "thank you" and "I love your work, Miss Angelou" to her as we passed them by on the highway, or scramble for pen and paper when we were stopped at a traffic light and ask for her autograph. Of course, I quickly gathered that she was well known and well liked, but the how and why of it all was still unclear. Nevertheless, I was proud and impressed.

That evening, when we returned to the house, I pulled my uncle aside and told him about the events of the day. "Who is she?" I wanted to know. "What does she do? Why is she so famous?" He walked over to the study, pulled a book off the shelf. "She's a brilliant author," he told me. "This is a book that she wrote." Then he handed me a copy of *I Know Why the Caged Bird Sings*. I opened it and looked at all the words, those small black letters grouped so neatly, permanently set against the stark white page. Maya Angelou was still there in the house. I could hear her voice being carried from some other room. Yet, at the same time, it was as if it was coming from inside those pages.

I thought of all those people whom we had encountered on our brief outing, and of the many more whom I would never know or meet, those people who had heard her voice, heard what she had to say, simply by reading those pages. And in that moment, I understood the power and the importance of words, of a Black woman's words.

⌣

Looking back over that experience, what I now realize is that as I was sitting in that car, I was not simply watching the public express its admiration for Maya Angelou; I was witness to its acceptance of a burgeoning movement that would ultimately place authors such as Toni Morrison, Alice Walker, Toni Cade Bambara, Paule Marshall, Gloria Naylor, and Jamaica Kincaid at the forefront of American literature. Never before had Black women gained so much mainstream attention and prominence for their writing—at the time of its publication and during the course of the writer's life.

I and so many young women of my generation who were born either in the midst, or on the heels, of the Civil Rights, Black Arts, Feminist, and Gay Pride movements grew up reading these authors. Through their books, we were able to hold in our hands both the pain and the glory of our history; we were able to mourn what was lost, and recognize the value of what remained. We were able to answer the question: What does it mean to be a Black woman?

The year that I read Judy Blume's *Are You There God? It's Me, Margaret* was the same year that I read Toni Morrison's *The Bluest Eye*. I took in Blume's book with a sort of envy that was as delicious as it was angry. Her main character, Margaret Simon, was close enough for me to touch, for me to feel. Many of her concerns were my own concerns: the relationship to one's newly changing body, the intersection of private spirituality and organized religion, the desire to feel a certain connectedness to the world. The themes were all so universal, there was a basic humanity there that made sense to me. Yet, the deeper that Margaret Simon drew me into her life, the more evident the distance between us became. We were strangers, Margaret and I.

And then there was Pecola Breedlove, with her desire for a certain connectedness, her relationship to a body that had been so violated, her painfully impossible prayers. *The Bluest Eye* told a story that was not readily familiar to me. Still, I was instinctively aware of its significance. I didn't just feel Pecola; there was a part of me that knew her. She seemed to be as close as my own breath, my own reflection.

Seeing Pecola Breedlove enabled me, in ways large and small, to see myself. Just as, I believe, reading the stories that were written by that generation of Black women writers enabled many of us in my generation to see ourselves as writers, to understand that it was possible, as Black women, to choose a writing life and to know that our stories, our voices do, in fact, matter.

"For the first time in my life," writes asha bandele in her memoir, *The Prisoner's Wife*, "a life which had been dominated by white history, white cultures, white literature, white music, white sensibilities, a life where Black was a metaphor for less than, I was reading books with characters and experiences that I understood. I was finally offered a history that went beyond slavery to include that which was Black and successful, Black and intelligent, Black and encouraging.

"Learning this left me with a range of emotions I think common to any conquered people. The greatest, the most profound one I had, was love, at last for myself, as a Black woman, a woman who indeed had a place in history, if not in high school textbooks. "

⌣

The purpose of this collection is to offer the literature of twenty-three young Black women writers whose voices are among those defining this new era of contemporary American literature. They are, most definitely, not the only ones; but dare I say that the writers featured here are a fair sampling of the best. These authors have produced work that has been critically acclaimed, hailed as "groundbreaking," and both nominated for and granted some rather prestigious awards. They are often referred to as "promising." But that word alone, as a description, seems to me to overlook all that these writers have already accomplished. They have already fulfilled so many of the promises that were made by those who came before them, particularly the promise of memory, and the promise of permanence.

All of the books from which these selections have been excerpted were published after 1990. Some of the pieces are fiction, a number of them are memoir, a genre that has gained tremendous strength and popularity over the last decade. But, from slaves narratives such as Harriet Jacobs's *Incidents in the Life of a Slave Girl* to Maya Angelou's *I Know Why the Caged Bird Sings*, this genre of writing has often been used to document Black women's lives. It is, also, part of our tradition—our way of speaking truth to power.

In the pages that follow, you will read stories that explore the issues, interests, and cultural and historical influences that have shaped our times, our imaginations. We are, after all, the children of Black Power; Fat Albert and the Cosby Kids; Roots; the Huxtables; the Carter, Reagan, Bush, and Clinton years. We are the latch-key kids who were bused crosstown, the ones who packed up and went off to prep schools, joined the army and the navy, attended Ivy League colleges, earned M.F.A. degrees. We are the immigrants who came by boats and planes, and the curious travelers who left the United States to visit foreign lands. We are biracial, bicultural, bisexual; we are constantly inventing ways to get past the boundaries, the binaries; we are constantly insisting upon the recognition of our individuality, our complexity.

In the early 1990s, when Lorene Cary's memoir, *Black Ice*, was first published, a friend of mine called to tell me about it. "You have got to read this," she said. "It's about being a Black girl in a predominately white boarding school. It's about us." That was all she needed to say. There are so few people, even among the mainstream, who attend boarding school. It's an exclusive experience. Purposely so.

I was excited to learn that someone—someone Black—who had "been there and done that," had mustered the courage and discipline to write about it. As soon as I got off the phone, I ran to the bookstore, anxious to find out about Cary's boarding school years and compare them to my own. Was she happy or miserable there? I wanted to know. Did she feel like she belonged, like she was welcome? How did she wear her hair? Did she date boarding school boys? Black ones or white ones?

Cary's book moved me into a modernity that had not existed in the books that I had been reading; not in the same way. It was as if her book opened the door to *today*. Thus, the question became: What does it mean to be a Black woman *today*? What does it mean to be a Black woman who grew up in the suburbs, to be a Black woman who grew up in a white family, a Black woman who was the first in her family to attend college, the first to choose a person of the same gender or a person of a different race as her life partner, to choose a professional career over parenting, to parent in nontraditional ways? What does it mean to be a Black woman *today*?

Or, more specifically; What does it mean for *us* to be Black women today—the *us* being my peers, those women who had grown up roughly around the same time as I had. How similar were our references, our realities? How similar were our interpretations of race, of class, of gender? How different, based on our varied backgrounds, were our expressions of self? Each time I found myself rushing around the corner to the neighborhood bookstore, standing in front of a towering wall of shelves, my index finger slightly grazing the spines of all the recently published books, these were the questions that swirled through my mind, the questions I hoped would be answered somewhere in those pages.

⌇

One of the things that struck me as I was going about the business of putting this collection together is how wonderfully the selections work as a whole. It is evident that these writers have bonds that extend beyond their fellowship as wordsmiths; they clearly read and draw inspiration from one another. Though each piece has its own singular charm, its own precise approach to the subject it addresses, the emotions it evokes, there is thematic continuity. There are the obvious connections, such as the themes of love, alienation, displacement, isolation; but beneath all of that, there are also mutual conceptual nuances, there are more subtle links.

ZZ Packer remembers her near-abduction from a local Atlanta camp during the same summer that Black children in that area were being found murdered. Similarly, as her community is grappling with the disappearance of a young girl to whom she bears an eerie resemblance, Birdie, the biracial heroine in Danzy Senna's story, imagines what it would be like to disappear from her own life, one that is caught in the divide of Black and white.

Rebecca Walker explores a childhood spent shifting between disparate racial, cultural, and geographical landscapes. The teenage narrator of Carolyn Ferrell's story is torn between her allegiance to her white mother, who is the victim of domestic violence, and her desire to locate and love the beauty that exists in her Blackness. The acceptance of that individual and communal beauty in a place like Shreveport, Louisiana, proves to be a religious experience for Yolanda Young.

Catherine E. McKinley reveals the pain and confusion of having been adopted into a white family and denied all legal access to information about her biracial background. "There was the funny confusion I was experiencing," McKinley confides, "of being talked about as 'Afro-American' and 'Black' and 'colored' and 'Negro' all at the same time and knowing those things had something to do with Africa, but what exactly? And when I was able to settle that confusion, someone was there to ask another question about being 'adopted,' or (different from my brother) being adopted 'transracially,' and having Black and white 'biological par-ents,' and being 'mixed race,' and that other list of things all at the same time. I felt tortured by my strange status and by my isolation and distance from so many things."

Boarding school is the setting for the excerpts from both Lorene Cary and Martha Southgate. Cary learns to place her presence at the school in a larger context, while Southgate's character Rashid learns that similarity does not automatically translate into solidarity, even when it comes to race.

Debra J. Dickerson confronts the racial prejudices and political beliefs that have placed her at odds with herself and her people. "As my formal and informal education continued simultaneously in the most intellectu-ally and politically pivotal year of my life, 1984," Dickerson writes, "I began to see myself, my family, my neighborhood, my people in historico-social context. Some things were our fault, some things were not. Oppressed people have a duty to fight back, work hard, and retain their dignity, but society also has a duty to acknowledge disadvantage and work to end it."

asha bandele and Veronica Chambers each talk about the impact that their love for a Black man who is incarcerated has had on their lives. For bandele, that man is her husband, the man she met and fell in love with while participating in a poetry program at a prison. For Chambers, that man is her younger brother, whose misconduct and manipulations have all but shattered the closeness they once shared in their youth.

The narrator of Dana Johnson's story surveys the emotional distance that her education, relationship, and other life choices have placed between her and her mother, and wonders how she can find her way back home. Meanwhile, Natasha Tarpley's search for her origins leads her to a slave fortress in Ghana, where she uncovers a web of betrayal and creates her own definition of home, a definition upon which she begins to rely in order to release the past and construct her future. "There was music now," Tarpley writes, "streaming over our heads. The locals in the crowd began to dance. A dance that was more like running, feet sliding along the pavement. Three steps forward, one back. On the one step back, the entire body would lean backwards, suspended, as though surrendering to a strong wind, then snap upright, curving slightly, head down, fighting this same wind to move forward. Three steps forward, one back. Us, I thought. This is us. History. The body remembers."

It is those memories, the ones that reside just below the surface of the skin, that Phyllis Alesia Perry chooses to examine. When Lizzie, the main character in Perry's novel, is given a quilt that was willed to her by her late grandmother, she suddenly finds herself sliding into trancelike states, during which she inhabits the bodies of her maternal ancestors and relives the physical and emotional tortures of slavery.

While the pieces by Tarpley and Perry carry readers through the legacy of Black enslavement, Patricia Powell gives us a glimpse of the Chinese-Jamaican population and how they were taken from their native country, transported through the Middle Passage, brought to Jamaica, and used to work the plantations of that land. Powell also examines the relationship between the Chinese and the Blacks on the island, the adversities they faced and the alliances they forged.

Edwidge Danticat draws a haunting parallel between those who were lost to the waters of the Middle Passage and those who were lost more recently to the very same waters during their escape from Haiti by boat. In the letters that are written by a young revolutionary who is headed toward America aboard a makeshift boat with thirty-six other people and by the childhood sweetheart he has left behind, we are pulled into the sustaining command of hope and devastated by the high, nonnegotiable price of freedom.

Leila, the immigrant girl whose world we visit in Nelly Rosario's excerpt, ghost-walks the thin line between memory and destiny as she escapes the watchful eyes of her Dominican grandparents and attempts to find a freedom that exists beyond the threshold of their New York City apartment.

There is also a healthy array of sex, seduction, and plain, old-fashioned love between these covers. Ouida Staples, the leading lady in Helen Elaine Lee's tale of kindred spirits, is a recently divorced manicurist who is independent and free willed. She is careful, when dealing with her many male admirers, not to mistake the call of passion for the cage of possession. One day Ouida spots an uninhibited Zella standing on the street outside the shop catching rainwater with her tongue, and the two women are swept into a romance that is as natural and effortless as it is empowering.

The two women in Lisa Teasley's story are in love with the same man. They are taking a road trip up the California coast to work it out, reach an agreement. Over the course of their escapade, it becomes apparent that these women's fiery obsession with one another is about more than just the man they both want; it is about the sensual desire that they share for each other.

Shay Youngblood's character, Eden, leaves her small, still-segregated Georgia town behind to journey across the ocean to Paris in search of James Baldwin and the inspirations that facilitated his creativity. Far away from the narrow-mindedness of her hometown, Eden becomes involved with Ving, a fellow expatriate, a white horn player from Louisiana whom she meets at a party. They both know that theirs is a union that would surely be frowned upon in their native southern states. Before long, the couple is confronted with the realization that where there is the possibility of love, there is also always the presence of a hate that is conspiring to kill it.

Itabari Njeri pays homage to the power and the pleasure of retribution by proving that while the pen may very well be mightier than the sword, a bottle of sugar and a sharp paring knife can also help ease the pain of heartbreak. If only a little, and for a brief moment. Meanwhile, Lisa Jones packs up some fascinating American stereotypes and travels to the Bahamas to see how they play out on those shores. "We found out a long time ago," Jones explains, "that everyone masturbates and that everyone wants to be rich. The new truth is that everyone is consumed with the same racial mythologies that made this country so great:

"Blondes have more fun if they're sleeping with black men; black women of all complexions prefer dark-skinned black men; white men love themselves exclusively, they invented masturbation; Puerto Rican women in Hartford have the hots for black men; women who love women want to make it with women of color; white men in leather want black men, also in leather; Asians of both countries want it bad with everyone; light-skinned black American women with money think they invented pussy; light-skinned Latin men, especially Colombians, love and marry dark-skinned women from all Latin countries; progressive black American men with money say color isn't an issue, yet are only seen in public with women with 'good hair'; progressive, dark-skinned black American women who get no play from color-struck brothers are experimenting with white men; the finest men in the world are all black and are usually from Zimbabwe, Atlanta, or Brooklyn; the finest women in the world are from Brazil, come in all colors, but usually have hair like Troy Beyer, Diahann Carroll's daughter on *Dynasty*. And if you think you don't fit into all this, you're lying."

My own work is consumed by the absolute notion that it is through our honesty and compassion, it is through our sisterhood, that we as Black women will begin to heal ourselves. That is the central idea that is expressed in my excerpt. It is the driving force behind this collection of work by writers whose curiosity, craftsmanship, and commitment to truth I greatly admire.

Given all this, I wanted to select a title for the collection that was fitting, one that spoke not only of the work but also if the writers and the impact that they are making. At the same time, I didn't want something that was too defining and, as a result, potentially limiting. I came up with a few ideas; I received suggestions from my editor, the contributors, and a few of my other colleagues. A couple of the ideas were interesting though not, for whatever reason, appropriate; most of them, however, were horrible. Fortunately, the perfect title was, if not within my grasp, certainly within earshot the entire time. I didn't realize that until I had already done quite a bit of searching.

"Shakin' the Tree" is the title of a song written by Peter Gabriel. There is a version of it, sung by Gabriel and Youssou N'Dour, that is at the top of my list of "liberation" music—songs that encourage, remind, and celebrate. I draw a lot of strength an inspiration from the lyrics, which urge women to challange the staus quo, to be the architects of our own futures. It was one of the songs that I reguarly listened to as I was working on this collection—which is how, at last, I was able to get the clue. And the rest, as they say, is history.

Meri Nana-Ama Danquah

Shaking the Tree

What can I share with the younger generation of Black women writers, writers in general? What can they learn from my experience? I can tell them not to be afraid to feel and not to be afraid to write about it. Even if you are afraid, do it anyway.

—AUDRE LORDE

asha bandele

The thing with writing is authenticity. Authenticity of the spirit. I've never quite known how to speak, how to say what I think in a world that seems to prefer the redacted version, the falsified version of our interior landscapes. People ask, "How are you?" And I know they mean well, but they also mean, "Don't tell me the real deal. Don't say what's honestly going on, what you're thinking, how you're feeling." If you do, when you do, so often they look at you like you're crazy, talk too much, are too emotional, wow, look at the time, bye . . .

So I have the page, the written word, and it's an oxymoron of sorts; this particular art form that must, at the end, give way to revision, give way to editing, is the one place where I don't feel edited down. Where I don't feel silenced or cut short.

Home

From *The Prisoner's Wife*, a memoir

WHEN PEOPLE HAVE asked me how could I have fallen in love with a man who was convicted of murder, where I begin is as a student who was volunteering time and hoping that my poems and willingness to talk would somehow change someone for the better. Then I tell about the man who would become my husband, how his spirit engaged me, engaged every one of us, and how by the openness of his spirit, it was I who would change.

Back then, during those early days of friendship, I learned something about taking in different points of view, listening carefully, reserving judgment, and not having to win an argument for winning's sake. I learned by watching Rashid, who always spoke in turn, and who spoke deliberately, and who admitted being wrong if he'd been shown to be wrong.

Prison, he told me one day, *will teach a man to be polite.*

The tension's so high here, you don't want to add to it by not saying "excuse me" if it's right to say "excuse me." And that's good. I wasn't always like that. I used to be so arrogant.

I've explained to people that I didn't, despite what it would seem, fall in love with a killer. I fell in love with a man who wanted to become his own more perfect creation, a man committed to the transformation of himself, of the world. And the world he imagined was like the world I imagined. It was a place that was just and fair and safe and livable. We could meet there, in that place. We could meet there as creators. We could meet there as equals.

He valued my opinions! I have said this to friends.

Can you imagine such a man? He wants to consult with me about every-thing. Everything! He takes my advice, I have said to whoever would listen.

When I talked about things Rashid had never heard of, he took notes. *But it's more than this,* I've said, trying to get in every point I could while they were still paying attention.

He respects me enough to argue with me. I told my girlfriend one afternoon.

I never used to be able to imagine that, I said to her. To be engaged in a debate, and I didn't mean the way men usually argue with women in that, *Okay, dear, whatever you say* kind of way. No! I meant the way men argue with men, as though the other person was a worthy opponent. Rashid listened to me and he challenged me. That's who I fell in love with, I said over and over. A man who believed I was a woman who was worth it.

Sometimes when I've told people these things, they say they just can't see it. *Where's the ugly stuff?* I've been asked over and over. And I've told them yes, it was true, that there were some women for whom ugliness and hurt was the texture of their story, but it simply was not the picture that I had to draw.

asha, some have argued, *girl, you have blinders on. He might be great now, but who is he going to be when he comes home?*

I don't know, I respond. *Who will I be?*

Rashid could come home and be horrible to you, I've been warned.

Yes, I tell them. *Of course that's true. But Rashid could also come home and be wonderful to me. None of us know tomorrow, only this moment, now, this time, already recorded in history.*

And this moment, when I am kissed, nurtured, rocked, and then set at ease by the love I have been given, this moment is the only real thing I know. That, and also this one other thing: that there are so many people who are lonely, without love and without passion in their lives, that I know that what I have, as difficult as it may be, is the most precious of all gifts.

And I couldn't just give it up without a fight, this rare, this desired thing, this thing which is life-sustaining. Could I? Could they, I ask? I want to know this. Could they reject the greatest love they've ever known just because it came from the worst place they've ever known?

⌣

Still I am aware that all things happen in a context, and so, Rashid's many charms notwithstanding, it is also true that there was this confluence of events in my life, and together they probably assisted in making him so significant to me.

The world is so magnificent, the way it keeps rebirthing itself to you, if you're amenable. And if you're amenable, the way the world comes will be exciting, new each time, in different colors, different shapes.

For me, a brand-new world was born when I became a student at the City University of New York. I majored in political science and Black studies, not realizing that within each classroom I would find pieces of myself, scattered pieces of Black female me just waiting to be scooped up and reattached.

For the first time in my life, a life which had been dominated by white history, white cultures, white literature, white music, white sensibilities, a life where Black was a metaphor for less than, I was reading books with characters and experiences that I understood. I was finally offered a history that went beyond slavery to include that which was Black and successful, Black and intelligent, Black and encouraging.

Learning this left me with a range of emotions I think common to any conquered people. The greatest, the most profound one I had, was love, at last for myself, as a Black woman, a woman who indeed had a place in history, if not in high school textbooks. For the first time in my entire academic history, I was studying the literature of Black people: James Baldwin and Zora Neale Hurston, Buchi Emecheta and Chinua Achebe.

I learned that there was more to my ancestry than slavery and the Civil Rights movement, which during my grammar and high school years were the only contexts in which I'd heard Black people being discussed. I could, at that pivotal juncture in my academic career, study Malcolm X, not as an extra-credit project, but as an extraordinary international political figure who had moved from prison to the Bandung Conference to the Organization of AfroAmerican Unity. I am embarrassed to admit this but I know it has to be said. For the first time in my life, I was truly and completely proud to be Black. I had never felt that before. Not once. Not all the way.

But at the same time that I was virtually falling in love with my history and culture, I was also feeling a huge sense of grief over what had been done to my people, what had been lost, who had been murdered. There was, certainly, a rage, a nearly unmitigated rage, at the people who made the policies and laws and institutions which could only be called evil.

I tell you this so that you understand how easy it was in those days to determine who was friend and who was enemy. Later, as I matured, took in more and more information, nothing stayed simple and clear. But it was, then, literally and figuratively, a black-and-white situation. And it was through this lens that I first saw not only Rashid, but all prisoners.

Back then I saw all prisoners as victims. I told Rashid this.

Yes, well, a lot of us also think like that in the beginning, he said to me.

And some people really are, straight-up, victims. At first we say we're all political prisoners because of the politics of the criminal justice system. And race is always an issue. But you know, as you get older, you want to take responsibility for all your life. Because if you live long enough, you do good things too. And I began to want to claim the good that I had done. But if I was responsible for that, then I had to be responsible for the bad, too, right?

Yet it wasn't only this emerging worldview which influenced my choices. There were indeed some tangible and devastating things which happened all at once, in the year just before I fell in love with Rashid. There were these departures. Suddenly everything in my life was shifting aside, seeking a fast exit, and I was just there, crouched on a curb, alone, unable to see across distances, unable to get perspective.

The initial blow came when I was put out of school for protesting against the steady tuition increases and budget cuts which were closing more and more students out of an education. We had rallied, marched, lobbied, and then occupied the administration building of our school. And it was for this final act that a few of us were brought up on internal charges, found guilty, and removed.

For two reasons, this was a bigger loss than I had anticipated. First of all, I was president of my student government, and therefore largely defined by school activities. But second, my own parents had been administrators at the university. And to be sure, they disagreed with the tuition increases and budget cuts as well, but more than anything, they wanted me to graduate. They said this to me then, and as much as I wanted to comply, I would in fact make them wait some five years before I paraded in black to the proud hum of *Pomp and Circumstance*.

Fourteen years before, when I was fifteen years old, I had walked in a similar parade to the same song down the aisle of my high school auditorium. There were many valleys, long drops, down and down further between those two days, and in all that time, despite my often hostile outward behavior, what had always been of greatest importance to me is what was of greatest importance to many children.

I wanted desperately to please my parents, to make them proud. My parents, I knew, had made incredible sacrifices for my sister and me, to have a nice home, to go to good schools, to be exposed to the arts. We were middle-class but never rich by any stretch of the imagination. Whatever we had, my sister and I, came as a result of long, often arduous hours my parents put in at their respective jobs.

And they were jobs that were not necessarily dream jobs—not my parents in jobs that nurture your soul. My mother and father worked so that my sister and I could have that sort of option, to work in any field we wanted. It would be a long time before I was old enough to understand this, to see my sister and myself as their legacies. And only then would my studies become an urgent matter. In my generation, it seems, most of us struggle for position and status. But my parents, their struggle was for us, their children, and I believed I owed them.

I knew I had been a very difficult teenager, more sullen, a worse student than the other young people my parents knew. My various misdeeds, the hanging out, the skipping school, the drugs, the drinking, they had stolen away the chance for my parents to be proud as I pondered which Ivy League school I would attend; in fact I only initially made it into college because of people my mother had known. And then just as I had settled down some four years later, just as I transferred into the City University and began making all A's, this: the protest, the charges, and finally, the suspension.

In a sense, losing my student status in the last half of my senior year meant losing something of my parents. I felt a bit like they had given up on me. I was, after all, in my twenties now. What more could they do?

⌣

Against the disastrous backdrop of being put out of school, my precariously situated marriage toppled. I was twenty-three and two years married.

It was not that we didn't love each other, my first husband and I. It was that love was all we had. And we needed so much more. All couples do. We needed common passions and interests and goals. We needed to enjoy speaking with each other. We needed, then, some great omniscient who could have explained him to me, me to him.

What we had, instead, was silence. And in the face of that hard, that unfriendly quiet, my husband ran to work and stayed there for sometimes twelve, thirteen hours a day. I ran to school and did the same. By the time we'd come home, what else was there to do but sleep?

And we did, we slept. We slept fitfully, angrily, accusingly, but most of all, we slept singularly. We slept until there was nothing left to do but crawl out of bed, separately, and go on out into those two distinct worlds we had created for ourselves, his on one side of the universe, mine on the other.

And again my parents, with their happy, healthy, four-decade long marriage, my parents did not agree with or understand, how, after only two years, it could all fall apart. Everything had been so carefully constructed. I had, all of us had, listened to the experts, and tried to follow suit.

My husband and I began life with an expensive, formal June wedding. I wore a white gown and veil. My father walked me down the aisle, and danced the first dance with me. We had joint bank accounts and credit cards. My husband said I didn't have to work, just go to school. I went to school. I cooked and cleaned. We had dinner parties. But in the end none of it worked because while we had the administrative part of it down, we were missing the creative. It didn't work because in the end, there were no words, no ongoing dialogues, no private jokes between us. And for many people, the absence of language is not enough reason to end a marriage. But for me it was the primary reason to do it. I know this now. I didn't know it then and this is why I could not run home to her, to my mother, who had, I'm sure, worked through and across silences to sustain her partnership with my father.

The bottom line was this: I wasn't running for my life from some kind of monster, a batterer, a raging alcoholic. I was running from a man everybody loved, a man I loved. And this was why things got blamed on me. I had destabilized my own life, and then had the audacity to want sympathy, a shoulder, a helping hand.

I couldn't stay in school. I couldn't stay in a marriage. I didn't have a job. So where could I stay? Who could I love? What could I do? What goal *could* I meet?

In the middle of the night, these questions would bang in my head. They would bang, like thick lead pipes against the sides of my dreams, bang and bang until I awoke. Awoke in fits of fear, sadness, isolation.

⌒

I wanted love in my life again. I wanted to be important to someone again. I wanted to be accepted by someone again. My parents' disappointment, and my husband's disinterest, those things pushed and pricked like a thousand tiny pins menacing the soles of my feet. Whenever I walked, the pain of their rejection, what I translated as their rejection, would contort me; I suspected I looked like a sideshow act. That, or else an obvious failure. And I didn't know how not to be these things, how not to appear freakish, how not to be an outcast in the eyes of my family, and yes, in the eyes of men. That's the way breakups always seemed to leave me, especially at first, feeling undesirable, unlovable, ugly.

It was then no one single thing, but this terrific twister of loss and need that carried me into loving Rashid. For a year or more, he had been consistently inviting me up to the prisons to be part of their various cultural heritage shows, and I had gone each time, bringing other young people with me. One summer afternoon, I brought two young men I knew with me to do hip-hop poetry. One of the young men, a brother with a beautiful, sharp, carved face, stepped up to the mike. His tiny dreds stood firm on top of his head and it seemed like he was looking at everyone in the audience all at once, me, the prisoners, the police, everyone. Then he said, and I will never forget this,

Feel the rage of my warrior's wrath, as I have a path of resistance. I want to put a head out. Now!

As soon as those words hit the air, the stage was surrounded by more police than I have ever seen at one time, before or since, in a prison.

All right! That's it! one of the police said, and we were told we were going to have to leave the facility for "attempting to start a riot."

Before we were shoved out, I gave Rashid my home phone number. If we were being put out, I thought, what will they do to Rashid since he invited us up here?

Call me, I told him. I closed his hand around the tiny scrap of paper I had scribbled my number on.

Call me if they give you any trouble because of this.

Weeks, eight, maybe nine, pass between that incident and the first time I would answer my phone and hear what has now become an urgent and familiar recording:

You have a collect call from . . . Rashid . . . an inmate at a correctional facility. If you wish to decline the call, hang up. To accept press three, now.

And I did it. I pressed three and every part of my life, how I think, how I love, how I set priorities, what I pray for, what I treasure, what angers me, what I appreciate, how I organize my time, my money, every little thing in my life, and every big thing, changed. And it changed before I had a chance to seek consultation or ask a question. It changed before I had a chance to pause or reconsider. Or run.

Lorene Cary

When I finished the first draft of Black Ice, *I took a day off and walked my dog by the river, ending up in the park where we took our daughter to play at least three times a week. On the bench sat a man I'd never seen before. He commented, in a Caribbean accent—close to Barbados or Trinidad, I figured—that he liked my T-shirt, which said, Howard: Black by Popular Demand. I didn't want to talk, so I made a tight smile and walked on. He lobbed an amused query at my back: "So when you're not walking your dog, what do you do?"*

"I'm a writer."

"Oh, you want to be a writer, how nice."

"No, sir, I am a writer. I've just mailed off my first book."

I began to tell him, perhaps because his accent sounded so familiar, but I don't know why, really, that I'd included in Black Ice *Barbadian folktales from my great-grandfather. Immediately he asked about them by name: "Did you put in 'Skin-skin'? 'Jump, Izzy'?"*

I told him yes, and I went on, as if unable to stop myself, that the book was two hundred pages longer than it ought to be, and that I was afraid my editor would want me to cut the folktales in order to keep the boarding school narrative. And he told me, this man I'd never seen before in my neighborhood park and have never seen since, that these stories would die if we didn't write and publish them, and that it was my job to figure out how to get it all in and not one I should foist onto my editor. "Who's story is it?" he asked.

As writer I was nothing but vessel. The story was mine and not mine. Figure it out; do the gig; do the whole gig, and no whining. I felt like a new mother who hasn't yet accepted that she must wake in the night, every night, to feed the baby. I went home and wrote on my wall, over my desk: Just tell the story.

From *Black Ice*, a memoir

DURING THE WINTER term Bruce Chan, who had drafted me to look after Fumiko on the first day of my Fifth Form, suggested that we begin tutoring some of the younger students in English. He also delegated me to write a letter of protest to the English department for what we thought was prejudice against the incoming students of color. (One teacher, by way of correcting a young student's paper, commented on the pattern of grammatical errors and warned the boy that he'd have to work to overcome his black English. We suspected, after reading several papers, that our teachers judged typically black "errors" more harshly than others, and that once obsessed by idiom they lost sight of black students' ideas.) A few days later I gritted my teeth as Bruce edited my letter in red pen. I remember delivering the rewritten version to the department chairman, who responded that he and the other teachers worked hard to be as sensitive as possible to the needs of all the students, but that he would urge his teachers, as he had been doing, to even greater consideration.

The tutoring was equally frustrating. Students brought us their papers during free periods before class. They wanted us to tidy things up, plug in big words. They did not come with a rough draft, as we asked, prepared to rethink and rewrite.

The best I could do, I decided, was to try to build their confidence rather than tear it down. I tried to pick out their original ideas and show them that these, the scary ones, were worth writing about.

"Forget your notes; put them away until exams. The papers are yours. It's how *you* read the same old story that that man has been teaching for twenty years. He's waiting for *you* to see it fresh. And you *can*. You've brought a whole bunch of new ideas that haven't been here until now."

When the girl left, I heard my own words. I had never said them before, never even thought them. I sat in my room grinning. More than anything I had said while I stood nervously trying to solicit discussion on blues lyrics, a half-hour with that girl and her no-thesis, no-introduction, no-proper-conclusion paper had shown me that I, too, had something to give to St. Paul's. I had come not just with my hat in hand, a poorly shod scholarship girl, but as a sojourner bearing gifts, which were mine to give or withhold.

No doubt, the appearance of Miss Clinton that year gave me new strength. The new black Spanish teacher was in her early twenties. She was dark and thin with high pockets and a high bark of a laugh if you caught her in a funny mood outside of class. In class was a different matter. She would step outside the classroom, kick the doorstop with one sensible shoe, and say clearly over her shoulder: "*¡Listos, ya!*"

Her mouth with its pointed top lip was beautiful when she spoke, and the language came out bright and precise: "Ready, now!" Those of us who were not in her class stood in the sunny hallway in the modern-languages wing of the Schoolhouse on purpose to hear her. We yelped when she said it—not *ahora*, meaning now, but *¡ya!* Immediately! She was tough.

"Hell, no, they're not ready," we'd say as we walked back to the Reading Room across the hall.

"They're not *even* ready."

"They will never be ready."

"They better get ready."

"Forget it. Those guys are smoked. *Smoked!*"

The other teachers did not treat Miss Clinton with condescending politeness (as many did another young black teacher). I could not tell whether they offered her friendship, but I could see that they gave her respect.

And no mistaking she was black. Now and then Miss Clinton drove into town to buy greens—fresh greens in Concord—and she'd boil a big pot. It stunk up her tiny dormitory; it seeped into the Indian tapestries on the students' walls. On Saturday evening I watched her dance to her new Marvin Gaye album, and I realized how lonely she might be, this energetic young woman, for a companion. But she neither hid it from us nor slopped it onto us to carry.

I took courage from her, as much as I dared, and yet I feared her, too. I feared judgment that never came.

"You should stop by more often," she said as I stirred her pot and moistened my face in the steam.

Buoyed up by Miss Clinton, my head crammed with the literature I was teaching under Mr. Lederer, who spent his sabbatical year teaching in a North Philadelphia high school, I began to feel more confident in the inevitable racial discussions in classes, at Seated Meal, after visitors' talks. I took the offensive and bore my gifts proudly. What the discussions concerned specifically, who was there, where they took place, I do not remember. I do recall hearing the same old Greek-centered European-centered assumptions of superiority. Might made right. I had my stories about Chaka Zulu from my Harvard evening course (and I knew they worshiped Harvard!). Nothing mattered. I was like a child again, trying to argue that I was still somebody—I am Somebody! As we shouted back to Jesse Jackson on the television—even though black people had been slaves, even though we hadn't had the dignity to jump off the boats en mass or die from tuberculosis like the Indians. More fact. I wanted more facts to show that it wasn't all fair now, that the resources that kept them here, ruddy and well-tutored, as healthy as horses, had been grabbed up in some greedy, obscene, unfair competition years before.

"Even if my great-grandfather did own slaves, it's not fair to hold me responsible."

Fair. Fair. Fair. They shouted fair, as if fair had anything to do with it, and I had no facts to wipe their words away. I had no words for their trust funds, capital gains, patrimonies, legacies, bequests. My mind screamed profanities. I had no other words. They had taken them and made them into lies.

That's how I felt the night I left a racial discussion with a girl named India Bridgeman. A group of black girls had once asked her to take the role of plantation overseer in a student-choreographed dance. I'd kept in my head the image of her as she danced around the slaves with a whip, her classical ballet training showing in every movement. She'd visited England as a member of St. Paul's varsity field hockey team. She was an acolyte who knew the rituals of high mass: where to walk, what to carry. I knew her through Janie, but mostly I envied her from a distance as a symbol, a collection of accomplishments that I did not possess.

We continued to debate into the Upper and then up the stairs to her room. She turned toward me, and I saw India the dancer. She pivoted on the balls of her feet, calf muscles bunched, sternum up. On her forehead was a light brown spot that I had thought she penciled on as an affected beauty mark. (It was a mole.) She had clear eyes, kissy lips, and big, dramatic movements. "Wait, wait a minute! Wait, wait, wait, wait!" India talked like that.

"I get it," she said. "I get it. You know how when you *get* something that you've never been able to know before?"

I nodded, but I resisted her enthusiasm, and the spontaneous humility of this sudden expansiveness. India translated what I had been saying into different words, and I listened, dumbfounded to hear them. It was clear that she, too, knew how it felt to be an outsider. I had never suspected it. India told me about her life growing up in Manhattan, and her own estrangement from many of our schoolmates. We talked until we grew hungry.

"Isn't there anything to eat, anywhere?" India jumped up from the floor, where we'd been sitting, and walked across the room to her stash. "All I've got is mayonnaise," she said as if the world would end. "Hold everything! I know I had some crackers, too. Do you think that's gross, just putting mayonnaise on crackers?"

"Are you kidding? I was raised on mayonnaise. And mayonnaise, not that cheap-ass salad dressing." I cut my eyes to the little jar in her hand. She whooped with laughter.

"What would you have done if I'd been holding some 'cheap-ass salad dressing'?"

"I would have died. But really, that stuff—"

"I know, I know, it's awful," she agreed.

"My mother makes mayonnaise sandwiches. My whole family does. And my grandmother! God forbid she should have a few drinks. You should see what she does. *That's* awful."

I had not talked to other girls at St. Paul's about my grandmother. India laughed with me, but solicitously, watchfully, as if to judge how much I could take, or how far beneath the surface of humor lay the shame.

"My *other* grandmother," I said, having risked as much as I dared just then, "sends me care packages, and I think I have some juice. Do you like pear nectar?"

"Not really."

"I used to love it. I don't have the heart to tell her I'm not so crazy about it now."

"I know. It's like they get one thing that they know makes you happy, and they'll buy it for you for the rest of your life." She stopped eating a cracker. "Oh, that's *so* dear. That's so beautiful that your grandmother does that. Do you have any more?"

"Sure. It's hot, though."

"Oh, let's get it. Let's drink to—what do you call her?"

"Nana."

"Let's drink to Nana."

We tiptoed to my room, and I pulled my pantry box out from underneath my bed. "Do you like sardines?" I whispered.

"Why not?"

India and I talked often and late into the night after that. We raged together at St. Paul's School—at its cliques and competitiveness; its ambivalence toward its new female members; its smugness and certainty and power. We talked about families and boyfriends, girls we liked and girls we didn't. We laughed at how we had appeared to each other the year before. Our talk was therapeutic, private, and as intense as romance. It was for me the first triumph of love over race.

Outside my personal circle, the school that term seemed to buzz, buzz. Class officers, it seemed, were often called upon to talk. We talked day and evening, in club activities and rehearsals, in the houses, in the hallways, in our rooms, in the bathrooms, and in meetings after meetings. We gossiped. We criticized. We whined. We analyzed. We talked trash. We talked race relations, spiritual life, male-female relations, teacher-student trust. We talked confidentially. We broke confidences and talked about the results. We talked discipline and community. We talked Watergate and social-fabric stuff.

I did not follow the Watergate hearings. I did not rush to the third floor of the Schoolhouse for the ten-thirty *New York Times* delivery to read about it; nor did I crowd around the common-room TV to watch the proceedings. I could not bother to worry about which rich and powerful white people had hoodwinked which other rich and powerful white people. It seemed of a piece with their obsession with fairness.

I was unprepared, therefore, to dine at the Rectory with Mr. Archibald

Cox, the St. Paul's alumnus whom President Nixon had fired when, as U.S. Special Prosecutor, Mr. Cox began to reveal the Watergate break-in and cover-up. Seated around him were the Rector and a handful of faculty members and student leaders. I said as little as possible in order to conceal my ignorance. Mr. Cox was acute. He referred to the Watergate players and major events in witty shorthand. I couldn't quite follow, so I ate and smiled and made periodic conversation noises.

Then he wanted to hear about St. Paul's School. There had been so many changes since his time. I found myself saying, in answer to his question, or the Rector's signal, that I was more aware of being black at St. Paul's than I was of being a girl. I used a clever phrase that I stole from somewhere and hoped he hadn't already heard: "Actually, we're still more like . . . a boys' school with girls in it. But black people's concerns—diversifying the curriculum and that sort of thing—the truth is that that's more important to me than whether the boys have the better locker room."

Pompous it was, and I knew it, but better to be pompous in the company of educated and well-off white folk, better even to be stone wrong, than to have no opinion at all.

Mr. Cox thought a moment. God forbid he should go for the cross-examination. I added more. "Black concerns here at school may look different, but are not really, from the concerns that my parents have taught me all my life at home." I put that one in just so he'd know that I had a family. "And believe me, sir, my mama and daddy did not put President Nixon into the White House. *We* didn't do that!"

Mr. Cox wrinkled his lean, Yankee face into a mischievous smile. His voice whispered mock conspiracy. He leaned toward me. "Do you know who Nixon hates worst of all?"

I shook my head no. I had no idea.

"Our kind of people."

My ears felt hot. I wanted to jump on the table. I wanted to go back home and forget that I'd ever come. I wanted to take him to West Philly, and drop him off at the corner of Fifty-second and Locust, outside Foo-Foo's steak emporium, right by the drug dealers, and leave him there without a map or a bow tie. Then tell me about our kind of people.

The Rector gave me a look that urged caution. I fixed my face. "What kind of people are those?" I asked.

"Why, the educated Northeastern establishment," he said.

The Rector smiled as if relieved.

Soon after, I received a note to meet another visitor: Mr. Vernon Jordan, president of the National Urban League. During his talk to students, Mr. Jordan referred to incidents in the history and current affairs of black and white racial relations that I had never heard. I felt the relief of a child after she has walked a very long way trying to be brave. Afterward I could not think of one intelligent question to ask him. It felt good simply to ride awhile. The next morning Alma and I met him at Scudder. Mr. Jordan was finishing breakfast when we arrived. He asked us about ourselves and the school. Alma described my involvement in Student Council and teased me about my reluctance to talk. "She's usually a big talker," she said.

I told him about Alma's athletic achievements, her varsity letters in basketball and lacrosse. We mentioned our Third World Coalition, and admitted our squabbles, our struggles: how at times we felt constricted, but could not figure out what to do.

He understood us. He caught up our words and showed us what we meant. "This is a new phase of civil rights," he said. "Just a few years ago, it was a lot clearer. You could point to outrageous racist laws. Now it's more subtle. You kids here are feeling the effects. I mean you're here—" he motioned his hand in the air to take in the graceful room. We could hear Mrs. Burrows washing dishes in the kitchen. "And it's hard not to become a part of all this. It's hard not to forget where we came from."

How could I tell him: forgetting wasn't the problem, it was finding a new way to fight. If we couldn't fight, we'd implode. I tried to say that. I tried to ask him what we should do now, in this new phase. It was time for him to go to Mem Hall, but he hadn't told us how to go on. I wanted to beg, to demand that he show us the way. "The most important thing," he said, "is to get everything you can here. You kids are getting a view of white America that we never ever got close to." He shook his head. "We couldn't even dream of it."

I thought of the scene in *Native Son*—I'd have to teach it soon to the Fourth Formers—where the two boys stand on the sidewalk looking at an airplane. Only white boys could fly, they said.

"You've got to get as much as you can here, be the *best* that you can, so that when you come out, you'll be ready. But you cannot forget where you've come from."

When I had been eleven years old, the year before Martin Luther King was shot, I had written to the Southern Christian Leadership Conference headquarters in Atlanta asking them what I could do to help the struggle. They had said the same thing. Stay in school. Prepare yourself. Then what?

"The fact is," he said, "there's no blueprint for what we're doing now. It's all uncharted water. We're going to need you. We're going to need every one of you."

Veronica Chambers

I wrote Mama's Girl *almost five years ago. At the time, I didn't know I was writing what would be termed a half-memoir, a genre that seemed to have exploded around the time of my publication date and that some considered, snidely, to be a too-early-told life story of someone too young to know anything worth telling. But I think that as a Black woman, I was instructed from childhood in the power of bearing witness. We may not all lead lives as magnificent and startling as Maya Angelou's or Josephine Baker's, but we all have eyes and we all have ears, we all have hearts. If I stand on the corner of Fifty-eighth Street and Ninth Avenue, and some crazy taxi driver runs you over, then I can be your witness. In the same fashion, if I stand at the intersection of my mother and my father, my husband and his brother, my friend and my enemy, there are things that I can see. There are stories I can tell. I can bear witness. And even now, as I write my first novel, this is what I'm trying to do.*

Veronica Chambers
Philadelphia, PA
July 11, 2002

From *Mama's Girl*, a memoir

IN TWO WEEKS, my brother Malcolm will be twenty-one. Right now, he is sitting in jail. I am sitting in my cubicle at *The New York Times* where I am an editor. If there is a worse place to receive this information, I can't think of it. When my twelve-year-old half brother calls me with the news, I must curl over my desk and whisper into the headset. All around me are white faces, no one that I can turn to and say, "You know, my brother's been arrested—I've got to go." Lucky, then, that it is almost five and I can just pack up my stuff and leave.

At home, I call my mother, who calls my father. I stopped speaking to my father three years earlier when I decided I had had enough of all the drama. My father still lives near Philadelphia, where my brother has been arrested. The week that my brother is in jail, we play this weird game of telephone—my brother talks to my father, who talks to my mother, who talks to me. At first my mother and I are extremely calm, we discuss the details with a clinical detachment. This is not the first time my brother has been arrested. It's about the millionth time that we've pow-wowed over Malcolm and wondered, What should we do, what should we do?

But the evening news sets me on edge—I see my brother in every young black man. Just as prejudiced as some white people, I find myself thinking, *They all look alike!* It amazes me that however many hundreds of years after the Diaspora and a splitting apart of a people, the family ties between black men and women are so visually evident. But that's too easy. The deeper issue is that the resemblance between my brother and all these other young black men bothers me because I'm wondering, *How will* they *know this is my brother? How will they know not to hurt him?* I think of another black man, Alexandre Dumas, and his tales of the Three Musketeers. Set within the context of the inner city, Dumas's motto, "All for one and one for all," has scary connotations for young black men. You go, I go. And every other street corner has a story about how Peter took the bullet for Paul. I spend the better part of the night crying, as I always do, hot and heavy, angry tears.

Just the week before, I'd spoken to Malcolm. He was living with his girlfriend, a twenty-year-old woman with two kids, neither of whom were his. "How are you eating?" I asked him. He told me that his girlfriend got food stamps. His answer implied that he wasn't dealing drugs anymore. I didn't like the idea of my brother living on welfare, but since he had a complete aversion to working for minimum wage, I decided not to push it.

Once I'd gotten out of college, I'd joined my mother in the crusade to save my brother. I grew up with the understanding that the world is a harder place for black men than it is for black women. That it is easier for a black woman to get a job than it is for a black man. I knew there was a way that the world made black men angry and that as a black woman, you worked around it, you kept your cool, you kept things together.

After five years of frustration, though, my mother and I had recently made a pact to restrict our efforts to words of support and guidance and not to give my brother any more cash because it never seemed to do any good and it might even have done some harm. If he wanted to live off his girlfriend's welfare, that was his business. But it turned out that was just another lie and now he was in jail. My mother and I guessed it was a drug offense and we were right: possession with intent to distribute. It was a charge that sounded familiar, like something I'd seen on a rerun of *Miami Vice*.

My cousin Guille, streetwise and familiar with the territory my brother had made his home, warned me to stop worrying about him. "He's out there doing what he wants to do," she said. "Malcolm doesn't care about anyone but himself. He'd take your last dollar, your rent money, your food money, and he wouldn't think twice about it. Look out for yourself."

But the success I had found in journalism made it hard not to wish my brother would find similar satisfaction in his life. Once again I was the super sister, thinking of what I could do to help him, and then I thought of the red winter coat and my heart hardened a little bit.

A year before I joined *The New York Times* I was living and working in Los Angeles. I hadn't heard from my brother for almost six months. He was hard to track down. He shuttled between Atlantic City and New York, living with different friends and different girlfriends. He wasn't good about letting me or my mother know his current phone number and address. The last phone number I had for him was a beeper that didn't work.

In early December, my brother calls me. He is in Atlantic City again. It's already begun to snow back East. My brother says he does not have a winter coat and is walking around in a denim jacket. He wants to know, could I send him money for a coat? I remember our pact and tell him that I will send him an actual coat instead.

It's odd to go winter-coat shopping in southern California. Not that it doesn't get cold at night, but it's never so cold that you have to bundle up in layers. As I walk through the mall, feeling coats for bulk, checking the labels to see if they are water-resistant, considering colors, I think about winters when I was small. My mother would get up first, shower, and get dressed. She would turn on the oven and leave the door open to warm up the tiny kitchen. Our apartments were always freezing and we couldn't afford space heaters. My mother would wrap my brother and me up in a blanket, walking us through the cold apartment into the bathroom. We'd take quick showers, then my mother would walk us back to the kitchen where she'd have our clothes laid out in front of the oven. I loved how warm the clothes felt against my skin, the turtleneck and jeans toasty from the oven's heat. It wasn't something I thought about, this ritual of warmth. I thought everyone got dressed in front of the oven in the winter and I assumed it was something I would do for the rest of my life.

It wasn't until college, my junior year, when I lived in an on-campus house, that I had the opportunity to adjust the heat in my room for the very first time. I kept the thermostat at 80°. My roommate was a white girl from the Midwest who loved the fresh air so much that she insisted on keeping the windows open, even during the brutal Massachusetts winter.

"You can always put on more clothes," she said, padding around in her Birkenstocks and socks.

"I *can't* get warm enough," I told her. I wanted it so hot that I was sweating. I wanted it so hot that I could sleep with only a sheet even in the middle of December. I wanted to explain to this girl about the cold apartments I grew up in, to tell her about getting dressed in front of the oven and the way my mother would boil tea for us at night so that we were warm enough to sleep. I wanted to explain what heat meant to me, how I had to have it, how I had to control it, but I never did. I didn't want her pity more than I wanted the heat.

I think of this girl and the oven and my mom when I am shopping for a coat for my brother. I buy him the biggest, most expensive red coat I can find.

I tell my mother about the coat, about the Christmas package I'd put together for Malcolm of CDs, a book, and the coat. My mother has just moved to Miami with my stepfather. She is still looking for a job and doesn't have much money. She asks if she can split the cost of the coat with me and make it a joint Christmas present. I agree and sign a card with both our names, though the truth is, I will never ask her for her half of the money.

I leave my office early and take the package to the post office the next afternoon. I circle the block until I can find a parking spot close to the front door. I lug the box out of the hatchback. A young guy dressed in a suit and tie holds the door for me. He looks like one of the budding studio execs that works in the mailroom at Columbia Pictures, just across the street. I push the package near the windows, then stand patiently in line. It is two or three weeks before Christmas, but I know that Christmas mail can be slow and I don't want my brother to be presentless on Christmas Day.

I am called to window #1. The thirtyish guy behind the counter is from South Central. He has a Gheri curl and a Snoop Doggy Dogg drawl. I like him because he keeps pictures of his beautiful daughters by his window and he calls me ma'am. He laughs when he sees the pitiful job I have done trying to seal the box with masking tape. "What did I tell you about this cheap tape?" he says, taking out the industrial-strength good stuff from beneath his desk. "You're lucky you got me and I'm gonna help you out. But do me a favor. Treat yourself to some good quality tape for Christmas, okay?" I laugh and agree.

"Malcolm X. Chambers," he says, reading the label. "That's a helluva name. Is this a present for a man out East?"

I shake my head. "Nah, it's for my little brother." I smile at him. There is something about this guy that just makes my day.

"Have a good one, ma'am," he says. I wish him the same and speed back to my office.

I remember it all so clearly even though it was just one of many gifts I was able to give that season, one of the many trips I took to the post office, one of a million errands to run before I took off for Christmas. It is so clear in my memory because it was one of those rare days when you just feel infused with love. I still believed that loving my brother would help see him through the mess he'd made of his life.

I spend Christmas in Miami with my mother. Not a word from my brother. Neither my mother nor I know how to get in touch with him. New Year's also goes by without a peep. Then sometime in early January, he calls me. "What's up, V?" he says, in that slow guttural delivery that so many guys like him have—an urban panther's growl.

"Malcolm!!!" I screech in what my brother calls my black Valley Girl speak. "Where have you been? What's going on? Why haven't you called?"

He pauses. "Yo, I've been busy. It's rough out here, V."

I don't want to ask because I don't want him to feel that I'm being obnoxious, but I can't help it. "Did you get the coat?"

He pauses again. "Yeah, the coat. Yeah, it was phat. But yo, it was too small so I gave it to my friend 'cause you know, he's smaller than me."

"You did what?" I hiss, barely audible.

"It was too small so I gave it to my friend." The tone in his voice warns me not to push the point any further.

I'm trying to think how not to turn this into a fight. I'm trying to think how to keep my cool. It's been almost a month since my brother's last call and if I piss him off, it could be months before he calls again. "Malcolm," I say as calmly as I can manage. "Malcolm, that coat was an extra-large. How could it not fit?"

My brother sucks his teeth. He knows this conversation is going to drag on and he's not pleased. "Yo, it fits in the shoulders and stuff, right?" he says, lapsing into a sweeter, more explanatory tone. "But the sleeves were too short. And V, I ain't got no gloves."

Whenever we were kids and we tried to outsmart my mom, she always used to turn to us and say, "I was small, too, you know. I wasn't born big. I was your same size and I had your same sneaky thoughts." Sitting on the phone with my brother, I'm thinking the same thing. He must take me for a real fool. Not only do my mother and I buy him this really nice coat that he says he needs badly, he doesn't call to wish us a Merry Christmas or a Happy New Year, let alone thank us. He gives the coat away. No gloves. Please. He lied. He wanted money and instead he got a coat he didn't need or want.

⌣

Now my brother is in jail and I am home in my apartment. I can't sleep. I'm having nightmares. I think about my brother all day, can't shut him off and do my work. I want to ask for a leave of absence at work, but I know that I can't. I am one of only two black editors. There is a constant and incredible pressure for me to succeed. A leave of absence opens the door for talk of incompetence. I can't explain to the people I work with where I've come from, what I'm dealing with. I don't think they would understand. Honestly, I don't think they want to know.

My brother's girlfriend calls to inform me of the prison's visiting hours. I tell her I'll try to make it, but I don't know how. This is one of those times I wish I worked at a factory or that I pushed papers at some nameless, faceless place where nobody cares where you came from or what you're about. But I don't. I have a career. So I am relieved at the end of the week when my brother is released from jail.

A month later, I go to visit my mother for the Fourth of July weekend. We are on the beach and we are wearing matching swimsuits. The day before, we were running around the mall like teenagers, trying to stay one step ahead of my stepfather and my boyfriend. We raced over to the swimsuits on sale. I had taken one over to my mother—cream with mesh netting that I thought would look good against my brown skin. "What do you think of this?" I'd asked her. She turned, laughing. She was holding the same suit. We'd each offered to choose another—dressing alike seems a little too Mommy Dearest—but we loved the design and after my mother pointed out that we live in separate states, we agreed to dress like twins, just for the day.

The waves are crashing hard. It is hurricane season and the ocean is temperamental. My mother still has not learned how to swim. Neither have I. The four of us—two men, two women—stand just a few feet in, jumping the waves when they come, splashing each other in between, until the rain forces us indoors.

In the house, my mother and I sit at the table and talk. The conversation turns inevitably to my brother. Despite all the things we have worked out, how we relate to my brother is the one thing that always makes me feel like I can't stand her. There is a saying that black women mother their sons and raise their daughters; when it comes to my mother, the saying is too true. My mother raised me—there were a lot of hard times, times when we both were hurt and angry; nevertheless I am the woman I am today because of her. But my mother let my brother walk all over her ever since he was a child. Her way of looking after Malcolm was something I'd emulated, not only out of concern for my brother, but to please my mother. Eventually, though, I became so fed up that I got tougher on him. I felt sympathy and wanted to support Malcolm and all the young brothers in his situation. But unlike my mother and the black women of my childhood, I wasn't going to support a black man at the expense of myself. This realization changed everything about how I viewed Malcolm, how I viewed my mother. And how I viewed my father. It was like we were all playing this black woman–black man game and then I moved my piece right off the board.

"If I could do things differently," she says, her voice small and helpless, "I would've been more strict with you children."

I cannot hide my frustration. My fists are clenched, my whole body is stiff. The same rain that we were dashing through a few moments before is giving me a migraine. Although he is twenty-one, she still considers him the measuring stick by which she will be judged as a mother. If he straightens up and does well, she will consider herself a good mother. If he never gets his act together, she will be a failure. So many times I've tried to explain to my mother that there is a difference between circumstances and choice. My brother and I grew up under the same circumstances, but we made a million different choices along the way. The circumstances we could not control, but the choices were ours to make.

"You do your best," my mother is saying. She doesn't listen to what I tell her, and I hate it when she ignores me like this. But the truth is, the same advice I give her, I still find hard to follow. This is one of the things that makes us so much alike. I tell her she's not a failure because of what my brother does or does not do. Yet I feel like I won't ever be able to enjoy my life fully, to enjoy my successes without guilt as long as my brother is out there dealing drugs and getting arrested and beginning to think of jail as a second home.

Once when I was in college, I went swimming alone. It was early spring, March, barely warm enough to go in the water, late in the day, sunset. I went swimming alone though I can barely swim, not knowing how deep the sublime campus river was. I waded into the cool water, deeper and deeper until I got a cramp in my leg and felt myself being pulled under. I was pulled under a footbridge as the dusk of late afternoon turned into the pitch black of night. I could not stay up. My wet palms slid along the mud wall of the riverbank. I felt myself falling and then resigned myself to falling, tired from the struggle. Then I decided to shout. I felt I had to try and shout. So I pushed up and screamed. I screamed again, though my head was full of water and it sounded like a whisper. I was screaming and whispering at the same time. Then I saw someone, then I couldn't see and only felt someone. Then I was lying on the side of the river. Wet and cold, but alive.

I know my brother is out there swimming. I know that he can barely swim. I know that the day is darkening on him. I know that he is sometimes tugged under because he can disappear for weeks on end. I know that he is resigned to falling in. I know that he thinks he will survive as a ghetto merman but he is falling in. I know that in water oxygen is finite. I know that he may come up this time or next, but there may come a time when he does not come up at all.

I know what it's like to nearly drown. When your arms are tired and your legs are dead weight. When your body betrays you and there is nothing and no one to hang on to. Even now I can still summon the fear. And what I fear more than anything is that if my brother spires to the surface, if in a moment of clarity he shouts and it only comes out as a whisper, will anyone hear him? Will anyone help him? Will I be able to hear or help? Or will he, resigned and tired, sink back to the bottomless bottom?

My brother at three was practically mute; he refused to speak until he was almost four years old. He spoke only through me, some strange gibberish that I cannot now recall. Now that my brother is a big strong black man, with big strapping black man problems, I long for our secret language. I imagine that I could whisper those words into his ears and I would become more powerful than his homeboys, that the call of our secret language would be more powerful than the call of the streets. But he is no longer three and I am no longer six, and the words we made up are lost forever.

Meri Nana-Ama Danquah

Writing, I think, is the next best thing to reading. When I was a child, you couldn't tear me away from my books. I would read anywhere and anytime I could. I would even read in the dark. Bedtime was always a problem. "Please, just one more chapter," I would beg. Long after I was supposed to be asleep, my mother would come in to check on me. Most of the time, she would find me crouched by the window with a book, trying to catch any sliver of moonlight that I could through the blinds. "You're going to ruin your eyes," Mum would warn. "Go to sleep. The book will still be there in the morning. The story's not going to change overnight."

My mother worked in a medical office and she would always bring home these free, promotional products that the pharmaceutical company reps used to give them—things like notepads, pens, and calendars, all of which displayed the name of some new drug that was being marketed. One day, when I was about twelve or so, she brought home a bunch of penlights. I thought it was just the most amazing invention. I took three and hid them under my pillow. After that, whenever my mother told me to turn off the bedroom light and go to sleep, I wouldn't complain or beg for more time. I would simply do as I had been told. When she came in to check on me, as she usually did, I would pretend to be fast asleep. As soon as she'd closed the door, I would pull out my book and my penlight and read until my eyelids were too heavy to lift. That went on for a while but, eventually, I got caught. I guess she must have figured out what I was doing because that night she came in to check on me twice. When she opened the door to my room that second time, she didn't seem surprised at all to find me propped up on my bed with my book in one hand and the penlight in the other.

That sense of urgency which I felt back then about reading has carried over into my writing. I want my work to feel seamless, fluid. I want my readers to fall so fully into the world that I have created on the page that they lose all track of their own reality. I want them to stay inside the story until the last page, the last word.

From *Willow Weep for Me: A Black Woman's Journey
Through Depression,* a memoir

DUSK IS MY LEAST favorite time. I favor night over day, but when I watch the orange sun melting into the shadows of the sky, a ball of loneliness rolls down my spine. When Jade arrived, the sun was setting; I was beside myself with grief. There was no room inside of me for conversation or laughter. Normally, I steered clear of social situations if I felt myself dropping into a "mood," but seeing as how Jade was standing in my doorway, that wasn't an option. Fortunately, depression teaches you the fine art of multiplicity. You become adept at wearing the right mask for the right person on the right occasion. I shut my eyes for a second, inhaled deeply through my nostrils and braced myself like an actor preparing to go on stage. After I opened my eyes, I slid my mouth into a perfect Colgate smile.

"Jade," I said enthusiastically. "Are you still up for eating and taking a drive? I wouldn't mind getting out of the house. And it'll probably put Korama right to sleep."

"Yeah," Jade beamed, returning the bright smile I had just given her. Her driver's license was four weeks new. She grew up in Manhattan, pedestrian capital of the world, so she had never felt a pressing need to learn how to drive. That is, until she moved into The Ivy.

"I feel like I'm celebrating my sixteenth birthday ten years too late," she said as she helped me fasten the safety belt to [my daughter] Korama's car seat.

The three of us stopped at a nearby restaurant for dinner. And then we drove around in circles until we ended up on a small, windy road in Rock Creek Park. Korama was still awake in the backseat. We didn't secure her car seat properly so each time Jade made a turn, the seat toppled over in the same direction. Jade's driving left much to be desired.

She and I didn't talk at all. Whenever I turned up the volume on the radio, she turned it back down. "I can't concentrate," she'd snap. The streets along Rock Creek Park were dangerous and it was so dark I couldn't see well through the windshield. I started backseat driving.

"Slow down," I'd yell whenever we hit a rough spot.

"Will you keep quiet?" she'd return.

Neither of us knew the city well enough to navigate along the back roads of the Creek. We got lost.

"Turn here," I'd advise.

"I think I should go straight," she'd demand.

"Go straight," I'd say.

"No, I think I should turn here," she'd protest.

We bickered and bickered until we landed in a narrow dead-end lane. I was afraid Jade wasn't skillful enough to reverse the car without dropping over the small cliff behind us or getting hit by a car coming from the opposite direction.

"Do you want me to turn the car around?" I asked.

"Just keep quiet, okay?" she warned. "You're making me jittery. I feel like I'm driving with my father."

Just as I was about to say something snide, I noticed that I wasn't apart from myself anymore. My mind wasn't tied up with [my sister] Paula, Mum, or some self-deprecating thought. I was fully in that moment, to the point where I was actually enjoying it. I started laughing hysterically.

Jade was not as amused. She didn't say a word. She didn't even look my way. I couldn't tell if she was angry or just pensive. As we neared my apartment, the feelings of sadness and loneliness returned.

"You're a good driver," I told Jade. "I'm sorry about freaking you out."

It was a peace offering. I didn't want her to go away mad. I didn't want her to go away at all. Korama was fast asleep and would probably stay that way through the night. There was nothing waiting for me at home except a stack of books and a few beers. Jade did not respond to my apology. She pulled up to the stop sign at the intersection nearest to my apartment, put on her turn signal and waited for two pedestrians to cross the street. After they were safely on the sidewalk, she started to make her turn but she didn't drive far enough forward before cutting the wheel. The right tires of the car skipped over the curb.

"Oh shit!" she gasped.

Startled, the two pedestrians stopped walking and gaped at us. Jade completed the turn and carefully parallel parked the car in a spot directly in front of [my neighbor] Scott's brownstone. She put on the emergency brake, removed the keys from the ignition, placed her foot on the seat, and leaned her back against the door so she was facing me. She was biting her lower lip, holding back a smile.

"Now, what was that you just said about my driving?"

I looked at Jade and offered her a heartfelt smile. This was the most comfortable I had ever felt with her. She had an air of confidence that usually made me uneasy and insecure.

Neither of us made a move to get out of the car, nor did we feel compelled to chat. I rolled down the window and took a pack of cigarettes from my purse. Jade had never seen me smoke before. Few people had. It was a nasty habit that I tried to hide.

"Do you mind?" I asked.

"Not if you let me bum one."

I had never seen her smoke either. She rolled down her window and took a cigarette from the pack. I held the lighter to her cigarette then lit my own.

"I didn't know you smoked."

She blew a billow of smoke from the side of her mouth out the window.

"I didn't know you smoked either. I think there are a lot of things we don't know about each other," she said.

She took another puff.

"Can I ask you a personal question?"

I shrugged my shoulders.

"Sure." She lifted her other foot up onto the seat and wrapped her free arm around her legs, just below the knees.

"Are you depressed?"

The question didn't register.

"What did you ask me?"

She repeated it.

"Do you suffer from depression?"

There was a certain safety in her eyes that urged me to take a leap of faith.

"Yes," I heard myself say softly. "Yes, I think I do. Why did you, I mean, how did you—"

"I recognize the masks."

"I need a drink," I mumbled, walking into my kitchen. I had just finished moving Korama's cot into the room I used as a work area so that Jade and I would not disturb her. I grabbed two beers and went into the living room. Jade was rummaging through her backpack. She pulled out a tattered green notebook, flipped through its pages until she found what she was looking for. I handed her a beer.

"Here. Read this," she said, pointing to the page.

It was her journal. I sat down, placed the book on my lap, and started to read. The entry was written in the summer, on Jade's birthday.

I am twenty-six years old today and I look at my life. I feel as if I have nothing to show for my entire life but at the same time I recognize that that's not true and that all the work I have done in terms of overcoming my depression and remaining functional within society or even functional for myself has been a great feat. I guess it's dangerous to read into the mainstream culture's definition of what success is. But at this age I had anticipated on being more, on having a lot more in my life. A lot more in terms of my own sanity, my own personal peace. In terms of my own financial status, my career, my own love for myself. Especially in terms of school and right now I don't have any of that. I am still not done with school. Ever since grade school I have had problems with school. And this is something I am just now dealing with. A great deal of the struggle has been in coming to terms with my depression. I have always felt that I just wasn't strong enough. That there was something wrong with me. I have always felt that maybe God hated me and that he chose me to carry a burden of pain for the rest of the world. And I think the hardest part of overcoming, or at least attempting to function within depression is learning how to love myself. This year I will learn how to love myself. I have to.

She had drawn a tiny heart at the end of the entry and placed a question mark beside it. I closed the book, gave her a hug.

"I don't know what to say."

"Do you feel that way, too?" she asked.

I didn't know how to answer so I returned her question with a question.

"Have you learned to love yourself?"

She balled her hands into a fist.

"Sort of, sometimes." She cocked her head to the side, pounded the fist into her thigh. "How about you? Do you love yourself?"

"Yes," I lied. "Of course I do."

The look on her face said that she didn't believe me. I bowed my head and picked at my fingernails.

"Well," I went on without looking up, "I love the me that I have created, you know, the persona, this assertive writer-person that everyone likes. I love being her. As far as the me that I really am deep down inside, I don't know."

I raised my head, met her gaze.

"I really don't know how to answer that question, Jade. I don't know if I love myself."

I grabbed the pack of cigarettes.

"Want one?"

She nodded and helped herself. I lit her cigarette and took a swig of my beer.

"What medication are you on?" she asked.

I pictured myself lying in a hospital bed while a blank-faced nurse stood over me holding out a Dixie cup full of pills.

"Medication?"

I got up to get an ashtray from the kitchen. Even though I had just admitted to Jade—and myself—that I suffered from depression, I suddenly found it difficult to accept the idea. I wanted to change my answer to "no," just like I had done on the hospital intake form. That's how deep my denial was.

"Oh no, girl," I laughed. "I'm not that far gone. There are days when I feel like you did on your birthday, like my life doesn't amount to much, but I hardly think that's cause for medication or a trip to the loony bin. Everybody gets that way sometimes, I suppose. I mean, I haven't had a nervous breakdown or anything."

The episodes I experienced in Los Angeles snuck into my mind, as did the emotional collapse I had when I first moved into my mother's home. I immediately cast them out and finished the point I was making.

"I mean, Jade. I'm just like you. We get down, we deal with it, we pick ourselves back up and we move on."

I put the ashtray on the floor. She rested her cigarette in one of the four grooves carved into its rim.

"I'm on Prozac," she sighed. "Forty milligrams a day."

Suddenly I felt embarrassed and frightened. People on Prozac were said to be unpredictable, even violent. On a television special I had seen, a man on Prozac had shot his wife and three children, then he turned the gun on himself. Another man had deliberately driven his car into a ravine. I wondered if Jade would get out of control. My heart was racing. What if she hurt me or Korama? The calmer part of my consciousness told me I was being paranoid. After all, she certainly had her chance to kill us all when we were on that dead-end road in Rock Creek Park.

"What . . . ," the words were stuck somewhere between my brain and my mouth. "W-w-what does the Prozac do? Does it, I mean are you, can you, h-h-how does it make you feel?"

She picked up on my anxiety and played with it.

"Like slicing my wrists. Got any razors around?"

The hair on my neck and arms stood straight. Jade laughed and touched my hand.

"It's alright, Meri. I'm not crazy. Well, no more than you."

She winked at me, pursed her lips, and picked her cigarette up from the ashtray.

My second wind caught up with me. The fear went away. It was as if I had entered my cool, calm, and collected persona. But I hadn't. I was still myself, the me that I am underneath the masks. From the first time Eugene suggested that I might be suffering from depression I knew he was right. Denying the truth seemed to me the most effective way to overpower it. What happened instead is that it consumed me. My every thought, my every move was either an affirmation ("*Why did I do/think that? That's how depressed people behave/feel.*") or a negation ("*See, I'm having fun. If I were really depressed, I wouldn't be having so much fun.*") of that truth.

Telling Jade that I was depressed did not leave me defenseless. Rather, it gave me a sudden surge of strength and determination. I wanted to know more.

"Tell me about your depression," I begged her. "When did you first realize you were depressed? What did you do? Does it ever go away for good?"

She went into the kitchen to get two more beers.

"Are you in therapy?" she shouted from the kitchen.

"No," I shouted back. When she returned to the living room, she sat down beside me and handed me a beer.

"When did *you* first realize that you were depressed?" Jade asked.

When did I? I scanned my life.

"I don't know. I've always been a sad person. I cry about the stupidest things. I cry at commercials, during cartoons, sometimes I cry about nothing at all. I cry for crying's sake."

"And you're not in therapy?"

"No way. I would never. Tonight was the first time I've ever told anyone. Well, my friend Eugene knew, but he figured it out on his own. He's been after me for months now to see a shrink. Someone in his family suffers from depression. Anyway, Eugene's convinced that my depression is clinical."

"As far as I'm concerned," Jade said, "all depression is clinical. People who are just having a bad day should use another word. They shouldn't say stuff like 'I'm so depressed because I failed a test' or 'I broke a nail and I'm depressed.' They're not depressed. They don't even begin to understand what real depression is."

"What is real depression? How did you know that's what you were feeling?" I wanted a concrete description from her. She swung her head back and studied the ceiling.

"How did I know? It's more like how did I not know? I knew before I knew, if you know what I mean. I was like you. I was always sad, always crying, always lonely, and nothing could change that. It was probably just my fate."

My spirits were waning.

"Do you think it will ever go away?" I asked. "Do you think that people like that, I mean, like us, can change the way we are?"

"Sure. I believe in change. But I don't know if I have the ability to change the fact that I have an illness."

Illness. It seemed like such a weighty word. Acceptance of my vulnerability to depression came in baby steps. Leukemia, cancer, heart disease, AIDS, even schizophrenia—*those* were illnesses. But depression? I wasn't buying it. Jade was slim and statuesque, with cinnamon-colored skin. Her hair was thick with tight, blue-black waves, and she wore it short, like a schoolboy. How could a woman so intelligent, so graceful, so *vibrant* describe herself as ill?

"Even if you were ill all of your life, there had to be one specific moment when you or someone else first realized it."

"There were a lot of those moments. Let's see, when was the first one?

Since I was most likely born this way, I might as well start from day one."
She lit a cigarette. "I was born in Cleveland. My mom got pregnant with
me while she and my dad were on vacation in—"

"Wait a second," I said getting up. "I need to check on Korama. Let
me do that now so I won't interrupt you later."

Jade used the phone to call home while I went into the back room.
Korama was breathing deeply. Her mouth was open and the thumb she
had been sucking was resting on her lower lip. It was cold in that room but
she had kicked the covers off. I pulled them up over her body and tucked
the sides under the mattress. When I touched her thumb to move it away
from her face, she plugged it back into her mouth and sucked heartily
without waking up. I went into the bathroom, threw cold water on my
face, and watched in the mirror as it drifted down my cheeks and along
my jawline.

"This is the face of a depressed person," I said to my reflection. "This
is *my* face." I didn't know how to react to my own words. It was as if I had
entered a trance. The whole evening was starting to feel surreal.

"Is everything alright?" Jade asked from the living room. Her voice
pulled me from my reverie.

"Yup. All done," I said, closing the door behind me. Jade had swiped
the comforter off the bed and wrapped herself in it. I sat across from her.
She offered me part of the comforter. I pushed my feet under the cloth.

"I think I'm going to drop out of college again," she said, more to herself than to me.

"The photography class? Why? I thought you liked it."

"Depression. That's always the reason. That's why I'm living in The Ivy
now. Remember I told you that I took a leave of absence from college?
That's because my depression got really severe . . ."

There was that word again. *Severe.*

"What exactly do you mean by severe?" I asked.

"I mean being totally incapacitated. I had to drop out and move back
in with my folks. It's funny, you know, when other people think of school,
they remember things like being in the band or a play or getting good
grades and awards. The things I remember are depression and therapy and
feeling like I didn't belong. It's gotten in the way of everything I've ever
wanted to be. At the rate I'm going, I'll never get through school."

She had a faraway look in her eyes, the kind people get when they lose themselves in themselves. Her eyes were shimmering but she didn't seem to be on the verge of tears. I propped my back against the wall, closed my eyes, and listened to her voice as if it was music, a sad, sad ballad.

Edwidge Danticat

I wrote "Children of the Sea" while in graduate school at Brown University in Providence, Rhode Island. It was 1992. Shortly after the coup d'état that unseated the constitutional government in Haiti, there was a flood of refugees from Haiti to the United States, most of them arriving in Miami by boat. A large number of the refugees had fled as a result of being persecuted by the de facto military government that had taken over. In spite of the political turmoil in Haiti, few of the refugees received asylum in the United States, something like 5 percent, even though the deposed president of Haiti was himself staying in the United States. While waiting for their asylum cases to be considered, the refugees were kept in the United States' military base in Guantanamo Bay, Cuba, where war prisoners from the world's most notorious terrorist groups would later be imprisoned following the terrorist attacks on the United States on September 11, 2001. Those few Haitian refugees who did receive asylum in the United States and had no family here were later turned over to the care of different Catholic charities throughout the United States, one of which was located in Providence,

Rhode Island, where I was in school. Having few Creole speaking staff, the head of the Catholic charity in Providence came to recruit Haitian students at Brown to spend time with some of the Haitian families and help them run errands. I signed up and "adopted" a family, consisting of a mother and two sons whose father had died at sea. It was while spending time with that family that I learned the details of their time at sea, the reasons they had fled, and why they had risked everything to come to the United States. And thus emerged the threads of the story that would later become "Children of the Sea." While I was with this family and other refugees in Providence, one thing kept coming up over and over again: when they were at sea, what they were most concerned about was disappearing without a trace. They were extremely worried that no one would remember them or think of them again. Their journeys kept reminding me of the Middle Passage, where our ancestors had been forced to board slave ships and cross the Atlantic to an unknown world. I imagined the dead of the Middle Passage reuniting with the dead of this new forced migration and the living descendants of both migrations reuniting on the other side. And thus the story flourished. What I wanted most to convey in this story was this intense fear of being forgotten, of not having one's memory honored, as well as the joy of being recognized on the other side, which both groups had faced. In some ways, we, the members of the African Diaspora, are all children of the sea, a sea that is as endless as our love for and, sadly enough at times, our fear of each other.

Children of the Sea

From *Krik? Krak!*, a short-story collection

THEY SAY BEHIND the mountains are more mountains. Now I know it's true. I also know there are timeless waters, endless seas, and lots of people in this world whose names don't matter to anyone but themselves. I look up at the sky and I see you there. I see you crying like a crushed snail, the way you cried when I helped you pull out your first loose tooth. Yes, I did love you then. Somehow when I looked at you, I thought of fiery red ants. I wanted you to dig your fingernails into my skin and drain out all my blood.

I don't know how long we'll be at sea. There are thirty-six other deserting souls on this little boat with me. White sheets with bright red spots float as our sail.

When I got on board I thought I could still smell the semen and the innocence lost to those sheets. I look up there and I think of you and all those times you resisted. Sometimes I felt like you wanted to, but I know you wanted me to respect you. You thought I was testing your will, but all I wanted was to be near you. Maybe it's like you've always said. I imagine too much. I am afraid I am going to start having nightmares once we get deep at sea. I really hate having the sun in my face all day long. If you see me again, I'll be so dark.

Your father will probably marry you off now, since I am gone. Whatever you do, please don't marry a soldier. They're almost not human.

⌣

haiti est comme tu l'as laissé. yes, just the way you left it. bullets day and night. same hole. same everything. i'm tired of the whole mess. i get so cross and irritable. i pass the time by chasing roaches around the house. i pound my heel on their heads. they make me so mad. everything makes me mad. i am cramped inside all day. they've closed the schools since the army took over. no one is mentioning the old president's name. papa burnt all his campaign posters and old buttons. manman buried her buttons in the hole behind the house. she thinks he might come back. she says she will unearth them when he does. no one comes out of their house. not a single person. papa wants me to throw out those tapes of your radio shows. i destroyed some music tapes, but i still have your voice. i thank god you got out when you did. all the other youth federation members have disappeared. no one has heard from them. i think they might all be in prison. maybe they're all dead. papa worries a little about you. he doesn't hate you as much as you think. the other day i heard him asking manman, do you think the boy is dead? manman said she didn't know. i think he regrets being so mean to you. i don't sketch my butterflies anymore because i don't even like seeing the sun. besides, manman says that butterflies can bring news. the bright ones bring happy news and the black ones warn us of deaths. we have our whole lives ahead of us. you used to say that, remember? but then again things were so very different then.

⌣⌐

There is a pregnant girl on board. She looks like she might be our age. Nineteen or twenty. Her face is covered with scars that look like razor marks. She is short and speaks in a singsong that reminds me of the villagers in the north. Most of the other people on the boat are much older than I am. I have heard that a lot of these boats have young children on board. I am glad this one does not. I think it would break my heart watching some little boy or girl every single day on this sea, looking into their empty faces to remind me of the hopelessness of the future in our country. It's hard enough with the adults. It's hard enough with me.

I used to read a lot about America before I had to study so much for the university exams. I am trying to think, to see if I read anything more about Miami. It is sunny. It doesn't snow there like it does in other parts of America. I can't tell exactly how far we are from there. We might be barely out of our own shores. There are no borderlines on the sea. The whole thing looks like one. I cannot even tell if we are about to drop off the face of the earth. Maybe the world is flat and we are going to find out, like the navigators of old. As you know, I am not very religious. Still I pray every night that we won't hit a storm. When I do manage to sleep, I dream that we are caught in one hurricane after another. I dream that the winds come out of the sky and claim us for the sea. We go under and no one hears from us again.

I am more comfortable now with the idea of dying. Not that I have completely accepted it, but I know that it might happen. Don't be mistaken. I really do not want to be a martyr. I know I am no good to anybody dead, but if that is what's coming, I know I cannot just scream at it and tell it to go away.

I hope another group of young people can do the radio show. For a long time that radio show was my whole life. It was nice to have radio like that for a while, where we could talk about what we wanted from government, what we wanted for the future of our country.

There are a lot of Protestants on this boat. A lot of them see themselves as Job or the Children of Israel. I think some of them are hoping something will plunge down from the sky and part the sea for us. They say the Lord gives and the Lord takes away. I have never given very much. What was there to take away?

if only i could kill. if i knew some good *wanga* magic, i would wipe them off the face of the earth. a group of students got shot in front of fort dimanche prison today. they were demonstrating for the bodies of the radio six. that is what they are calling you all. the radio six. you have a name. you have a reputation. a lot of people think you are dead like the others. they want the bodies turned over to the families. this afternoon, the army finally did give some bodies back. they told the families to go collect them at the rooms for indigents at the morgue. our neighbor madan roger came home with her son's head and not much else. honest to god, it was just his head. at the morgue, they say a car ran over him and took the head off his body. when madan roger went to the morgue, they gave her the head. by the time we saw her, she had been carrying the head all over port-au-prince. just to show what's been done to her son. the macoutes by the house were laughing at her. they asked her if that was her dinner. it took ten people to hold her back from jumping on them. they would have killed her, the dogs. i will never go outside again. not even in the yard to breathe the air. they are always watching you, like vultures. at night i can't sleep. i count the bullets in the dark. i keep wondering if it is true. did you really get out? i wish there was some way i could be sure that you really went away. yes, i will. i will keep writing like we promised to do. i hate it, but i will keep writing. you keep writing too, okay? and when we see each other again, it will seem like we lost no time.

Today was our first real day at sea. Everyone was vomiting with each small rocking of the boat. The faces around me are showing their first charcoal layer of sunburn. "Now we will never be mistaken for Cubans," one man said. Even though some of the Cubans are black too. The man said he was once on a boat with a group of Cubans. His boat had stopped to pick up the Cubans on an island off the Bahamas. When the Coast Guard came for them, they took the Cubans to Miami and sent him back to Haiti. Now he was back on the boat with some papers and documents to show that the police in Haiti were after him. He had a broken leg too, in case there was any doubt.

One old lady fainted from sunstroke. I helped revive her by rubbing some of the salt water on her lips. During the day it can be so hot. At night, it is so cold. Since there are no mirrors, we look at each others faces to see just how frail and sick we are starting to look.

Some of the women sing and tell stories to each other to appease the vomiting. Still, I watch the sea. At night, the sky and the sea are one. The stars look so huge and so close. They make for very bright reflections in the sea. At times I feel like I can just reach out and pull a star down from the sky as though it is a breadfruit or calabash or something that could be of use to us on this journey.

When we sing, *Beloved Haiti, there is no place like you. I had to leave you before I could understand you,* some of the women start crying. At times, I just want to stop in the middle of the song and cry myself. To hide my tears, I pretend like I am getting another attack of nausea, from the sea smell. I no longer join in the singing.

You probably do not know much about this, because you have always been so closely watched by your father in that well-guarded house with your genteel mother. No, I am not making fun of you for this. If anything, I am jealous. If I was a girl, maybe I would have been at home and not out politicking and getting myself into something like this. Once you have been at sea for a couple of days, it smells like every fish you have ever eaten, every crab you have ever caught, every jellyfish that has ever bitten your leg. I am so tired of the smell. I am also tired of the way the people on this boat are starting to stink. The pregnant girl, Célianne, I don't know how she takes it. She stares into space all the time and rubs her stomach.

I have never seen her eat. Sometimes the other women offer her a piece of bread and she takes it, but she has no food of her own. I cannot help feeling like she will have this child as soon as she gets hungry enough.

She woke up screaming the other night. I thought she had a stomach ache. Some water started coming into the boat in the spot where she was sleeping. There is a crack at the bottom of the boat that looks as though, if it gets any bigger, it will split the boat in two. The captain cleared us aside and used some tar to clog up the hole. Everyone started asking him if it was okay, if they were going to be okay. He said he hoped the Coast Guard would find us soon.

You can't really go to sleep after that. So we all stared at the tar by the moonlight. We did this until dawn. I cannot help but wonder how long this tar will hold out.

⌒

papa found your tapes. he started yelling at me, asking if i was crazy keeping them. he is just waiting for the gasoline ban to be lifted so we can get out of the city. he is always pestering me these days because he cannot go out driving in his van. all the american factories are closed. he kept yelling at me about the tapes. he called me selfish, and he asked if i hadn't seen or heard what was happening to man-crazy whores like me. i shouted that i wasn't a whore. he had no business calling me that. he pushed me against the wall for disrespecting him. he spat in my face. i wish those macoutes would kill him. i wish he would catch a bullet so we could see how scared he really is. he said to me, i didn't send your stupid trouble maker away. i started yelling at him. yes, you did. yes, you did. yes, you did, you pig peasant. i don't know why i said that. he slapped me and kept slapping me really hard until manman came and grabbed me away from him. i wish one of those bullets would hit me.

⌒

The tar is holding up so far. Two days and no more leaks. Yes, I am finally an African. I am even darker than your father. I wanted to buy a straw hat from one of the ladies, but she would not sell it to me for the last two gourdes I have left in change. Do you think your money is worth anything to me here? she asked me. Sometimes, I forget where I am. If I keep day-dreaming like I have been doing, I will walk off the boat and go for a stroll.

The other night I dreamt that I died and went to heaven. This heaven was nothing like I expected. It was at the bottom of the sea. There were starfishes and mermaids all around me. The mermaids were dancing and singing in Latin like the priests do at the cathedral during Mass. You were there with me too, at the bottom of the sea. You were with your family, off to the side. Your father was acting like he was better than everyone else and he was standing in front of a sea cave blocking you from my view. I tried to talk to you, but every time I opened my mouth, water bubbles came out. No sounds.

they have this thing now that they do. if they come into a house and there is a son and mother there, they hold a gun to their heads. they make the son sleep with his mother. if it is a daughter and father, they do the same things. some nights papa sleeps at his brother's, uncle pressoir's house. uncle pressoir sleeps at our house, just in case they come. that way papa will never be forced to lie down in bed with me. instead, uncle pressoir would be forced to, but that would not be so bad. we know a girl who had a child by her father that way. that is what papa does not want to happen, even if he is killed. there is still no gasoline to buy. otherwise we would be in ville rose already. papa has a friend who is going to get him some gasoline from a soldier. as soon as we get the gasoline, we are going to drive quick and fast until we find civilization. that's how papa puts it, civilization. he says things are not as bad in the provinces. i am still not talking to him. i don't think i ever will. man-man says it is not his fault. he is trying to protect us. he cannot protect us. only god can protect us. the soldiers can come and do with us what they want. that makes papa feel weak, she says. he gets angry when he feels weak. why should he be angry with me? i am not one of the pigs with the machine guns. she asked me what really happened to you. she said she saw your parents before they left for the provinces. they did not want to tell her anything. i told her you took a boat after they raided the radio station. you escaped and took a boat to heaven knows where. she said, he was going to make a good man, that boy. sharp, like a needle point, that boy, he took the university exams a year before everyone else in this area. manman has respect for people with ambitions. she said papa did not want you for me because it did not seem as though you were going to do any better for me than he and manman could. he wants me to find a man who will do me some good. someone who will make sure that i have more than i have now. it is not enough for a girl to be pretty anymore. we are not that well connected in society. the kind of man that papa wants for me would never have anything to do with me. all anyone can hope for is just a tiny bit of love, manman says, like a drop in a cup if you can get it, or a waterfall, a flood if you can get that too. we do not have all that many high-up connections, she says, but you are an educated girl. what she count for educated is not much to anyone but us anyway. they should be announcing the university exams on the radio next week. then i will know if you passed. i will listen for your name.

~

We spent most of yesterday telling stories. Someone says, Krik? You answer, Krak! And they say, I have many stories I could tell you, and then they go on and tell these stories to you, but mostly to themselves. Sometimes it feels like we have been at sea longer than the many years that I have been on this earth. The sun comes up and goes down. That is how you know it has been a whole day. I feel like we are sailing for Africa. Maybe we will go to Guinin, to live with the spirits, to be with everyone who has come and has died before us. They would probably turn us away from there too. Someone has a transistor and sometimes we listen to radio from the Bahamas. They treat Haitians like dogs in the Bahamas, a woman says. To them, we are not human. Even though their music sounds like ours. Their people look like ours. Even though we had the same African fathers who probably crossed these same seas together.

Do you want to know how people go to the bathroom on the boat? Probably the same way they did on those slaves ships years ago. They set aside a little corner for that. When I have to pee, I just pull it, lean over the rail, and do it very quickly. When I have to do the other thing, I rip a piece of something, squat down and do it, and throw the waste in the sea. I am always embarrassed by the smell. It is so demeaning to have to squat in front of so many people. People turn away, but not always. At times I wonder if there is really land on the other side of the sea. Maybe the sea is endless. Like my love for you.

⁓

last night they came to madan roger's house. papa hurried inside as soon as madan roger's screaming started. the soldiers were looking for her son. madan roger was screaming, you killed him already. we buried his head. you can't kill him twice. they were shouting at her, do you belong to the youth federation with those vagabonds who were on the radio? she was yelling, do i look like a youth to you? can you identify your son's other associates? they asked her. papa had us tiptoe from the house into the latrine out back. we could hear it all from there. i thought i was going to choke on the smell of rotting poupou. they kept shouting at madan roger, did your son belong to the youth federation? wasn't he on the radio talking about the police? did he say, down with the tonton macoutes? did he say, down with the army? he said that the military had to go; didn't he write slogans? he had meetings, didn't he? he demonstrated on the streets. you should have advised him better. she cursed on their mothers' graves. she just came out and shouted it, i hope your mothers will never rest in their cursed graves! she was just shouting it out, you killed him once already! you want to kill me too? go ahead. i don't care anymore. i'm dead already. you have already done the worst to me that you can do. you have killed my soul. they kept at it, asking her questions at the top of their voices: was your son a traitor? tell me all the names of his friends who were traitors just like him. madan roger finally shouts, yes, he was one! he belonged to that group. he was on the radio. he was on the streets at these demonstrations. he hated you like i hate you criminals. you killed him. they started to pound at her. you can hear it. you can hear the guns coming down on her head. manman whispers to papa, you can't just let them kill her. go and give them some money like you gave them for your daughter. papa says, the only money i have left is to get us out of here tomorrow. manman whispers, we cannot just stay here and let them kill her. manman starts moving like she is going out the door. papa grabs her neck and pins her to the latrine wall. tomorrow we are going to ville rose, he says. you will not spoil that for the family. you will not put us in that situation. you will not get us killed. going out there will be like trying to raise the dead. she is not dead yet, manman says, maybe we can help her. i will make you stay if i have to, he says to her. my mother buries her face in the latrine wall. she starts to cry. you can hear madan roger screaming. they are beating her, pounding on her until you don't hear anything else. manman tells papa, you cannot let them kill somebody just because you are afraid. papa says, oh yes, you *can* let them kill somebody because you are afraid. they are the law. it is their right. we are just being good citizens, following the law of the land. it has happened before all over this country and tonight it will happen again and there is nothing we can do.

⌣

Célianne spent the night groaning. She looks like she has been ready for a while, but maybe the child is being stubborn. She just screamed that she is bleeding. There is an older woman here who looks like she has had a lot of children herself. She says Célianne is not bleeding at all. Her water sack has broken.

The only babies I have ever seen right after birth are baby mice. Their skin looks veil thin. You can see all the blood vessels and all their organs. I have always wanted to poke them to see if my finger would go all the way through the skin.

I have moved to the other side of the boat so I will not have to look *inside* Célianne. People are just watching. The captain asks the midwife to keep Célianne steady so she will not rock any more holes into the boat. Now we have three cracks covered with tar. I am scared to think of what would happen if we had to choose among ourselves who would stay on the boat and who should die. Given the choice to make a decision like that, we would all act like vultures, including me.

The sun will set soon. Someone says that this child will be just another pair of hungry lips. At least it will have its mother's breasts, says an old man. Everyone will eat their last scraps of food today.

⌣

there is a rumor that the old president is coming back. there is a whole bunch of people going to the airport to meet him. papa says we are not going to stay in port-au-prince to find out if this is true or if it is a lie. they are all selling gasoline at the market again. the carnival groups have taken to the streets. we are heading the other way, to ville rose. maybe there i will be able to sleep at night. it is not going to turn out well with the old president coming back, manman now says. people are just too hopeful, and sometimes hope is the biggest weapon of all to use against us. people will believe in anything. they will claim to see the christ return and march on the cross backwards if there is enough hope. manman told papa that you took the boat. papa told me before we left this morning that he thought himself a bad father for everything that happened. he says a father should be able to speak to his children like a civilized man. all the craziness here has made him feel like he cannot do that anymore. all he wants to do is live. he and manman have not said a word to one another since we left the latrine. i know that papa does not hate us, not in the way that i hate those soldiers, those macoutes, and all those people here who shoot guns. on our way to ville rose, we saw dogs licking two dead faces. one of them was a little boy who was lying on the side of the road with the sun in his dead open eyes. we saw a soldier shoving a woman out of a hut, calling her a witch. he was shaving the woman's head, but of course we never stopped. papa didn't want to go in madan roger's house and check on her before we left. he thought the soldiers might still be there. papa was driving the van real fast. i thought he was going to kill us. we stopped at an open market on the way. manman got some black cloth for herself and for me. she cut the cloth in two pieces and we wrapped them around our head to mourn madan roger. when i am used to ville rose, maybe i will sketch you some butterflies, depending on the news that they bring me.

Célianne had a girl baby. The woman acting as a midwife is holding the baby to the moon and whispering prayers. . . . *God, this child You bring into the world, please guide her as You please through all her days on this earth.* The baby has not cried.

We had to throw out extra things in the sea because the water is beginning to creep in slowly. The boat needs to be lighter. My two gourdes in change had to be thrown overboard as an offering to Agwé, the spirit of the water. I heard the captain whisper to someone yesterday that they might have to *do something* with some of the people who never recovered from seasickness. I am afraid that soon they may ask me to throw out this notebook. We might all have to strip down to the way we were born, to keep ourselves from drowning.

Célianne's child is a beautiful child. They are calling her Swiss, because the word *Swiss* was written on the small knife they used to cut her umbilical cord. If she was my daughter, I would call her soleil, sun, moon, or star, after the elements. She still hasn't cried. There is gossip circulating about how Célianne became pregnant. Some people are saying that she had an affair with a married man and her parents threw her out. Gossip spreads here like everywhere else.

Do you remember our silly dreams? Passing the university exams and then studying hard to go until the end, the farthest of all that we can go in school. I know your father might never approve of me. I was going to try to win him over. He would have to cut out my heart to keep me from loving you. I hope you are writing like you promised. Jésus, Marie, Joseph! Everyone smells so bad. They get into arguments and they say to one another, "It is only my misfortune that would lump me together with an indigent like you." Think of it. They are fighting about being superior when we all might drown like straw.

There is an old toothless man leaning over to see what I am writing. He is sucking on the end of an old wooden pipe that has not seen any fire for a very long time now. He looks like a painting. Seeing things simply, you could fill a museum with the sight you have here. I still feel like such a coward for running away. Have you heard anything about my parents? Last time I saw them on the beach, my mother had a *kriz*. She just fainted on the sand. I saw her coming to as we started sailing away. But of course I don't know if she is doing all right.

The water is really piling into the boat. We take turns pouring bowls of it out. I don't know what is keeping the boat from splitting in two. Swiss isn't crying. They keep slapping her behind, but she is not crying.

⌒

of course the old president didn't come. they arrested a lot of people at the airport, shot a whole bunch of them down. i heard it on the radio. while we were eating tonight, i told papa that i love you. i don't know if it will make a difference. i just want him to know that i have loved somebody in my life. in case something happens to one of us, i think he should know this about me, that i have loved somebody besides only my mother and father in my life. i know you would understand. you are the one for large noble gestures. i just wanted him to know that i was capable of loving somebody. he looked me straight in the eye and said nothing to me. i love you until my hair shivers at the thought of anything happening to you. papa just turned his face away like he was rejecting my very birth. i am writing you from under the banyan tree in the yard in our new house. there are only two rooms and a tin roof that makes music when it rains, especially when there is hail, which falls like angry tears from heaven. there is a stream down the hill from the house, a stream that is too shallow for me to drown myself. manman and i spend a lot of time talking under the banyan tree. she told me today that sometimes you have to choose between your father and the man you love. her whole family did not want her to marry papa because he was a gardener from ville rose and her family was from the city and some of them had even gone to university. she whispered everything under the banyan tree in the yard so as not to hurt his feelings. i saw him looking at us hard from the house. i heard him clearing his throat like he heard us anyway, like we hurt him very deeply somehow just by being together.

⌣

Célianne is lying with her head against the side of the boat. The baby still will not cry. They both look very peaceful in all this chaos. Célianne is holding her baby tight against her chest. She just cannot seem to let herself throw it in the ocean. I asked her about the baby's father. She keeps repeating the story now with her eyes closed, her lips barely moving.

She was home one night with her mother and brother Lionel when some ten or twelve soldiers burst into the house. The soldiers held a gun to Lionel's head and ordered him to lie down and become intimate with his mother. Lionel refused. Their mother told him to go ahead and obey the soldiers because she was afraid that they would kill Lionel on the spot if he put up more of a fight. Lionel did as his mother told him, crying as the soldiers laughed at him, pressing the gun barrels farther and farther into his neck.

Afterwards, the soldiers tied up Lionel and their mother, then they each took turns raping Célianne. When they were done, they arrested Lionel, accusing him of moral crimes. After that night, Célianne never heard from Lionel again.

That same night, Célianne cut her face with a razor so that no one would know who she was. Then as her facial scars were healing, she started throwing up and getting rashes. Next thing she knew, she was getting big. She found out about the boat and got on. She is fifteen.

⌣

manman told me the whole story today under the banyan tree. the bastards were coming to get me. they were going to arrest me. they were going to peg me as a member of the youth federation and then take me away. papa heard about it. he went to the post and paid them money, all the money he had. our house in port-au-prince and all the land his father had left him, he gave it all away to save my life. this is why he is so mad. tonight manman told me this under the banyan tree. i have no words to thank him for this. i don't know how. you must love him for this, manman says, you must. it is something you can never forget, the sacrifice he has made. i cannot bring myself to say thank you. now he is more than my father. he is a man who gave everything he had to save my life. on the radio tonight, they read the list of names of people who passed the university exams. you passed.

⌒

We got some relief from the seawater coming in. The captain used the last of his tar, and most of the water is staying out for a while. Many people have volunteered to throw Célianne's baby overboard for her. She will not let them. They are waiting for her to go to sleep so they can do it, but she will not sleep. I never knew before that dead children looked purple. The lips are the most purple because the baby is so dark. Purple like the sea after the sun has set.

Célianne is slowly drifting off to sleep. She is very tired from the labor. I do not want to touch the child. If anybody is going to throw it in the ocean, I think it should be her. I keep thinking, they have thrown every piece of flesh that followed the child out of her body into the water. They are going to throw the dead baby in the water. Won't these things attract sharks?

Célianne's fingernails are buried deep in the child's naked back. The old man with the pipe just asked, "Kompé, what are you writing?" I told him, "My will."

⌒

i am getting used to ville rose. there are butterflies here, tons of butterflies. so far none has landed on my hand, which means they have no news for me. i cannot always bathe in the stream near the house because the water is freezing cold. the only time it feels just right is at noon, and then there are a dozen eyes who might see me bathing. i solved that by getting a bucket of water in the morning and leaving it in the sun and then bathing myself once it is night under the banyan tree. the banyan now is my most trusted friend. they say banyans can last hundreds of years. even the branches that lean down from them become like trees themselves. a banyan could become a forest, manman says, if it were given a chance. from the spot where i stand under the banyan, i see the mountains, and behind those are more mountains still. so many mountains that are bare like rocks. i feel like all those mountains are pushing me farther and farther away from you.

⌒

She threw it overboard. I watched her face knot up like a thread, and then she let go. It fell in a splash, floated for a while, and then sank. And quickly after that she jumped in too. And just as the baby's head sank, so did hers. They went together like two bottles beneath a waterfall. The shock lasts only so long. There was no time to even try and save her. There was no question of it. The sea in that spot is like the sharks that live there. It has no mercy.

They say I have to throw my notebook out. The old man has to throw out his hat and his pipe. The water is rising again and they are scooping it out. I asked for a few seconds to write this last page and then promised that I would let it go. I know you will probably never see this, but it was nice imagining that I had you here to talk to.

I hope my parents are alive. I asked the old man to tell them what happened to me, if he makes it anywhere. He asked me to write his name in "my book." I asked him for his full name. It is Justin Moïse André Nozius Joseph Frank Osnac Maximilien. He says it all with such an air that you would think him a king. The old man says, "I know a Coast Guard ship is coming. It came to me in my dream." He points to a spot far into the distance. I look where he is pointing. I see nothing. From here, ships must be like a mirage in the desert.

I must throw my book out now. It goes down to them, Célianne and her daughter and all those children of the sea who might soon be claiming me.

I go to them now as though it was always meant to be, as though the very day that my mother birthed me, she had chosen me to live life eternal, among the children of the deep blue sea, those who have escaped the chains of slavery to form a world beneath the heavens and the blood-drenched earth where you live.

Perhaps I was chosen from the beginning of time to live there with Agwé at the bottom of the sea. Maybe this is why I dreamed of the starfish and the mermaids having the Catholic Mass under the sea. Maybe this was my invitation to go. In any case, I know that my memory of you will live even there as I too become a child of the sea.

today i said thank you. i said thank you, papa, because you saved my life. he groaned and just touched my shoulder, moving his hand quickly away like a butterfly. and then there it was, the black butterfly floating around us. i began to run and run so it wouldn't land on me, but it had already carried its news. i know what must have happened. tonight i listened to manman's transistor under the banyan tree. all i hear from the radio is more killing in port-au-prince. the pigs are refusing to let up. i don't know what's going to happen, but i cannot see staying here forever. i am writing to you from the bottom of the banyan tree. manman says that banyan trees are holy and sometimes if we call the gods from beneath them, they will hear our voices clearer. now there are always butterflies around me, black ones that i refuse to let find my hand. i throw big rocks at them, but they are always too fast. last night on the radio, i heard that another boat sank off the coast of the bahamas. i can't think about you being in there in the waves. my hair shivers. from here, i cannot even see the sea. behind these mountains are more mountains and more black butterflies still and a sea that is endless like my love for you.

Debra J. Dickerson

*I will always wonder whether if I had been born to privilege, I would
be a writer. There is contempt and snobbery there, true, but there is also
something real and unpolitical. That something is the knowledge that
my writing springs from a sense of confused displacement and anger.*

*In the early 1970s, growing up in a world, a country, a household
that told poor, black girls to keep quiet and keep cleaning, I thought I
was a freak whose head was going to explode. I was an A student: I
knew that America was the land of the free, the home of the brave. But
how could I be free when I was confined to a ghetto? If I had to defer to
everyone, and God knows I had to, how could I ever exhibit bravery?
I read the canon hungrily—it being all the writing that I knew
existed—and I accepted that it encompassed all of human experience.
This I would legibly, painstakingly spout on all my A+ composition
papers. So why wasn't my Afro'd self encompassed in Melville or Brontë
or Dickens? I knew I didn't live there, and it broke my heart. I wanted
nothing so much as for all the stories to be true.*

Grown up, I realized that I felt confused and displaced and bro-

kenhearted because I was continually lied to and pressured to repeat the lies. I was airbrushed from a world that nonetheless required my obedience, my quiescence, my labor, my gratitude, and my self-hatred. I was told I was free, but I was herded like a cow to the back of every line. I was told I was equal, but knew better than to approach a white man in a suit or a black man in anger. I had as much opportunity as anyone else but was encouraged to go vo-tech rather than college prep. The biggest lie was that being free and equal, all of my problems were my fault and my fault alone. It's worse than a lie: it is a sin.

And that's why I write: to stop being complicit in the sin.

Beginning Again

From *An American Story*, a memoir

My Left Turn

At that point, I'd rarely read a magazine, a newspaper, or a work of (non-Randian) nonfiction. The 1984 elections were coming up, so I assigned myself the task of following the election closely. A staunch Reagan supporter, I relished the notion of following his every move. I began reading the *Washington Times* and the *Washington Post* every day, very much looking forward to using the former to prove how duplicitous was the latter.

Reagan was the first president I was fully aware of, and his decision to bomb Grenada, instead of merely yelling at it, impressed me greatly. In my simplistic mind, the president came as a package deal with the military, the institution I lived and breathed, the institution that saved my life. His conservatism and blame-the-victim ethos resonated squarely with my GI world. Based solely on the word of mouth of those around me, I bought his whole tough-talking, lock-em-up, cut-em-off-welfare shtick. Or, I did before I paid anything like close attention to him. A month later I was reeling with confusion. A month after that, I was howling with anger. Another month—I was laughing uncontrollably. The man was a moron. A sexist, a racist, and a howling elitist to boot, but by far his biggest crime was his imbecility. I was learning that my hero was neither honest nor bright.

I went out of my way to see him on television, the vaunted Great Communicator, hoping that would change things for me, but that actually made it worse. Though it would take more time before I gave up the ghost of my conservatism, I scoffed at the notion of his communicative genius. He talked to the nation like we were idiots or toddlers or toddling idiots. It was so obviously contrived, so obviously the grade B ham reciting the lines his controllers wrote for him.

The *Times* and the *Post* were not enough; I had to have more.

After I sucked all the knowledge I could out of my textbooks, I got recommendations from my professors for extracurricular nonfiction reading. Soon, I couldn't get enough news and analysis. I began reading newsmagazines. I was appalled by the state of the world. I'd had no idea.

Shielded by my parents, lost in books and my own misery as I grew up, overseas for two years, and insulated from the Reagan recession by my government job, I'd had no idea how bad things were for working people. With my new wide-focus perspective and all those pesky facts, as a college student in 1984 and finally thinking for myself, I began to see my relatives' layoffs and evictions differently. Maybe every detail of life was *not* completely within the control of the individual. Not that I gave in easily. There were spirited, even book-throwing arguments in my classes between us military conservatives and the civilian liberals. For the first time, none of the right-wing things I spouted went uncontested. My professors and classmates made points I had never considered before and could not easily dismiss. I had to fight for my rhetorical life in the classroom, and I argued the conservative cause far longer than I actually wanted to simply because I was still a bad loser. A prelaw course, especially, made it impossible to argue that individuals exercise anything like the unfettered freedom of will which justifies leaving every man for himself.

I began to view my relatives' struggles with more complexity. Every time I called home, another one of them would have been summarily let go from a job and be frantically scrabbling for a new one. They wanted to work, even though the jobs they were able to get barely afforded them a decent living. The long lines to apply for menial jobs that I saw on TV and in the papers told me that most people want to work. It maddened me that they wouldn't break the cycle with a degree, investments, or entrepreneurship, but for the first time, it occurred to me that some people just want jobs. You need money to live, so they work simply for money and look elsewhere to find the meaning that humans need to survive. They don't aspire to be CEOs, they don't aspire to work that fulfills or challenges—some people just want to exchange labor for money in a pleasant environment and get back home to their families.

One of the most arresting images I've ever seen was of those thousands of people shivering in a Chicago snowstorm as they waited to apply for hotel lackey jobs. Soon after, when the millionaire aristocrat Reagan thumbed through the want ads to prove that people could work if they really wanted to, I almost had an aneurysm. How could an honest person say such a thing? It was patently obvious that people were being buffeted by forces much larger than themselves, but I couldn't get my military friends to make that simple acknowledgment. We could disagree about what our social response to that should be, I argued, but not about that basic reality.

But no, I had to sit through pious stories about their poor immigrant parents who came here with nothing, or about the guy from their home-town who sold tomatoes door to door from a little red wagon rather than accept government handouts. They posited a world wherein every individual was completely autonomous and in control of his environment. Their analysis was that some people just don't want to work or that people have to live with the consequences of their actions. It was Joe Six-pack's fault that Reagan ballooned the deficit, that he broke the unions, that he deregulated everything? Even if some people chose poorly and, for example, dropped out of high school or had an illegitimate child—should one teenage mistake doom them for the rest of their lives? Is that really what's best for America? I could never understand liberal opposition to work-fare—there is no dignity in handouts, I've always believed. Also, people are rational; they'll factor the specifics of any given welfare regime into their choices. However, workfare, as usually espoused, is more punitive and humiliating than loving but strict. If a welfare mom has the brains to be an astrophysicist, are we really better off forcing her to pick up trash on the highway in exchange for her welfare pittance each month? Some will aspire no further than manual labor and every society needs manual labor-ers—but others pine for more. People from the lower socioeconomic classes need direction and support to aim high; they don't need the government to help them underachieve. Why not help as many citizens as possible maximize their potential and then require them to pay the cost of it back either monetarily (like my college loans) or through substantive community service (like working for low pay in underserved areas)? My conservative coworkers just rolled their eyes, called me a bleeding-heart liberal, and sermonized about giving people "something for nothing."

Even if your marginal existence is your own fault, I couldn't help wondering, is it really in our societal best interest to let people starve, to poorly educate them? Hopeless people commit crimes, so let's feed and educate them so they don't climb through our windows at night. Incarceration is so much more expensive and just about guarantees that the incarcerated will remain predators unable to support themselves legally: educated people commit white-collar crimes, the illiterate draw blood. What could be more conservative than crime prevention? But in response to my arguments about the relationship between lack of education and crime, all I'd get were sanctimonious non sequiturs like, "Nobody ever gave me anything" and "Build more prisons." I couldn't even get them to concede the bare-bones notion that crime reduction and prevention were preferable to high prison occupancy. Some people belong in prison, they'd sniff. I actually had a four-against-one debate once wherein my coworkers argued that inmates should be offered only the Bible during their incarceration. No exercise, no classes, no TV, no work—just sitting on their beds reading the Bible from five to ten. The fact that prison guards would resist such a regime more than any goo-goo liberal fell on deaf ears. My continued reading of the right-wing press only hastened my looming defection. I was used to the intellectual dishonesty of the left and black apologists—they pushed me right. But then, the intellectual shamelessness and moral clay feet of conservatives pushed me left. The left annoys me but the right insults my intelligence.

I was in a constant state of intellectual and emotional turmoil. It was my college angst all over again: who am I? What's my relationship to other blacks, to America? How am I supposed to figure out what to do with my life? Why can't I stop thinking about politics? I felt strong and confident but . . . toward what end? All I had were questions; I needed answers. When my commander called to tell me I'd been accepted into Officers' Training School, all I could think was, Now what? My coworkers were cheering and clapping and tossing papers at me like oversized confetti. I was faking a smile and thinking, Now what do I shoot for? Why isn't this enough? I was happy, just not satisfied.

I lay in my bed one night all alone, my mind whirring with plans and counterstrategies, when a sudden thought imprinted itself on my brain. Apropos of nothing, I said aloud, "I feel like I've been mugged." I realized what my Osan malaise had truly been about. I was exhausted. Worn out by my own life. The effort of dragging myself from the working class to the middle class, though successful, had nearly killed me. Even my fixation on physical fitness had been just another way of simultaneously gaining control over my life and expressing a deep-seated anger. I never had to consciously decide between conventional attractiveness and the female bodybuilder's stylized look because once I started dealing with the root of my behaviors, I never again worked out with the same intensity. I couldn't.

Where I'd once had a "let them eat cake because it's their own fault they don't have bread" attitude about those I'd left behind, by the time I graduated in 1984 I was feeling not so much vindicated as humble. No wonder so many people give up or never try at all; it shouldn't have to be this hard, I realized. But even if it was to be this hard, society should acknowledge the structural disadvantages so many face and ameliorate them as much as possible. What could be more conservative than abetting each citizen in maximizing her potential so she can contribute as much as possible? I tried and tried, but I just couldn't be satisfied with my own individual success. I knew I'd just been lucky.

DRIVEN TO ACTION

If a conservative is a liberal who's been mugged, a liberal is a conservative who realizes that she can't have what's being conserved. The final experience that changed my worldview was buying my first new car.

Military bases are full of concessions. As I planned to rotate back from Korea at the tail end of 1983, I bought, sight unseen, a Chrysler/Renault Alliance, the 1983 Car of the Year. That and the implicit military seal of approval were enough for me.

As I drove home from the dealership, the car died in the middle of the highway. It continued to die, for no discernable reason, for the rest of the time I owned it. The dealership tried repeatedly to locate the problem, but couldn't. Finally, they told me to have my car towed off their premises. The Chrysler representative laughed at me when I asked for a refund.

I was frantic. The car payment and insurance consumed most of one biweekly paycheck; I couldn't afford to buy another car, nor was Laurel, Maryland, an area well served by public transportation. How was I going to get to school?

I appealed to the military for assistance but was told it was none of their affair. I was, however, ordered to continue making the payments and reminded that I'd lose my security clearance for "financial irresponsibility."

Those were the days just before lemon laws; I was booted out of one lawyer's office after the other. Not only that, they did so in a manner which suggested personal disapproval of me. Just as had Lieutenant Colonel Davis when punishing me for having been raped, several of these lawyers failed to offer me a seat and snapped at me.

What was most remarkable to me about this experience was the vehemence with which everyone who refused to help me insisted that I keep up my car payments—not for my own good but because it was my duty. I was struck by everyone's deference to big business's interests, as if they were a proxy for morality; they could just as easily have been in my shoes. How brainwashed we all are, I thought.

It was January 1984. I'd been making payments since September. I'd only had the car a month. The last lawyer had just finished telling me I'd be better off buying another car. I couldn't take any more. What was I supposed to do, have someone "steal" the car or make four years of payments on a car that didn't run? I couldn't believe that these were my only options, I, who so believed in America. I felt like a rat in a maze with no outlet, like a speck of dust on a tabletop, like a thing unworthy of the least consideration. There was no way out of this situation, no matter how willing I was to work hard and play by the rules. This, I thought, is where outlaws come from.

I made for the door, blinded by tears and racked with sobs. Frantic for something to say, the lawyer sputtered about how his mother-in-law had gotten a couple hundred dollars' refund with a letter-writing campaign and maybe I should try that. I didn't even bother to respond, just dragged myself out to my friend's car and back to my one-sided responsibilities.

I was trapped. My only option was the letter-writing campaign. As I worried my situation around and around in my head, I stopped crying and started to get mad. Really mad. I hadn't done anything wrong, I always played by the rules, yet I was being abused.

I didn't just want out of my contract. I didn't just want my money back. I wanted acknowledgment of the wrong being done to me and I wanted revenge. So I took three days off from work and waged war on Chrysler.

At the base library, I explained my situation to the librarian. Unlike the lawyers, this lowly government worker was energized and outraged. We explored the government committee structure, which regulatory bodies did what, the structure of the automobile industry. I learned how to research corporate hierarchies and trace ownership.

In the end, I sent out a mass mailing of two hundred letters to everyone from Reagan and Bush (neither of whom responded with even so much as a form letter), Tip O'Neill, every female and/or black in Congress or the Senate, all the way down to my local Better Business Bureau. I swamped the federal government, the Missouri and Maryland governments, business, military, and women's groups.

I also mass-produced letters addressed to the chairman of Chrysler's board reading: "I am aware of the situation between you and Debra Dickerson regarding the car she bought from you which does not run and cannot be fixed but for which she must still pay. As a consumer, I will be following this situation closely and telling as many people as possible." They were to sign and include their city and state, then mail them to Chrysler's chairman in the pre-addressed envelopes I provided. I sent them to relatives all over the country and friends all over the world to disperse. Each letter I wrote made me feel less like crying and more like challenging the chairman of Chrysler to a duel. It's a dangerous thing to leave a person no way out.

Two weeks later, my office at the NSA had dedicated a phone line for me to answer all the calls I was getting. It was a populist uprising. People were furious on my behalf, which they saw, correctly, as theirs. I had taken a scattershot approach, writing groups even only loosely related to my issue; many of the calls and letters I received began, "I can't help you with your problem, but I was just blown away by your letter. Have you tried this group or that senator?" Some of the callers were still shaking with indignation, my letter still in their hands. Many pleaded with me to keep them informed.

A lawyer with the Federal Trade Commission called to explain the warrant of merchantability and how any of the lawyers I'd seen could have gotten Chrysler to cave if they'd given it half a try, especially with lemon laws pending all across the country. But they just didn't give a damn about a mousy little black girl with no money, even though I went to all those meetings in uniform. Not one of them mentioned this concept of merchantability (that a thing sold will be fit for the purpose for which it was intended). Not one of them.

Shortly thereafter, I got a call from the Chrysler chairman's lackey. He apologized for the "mixup," made it my fault because "I hadn't sufficiently explained the situation before," and asked with feigned nonchalance how many miles were on the car. I said, "Twenty-seven. Mostly from towing." "Jeee-sus!" the man muttered. Again, with feigned nonchalance, he asked,

"By the way, just how many people did you write?" That was when I knew I'd won.

Two weeks after that, in March, a very embarrassed Chrysler rep called and begged to know who else he should expect to hear from. You can actually hear an oppressor sweat when you turn the tables on him. We worked out the details of the buyback. Though my mother would have been able to, I couldn't help myself. My last words to him were, "Is it still funny?"

People from all over the NSA and the country asked for copies of the notebook I'd compiled or for me to act on their behalf. Unsurprisingly, a great many people had been victimized by car companies and had nowhere to turn. Had I been less well educated or had a less flexible job, I'd probably have been jailed for insurance fraud.

The magnitude of what I'd accomplished without lemon laws (or word processors) didn't really hit home until I was deferring to my insurance agents on the details of winding up the insurance, saying, "Just do what you normally do when a car company buys a car back."

"Debra," he said, "in twenty-five years, I've never seen a car company do this. We're in virgin territory." The Chrysler rep, as well, was at a loss as to how to proceed.

Including licensing fees, insurance costs, and payments on a car I couldn't drive, I lost nearly two thousand dollars and nine months' worth of peace on that deal, and with it, the last vestiges of my political innocence. Instead, I gained an appreciation of my own power as well as of the helplessness of the unsophisticated and uneducated.

⌒

That experience made it crystal clear to me whose side society was on and how much contempt the ruling class has for the masses. If a blameless person in uniform in the Reagan eighties couldn't get respect, who could?

I was appalled by the legal profession all over again when Chrysler refused to reimburse me for the money I'd lost on the deal (known legally as consequential damages). I saw the same lawyers again only to be subjected to their inexplicable fury. They accused me of trying to "steal from Chrysler," of "trying to get money I didn't deserve," of "trying to take advantage." None advised me calmly that it would cost me more to sue than I could hope to win. Instead, they lit into me. "You should be grateful instead of begging for more," one lectured. Where did we all learn to cringe before capitalism?

The last lawyer I spoke with was so vicious I hung up on her. Weren't they supposed to be technicians really, simply saying yea or nay to the facts laid out before them? Why the emotion? Why the identification with Chrysler and not the person they might wrest some money from? I think it made them uncomfortable that I was self-assured, well educated, and successful. I'd made them look foolish. I was uppity.

Perhaps because of the similarity, that distasteful memory of my long-forgotten run-in with State Farm resurfaced and I had another of those moments which reshaped my life.

Chrysler made me realize that I'd been wrong in my earlier dismissal of lawyers, after my Flo Valley accident. The vision I had for myself was this: to tackle the power structure head-on rather than to hold my nose and suffer nobly while it ravaged me and everyone else. I had to go to law school and perhaps to government office, though I still believed the law to be the tool of the ruling class, because ignorance comes with too high a price tag.

I stopped seeing these brutalizing experiences as particular to me. I could see now that all the little people got treated this way and would continue to be as long as we remained passive. It was clear to me that though with each passing year I became less vulnerable to exploitation, that was not true for most Americans. Few had the resources or personalities to engage in this type of work. The conviction grew in my mind that people like me have to fight for the masses who are unable to fight for themselves. It's just not enough that I, personally, got out of a car contract. It's not enough that I got a decent education, that I was able to haul myself up from the working class.

As my formal and informal education continued simultaneously in the most intellectually and politically pivotal year of my life, 1984, I began to see myself, my family, my neighborhood, my people in historico-social context. Some things were our fault, some things were not. Oppressed people have a duty to fight back, work hard, and retain their dignity, but society also has a duty to acknowledge disadvantage and work to end it. It was the second prong of that analysis that forced me to disavow conservatism. Liberals, with their condescension and lack of common sense, are wrong a lot, but at least they err while giving a damn about people.

Liberal concepts like "internalized oppression," "self-hatred," and "false consciousness" had always made me roll my eyes, but by 1984, I had to revisit them. I knew I suffered from all three, as do a great many blacks—from the overachievers to the troublemakers and the apologists for both groups. Self-hatred is the number one problem among black people; all our counterproductive behaviors stem from it.

I had a dream right about then. Really, it was a memory, but it came to me while I was sleeping. When I'd come back from Korea in November 1983, I'd been taken, as usual, to the same tacky, beer-sodden club in east St. Louis we'd always gone to. In my dream, I stood again in the back of the room on a riser, just looking at that room full of black people. Perhaps it was two years in Asia that made the sight of all that blackness swirling around me so arresting. I couldn't take my eyes off us. I watched us dance and flirt and drink and talk and cuss each other out, and for once, I hadn't felt afraid or annoyed. What I felt was wistfulness because I wasn't part of it. Even so, it was a soothing dream, one that filled me with hope and humility. I envied my oblivious brethren their places at the table and I wished I could move so unselfconsciously among them. For the first time, I also knew that anyone in that room who was wasting his time judging me and critiquing my every move wasn't worth worrying about. I even considered the possibility that nobody was paying me the least attention. How self-absorbed to carry on as if no one but me had mastered mainstream English or ever cracked the covers of serious literature. The weight of the community off my shoulders, I woke up smiling. It hit me like a thunderbolt. I was alone. Truly alone.

I didn't like it.

I wanted to be black.

I admitted to myself how ashamed I'd been of us and I simply let it go. I just walked away from it.

It was much easier than I would have imagined it would be. Once I stopped kidding myself about my true feelings, I just stepped out of that shell of self-hatred and felt a hundred pounds lighter. Once I did, my overwhelming emotion was—foolishness. I felt silly. How could I hate black people? That's like hating my elbows. If black people were no good, then I was no good. My mother, my sisters, strangers on the street. That couldn't be. I had a lot more thinking to do, but the more I lived, the more all my old assumptions were crumbling.

Carolyn Ferrell

One Christmas, as my family gathered together after dinner, my mother suggested I read aloud a story I had recently published. So I began to read "Wonderful Teen," all the while feeling a mixture of shame, fear, and a little pride; wasn't the story of a mother taking her children and fleeing her abusive husband one we had all lived through some years before? Tremendous drama and conflict, yes, but now there were new, nagging thoughts: Had enough time gone by to hear the story again? Were the characters enough removed from my own family that I wouldn't have to worry about offending anyone? "Wonderful Teen" was probably my most autobiographical work to date, truthful (I believed) in its pain and immediacy, but as I read the story out loud, no one was angry, no one laughed, no one commented. They were all immersed in the words: digesting turkey and sweet potato pie and returning to those sad, olden days. Back at the motel, the blare of Divorce Court *on the television, the relentless crash of surf and highway. Remembering the part of the story that had escaped my telling; wanting more, wanting just what was there.*

Wonderful Teen

From *Don't Erase Me* a short-story collection

It seemed to me that our motel room in Laguna Beach was only big enough for two people, like a mother and father, and here we were five. Mother picked up the phone and dialed for a plain cheese pizza. We protested, saying that we wanted a pizza with mushrooms and little fishes on it, and a bottle of orange soda as well, since it was so hot. The sun outside was turning roads back into tar, and the pool at the motel was as hot as a bath. A few minutes outside, and we could feel the light brown of our skin bake darker, like brownies with nuts in them. There was my baby sister Tess and me and the twins, Todd and Lee. Lee was named after my father, who was back at the house, probably cursing out loud to no one. We ran the bathroom sink full at the motel and soaked our arms up to the elbows in the cold hard water. Sometimes someone would say, "It's too hot here in this stinking room" or "I wish we were back at home." Mother would tell us to think about something else and to behave ourselves. That, and "I'm not made out of money! You eat what I say! If you're thirsty, fill yourself up a glass from that water you're playing with!"

Mother picked up the phone again and told us to be quiet. We all sat on the edge of the bed. I held Tess on my lap. I knew that she would be the first one to start bawling, no matter what. Mother twisted a strand of her ash-blond hair around her finger and put it in her mouth. The swelling around her eye had turned dark purple from the sky-blue it had been in the morning. When we walked into the motel office at eight A.M., Mother took off her sunglasses automatically, forgetting. The old lady behind the desk stared at us. Mother asked, "Do you give discounts for black eyes?" Then she started to cry, which made us all feel very wobbly. Mother put her sunglasses back on and touched each of us, one by one, with the tip of her hand, like she was making sure we were there. The old desk lady said, "Honey, we've seen everything." She gave us the room closest to the old highway because she said she didn't want to hear no trouble. She asked my mother if she was babysitting us kids. "They are mine," Mother announced. The old desk lady said she had never seen four colored kids come in with a white lady with a black eye before. She said she wasn't looking for no trouble. Mother sucked in her teeth and moved us out the door.

In the last issue of *Wonderful Teen*, it had said that most people don't really realize how grown-up and responsible their teens really are. "Today's youth," it said, "tomorrow's *you*." That made me feel different after I'd read it, even though I was only twelve. Now, on the way to our motel room, my hand was on Mother's shoulder, not like it used to be when I was a girl, when I used to hold on to her fingers with my whole hand. I'd brought the last issue of *Wonderful Teen* with me, because before we left, Mother made it clear to us: we will stay gone.

She was trying a new number. She said to me, "Hannah, get me a cigarette out of my bag." I pushed Tess off my lap and dug into her pocketbook for the twisted pack of Slims. *Wonderful Teen* was against cigarettes: it said that smoking could turn youthful skin not only older but darker as well. I knew this fact, and still, I never gave up my prayer with the pack of Slims in my hand that six years would hurry up and pass so that I would be able to smoke cigarettes legally, like Mother promised. It happened around the same time you could drink a chaser before your main drink and join the army and get married. My prayer was the same lines over and over: "And when I am a full woman . . . And when I am a full woman . . . thank you, heavenly God." I would start smoking nonfilters and I would be exactly like Mother anyway, who smoked all the time, and look: her skin was soft and youthful and not dark at all.

Mother lit up a cigarette and said, "Is that you, Lee?" Tess's lips began to shake so I whacked her on the head with Mother's bag, gently. Mother said, "You can't push me around now, Lee. You can't do that now! We're on the coast. Never mind where! One more word like that and I'll hang up for good!" The boys put their heads underneath the bedspread and began to howl like baby dogs. Tess was full-steam-ahead crying, just as I had predicted. I said, in the most mature adult whisper I could manage, "Shut up, you disgusting brats!"

Mother's voice was scratchy, like she was gargling with saltwater. She said, "You can't push me around now! No sir, there's not going to be a next time! There's a point I've reached, Lee, and that's called: *self-respect*." She slammed down the phone and told us to go outside and wait for the pizza delivery truck. I shoved my brothers and sister out the door and said to my mother, still in that grown-up whisper, "You know I'm here if you need me, Ella." Mother put out her cigarette in the ashtray and said, "Just where did you learn talk like that? Go out and close the door!"

‿

In the sun, our game was to put our hand on each other's foreheads to see who had the hottest skin. Tess wanted to change after a few minutes; she said she wanted to be a little white cloud that floated above the motel and looked at itself in the pool mirror. My brother Todd, who was only ten years old and just naturally thought he was the absolute Panama Cigar, said, "That's only something deluded baby girls think of. Me, I've had enough of delusions." Lee, still in the old game, jumped up and down and announced that his skin was on fire. I looked at them and folded my arms over my chest. Tess, Todd, and Lee were nothing but babies when you faced the cold, hard facts. I had been born two years before any of them, and in *Wonderful Teen* it had said, "Every year marks a difference." Lee said he wanted to go back in and tell Mother that he had a fever, but I said not to. I said she needed time to herself, and Todd said, "Why, is she lost?" and he horse-laughed. I ignored him and pushed the others over to the pool.

There was a colored lady sitting next to the pool in a lounge chair. She was the first black person I'd seen all day, ever since we drove into Laguna Beach on the lam. She saw us and cried out, "Come and play your games over here by me!" She smiled. Her voice sounded like our grandma from the South, the one who wore an undershirt instead of a bra and who ate squirrel meat. The colored lady was beautiful. She had the same skin as Dad, the kind Mother had called "day-old coffee" in the old times when they used to laugh about it. The colored lady was just sitting there in broad daylight. She didn't have her arms or legs covered up in the sun. She kept batting her eyes. The look on her face was the kind that said *I'm never lonely*.

Todd and Lee went over to her and did cartwheels and rode upside-down bicycles with their legs. This colored lady's hair was made up into a thousand braids wrapped in one big twist at the back of her head. There were blue and gold beads woven into the braids. Blue and gold were my favorite colors. I suddenly remembered. Blue and gold were the national colors of *Wonderful Teen*. Todd and Lee were playing the Injured Cowboy and the Horse Who Could Dial for Help. She threw her head back and laughed. Her teeth could have been a full-page ad in *Wonderful Teen*; they had that unmistakable teen shine, although I guessed her to be a bit older. She looked over at Tess and me and said, "Are you feeling blue, girls?" Her voice was like a love story in the movies.

I shoved Tess behind me and said, "Our mother is under the weather. I am here to keep an eye out on the kids. You see, I'm almost a teen. And I'm here to keep an eye out."

The way the colored lady leaned forward in her chair, you could really see things if you looked. She tied the knot of her two-piece white-and-gold swimsuit tighter and said, "If you're going to be a teen, then you probably have all the reasons in the world for feeling blue." She winked at me. The boys ran to the highway edge to check for the delivery truck. My arms were hanging at my sides like long noodles, and suddenly I realized how amazing it was that I was going to be a teen.

The colored lady took Tess by the hand and said, "With this kind of hair, she'll have all the boys. All the boys who wouldn't want *us*." Tess had Mother's hair, the kind that was soft and went straight down. Not like mine, which didn't flow to the back when the wind hit it. My hair just stayed.

Then the colored lady asked, "What does your mother have?"

Tess said, "Dad slammed the phone down on Mother's hand, so that's why we're all here." She put her face in her hands, just like a grown-up, even though she was only five.

The colored lady turned and said to me, "Do you want me to start showing you the right way to be a teen?"

⁓

The boys came back and hung their legs over the side of the pool. The colored lady was braiding my hair. I sat on the ground in between her legs and looked into her compact mirror. She made five rows of braids on my head from front to back instead of the two that Mother usually did. She took out a jar of light blue grease and smoothed it through the rows over the hair that wouldn't stay put. I smelled like Dad in the morning. Tess said I looked like a star. I sat between the colored lady's legs on the hot cement and felt what *Wonderful Teen* would have called "The Evolution" come out.

The colored lady asked me, "Does your mama know what a beautiful baby she has here? You're going to get all the boys with your charm."

I said, "But what about my hair?" I asked her if I would still get all the boys with my hair. She smiled. Mother called for us from the door of the room. The colored lady wanted a goodbye kiss from the boys. I looked at myself one last time in the compact. I said to myself, "And when I am a full woman, I will always look like this. And when I am a full woman, I will always look like this. Thank you, heavenly God." Remembering our game, I shouted out to the others racing back, "Has anyone's skin reached the boiling point yet?"

⌒

Todd and Lee ran back into the bathroom to play with the water. Mother was flopped on the bed. Tess was flopped on Mother's chest and was trying to hide her face inside Mother's blouse. There were three cigarettes, all lit, in the ashtray. Mother's face looked tired and had red blobs all over it. She was wearing her sunglasses again, even though it was just us. When I sat next to her on the bed, I could smell the way our home smelled at night, when Mother smoked and cooked in the kitchen. The TV was on: it was our favorite show, *Day in Court.*

A man had returned home after twelve years of amnesia and now his wife's new husband was feeling pretty disgusted and filing for divorce. The new husband called his wife a "black plague," and that made Todd laugh like crazy. The wife sat in the witness stand like a stone with its mouth open. She said she hadn't known. The judge said it was a clear-cut case of bigamy. The old husband just woke up in Las Vegas and adjusted to life as a children's librarian there. He'd married again, had a son, and gotten arrested for bad checks. But all that didn't matter now, now that he remembered who he really was. The new husband rolled his eyes at the camera and said, "Plague is right." The judge said it was a clear-cut case of mistaken identity.

When it came time for the wife to speak, Mother said, "Turn the set off. It's too damn late for her."

⌒

There was this ad in the last *Wonderful Teen* that I loved: a lady in a tanning studio applying a bottle of Wild Thing tanning oil to her silky legs. And she was dreaming of a man who had sun-streaked hair and closed eyes with a heavenly smile on his face. The ad said, "True Happiness."

That was it. I tore it out of the magazine and kept it in my slacks pocket. Whenever I looked at it, I wanted to take off my shirt. Whenever I looked at it, first I would feel sexy, then sad.

I thought about the colored lady at the pool. I said to Mother, "Do you notice anything different about me?" I twirled the ends of my braids in my fingers.

Mother closed her eyes and said, "Not now, Hannah. Can't you see I'm thinking?" One of her eyes was glued together by the lids in a purple ball.

I told her what I was thinking, though: that now I didn't look exactly like her anymore, but still, when people looked, they would be able to tell that I was hers. Mother laughed, "Oh yeah? You sure you're not shitting me?" Then after a minute she said, "To me, you're looking more like your father's side. Are you *sure* you're still mine?" And she laughed. And her laugh was the kind that meant: I might be serious.

I ran into the bathroom and looked into the mirror. I wanted to pull all the braids out. I wanted a hat or a scarf: I was ashamed. There were five braids where there used to be two and everything felt like it was gone and I was ashamed to death. Todd walked past the bathroom and whispered, "Plague" and with both hands I slammed the door. Shut.

⌇

Todd and Lee had been playing with the water, but now they came running out of the bathroom. The sink was overflowing. Todd announced, "I want to go home now."

Mother replied, "We can't right now, honey. Be good for a while. We'll check in on Dad later."

Lee said, "I want Dad to bring me my bike."

I said, "Now you two boys *behave!* I don't want to have to tell you again." I turned to Mother and I sighed. "What's a woman to do?"

Todd said, "Shut your face, black bitch." His voice was high and shaky. He kept his eyes on Mother's feet, lying on the bed.

"Yeah, black bitch," Lee copied. He was smiling like an angel. He was clearly such a baby.

I shouted, "Mother! We don't have to stand for this!" I began to think of punishments for the boys.

She rubbed her eyes under the sunglasses and said, "Kids! That's the last thing I need! Nobody calls anybody else a black anything! Far as I'm concerned, we are all *black*."

She slid off the bed and put on her slippers and walked into the bathroom. No one said anything because it was just a feeling. Mother clicked the bathroom door locked. The only noise was from the highway. You could tell that inside, everything went frozen, frozen stiff, even our teeth hurt. You could tell we were alone.

Todd fell on the bed next to Tess and started bawling. Then Lee started in. Todd wriggled his body in the covers like a desert soldier. Mother shouted after a minute, "I have so many things to worry about, don't give me anything else on my plate, you hear?"

The toilet flushed. Then Mother resumed saying, "Boys, I'm doing all I can. Ask Hannah to read you a story."

I looked at my brothers on the bed. I was thinking: Yes, it was true. Even Mother had to admit I was the natural-born leader of the children. It was all up to me. I moved over and touched Todd's back with the flat of my hand and I let it stay there for a minute. Yes, it was true. He screamed at me to get my black bitch hand away. The toilet flushed again. I moved back for a moment. Then I slid underneath the bed like a sideways crab.

⌒

The doorbell to our room rang, and it was the old desk lady. She wanted to know whether Mother was interested in buying something to drink. She was selling bottles of Old Country Gentleman at a discount price. This was the stuff that would be good for someone like our mother, she said. I told her, "We are probably going to order a bottle of orange soda, which is rich in vitamin C."

Mother was back on the phone. "I told you how to get here," she was shouting. "Are you going to keep me waiting all damn day?" She slammed the phone down. We were all listening. "Who was that at the door?" Mother asked, going back into the bathroom.

⌒

Later, she made us wash our faces and brush our teeth even though it wasn't dark outside yet. She sat us down in a row in front of the TV and told us we could watch *Nature's Glorious Kingdom* and *The Gentle Giant*. We had to put on our pajamas. Mother combed out our hair. She asked me why mine was so greasy, but that was all. She didn't ask me where the braids came from. The doorbell rang. Lee said, "Maybe that's Dad." Todd replied, "Shut up, stupid dope."

It was the colored lady from the pool. Mother was peeking out from behind the front door. The way the lady stood in the doorway with her short white robe covering almost every important thing, I just knew she was a star. We were in Laguna Beach. That was home to the stars. The colored lady said she was selling cosmetics, natural cosmetics that didn't have any unnecessary chemicals or animal tests. They enhanced a woman's natural beauty without covering up or polluting what nature had put there in the first place.

Mother said she wasn't interested. The colored lady took out a small case from a huge bag that had "Only One You" on the side. It was a dark blue eye shadow. She said, "That one goes over big with ladies of your hue." She dabbed Mother's eyes, including the purple one. Then she said, "You'd be surprised to discover all the treasures that this particular tone can bring out." She showed Mother an orange lipstick called Debonair and a bottle of pink foundation. The colored lady said it would bring out the secret most beautiful woman that Mother had inside of her. Mother said, "I ain't in the market for that today, honey."

The colored lady gave her an eye pencil called Fire and Smoke and a mascara with a special lash-separating comb. She saw us through the door and waved. She pointed to my head and smiled. I felt my throat get thick. Mother kept her eyes down. She thanked her for the samples and then closed the door. Then the colored lady was gone, like that was all there was to it. Mother was silent. I knew that that meant *We are back in here together alone.*

She went back into the bathroom. When she came out, she had on the lipstick and the eye pencil. Her eyes looked like two wonderful stones. She asked us, "Is the treasure out?" and then burst into tears. We were all frozen again, but still we could run and put our arms around her.

⌣

Nature's Glorious Kingdom came on. I could tell that the day was ending because out the window, the bottom of the sky was turning pink. Tiny stars were popping out everywhere. *Wonderful Teen* said that the evening-time would become a teen's best friend, what with the promise of corsages, candy, dates arriving at the door, cars, limousines, evening dresses. I sat on the edge of the bathtub and anticipated the universe as Mother scrubbed her feet and hands. She took moments out to dry her hands and smoke a cigarette. I said to her, "I wish I was eighteen already."

She answered, "Hannah, baby, when you're eighteen, you're going to wish yourself right back to twelve, believe you me." She smiled at me for the first time in days.

I thought about the car I would start driving when I hit the wonderful age, and all the men standing at street corners waiting for me to pick them up and drive them around. I would have on nylons, and instead of underwear, I would wear a white-and-gold bikini bottom. The men's hair would blow in the wind and they would have the best suntans. I would show Tess how to drive way before her time and how to hold a penny between her legs for posture. I would use Debonair.

I said, "I only want to keep getting older, Mother. I want to be exactly like you."

Mother said, "By the time I was twenty-nine, I had had all of my children. Grandmother used to call me and tell me that it was never too late. It didn't matter what I'd thought I wanted before. She just wished it could have been anything else—South American, Russian, even Chinese, for Christ's sake. I had four children, but my own freaking mother told me it was never too late to leave and come back and be twelve again."

Then Mother said, "Dad could've been anything, and still I would've fallen in love. It's not that love is blind, for Christ's sake. It's that love closes your eyes out of spite. Dad could've been anything, and still I would've gotten to right here." And then her cigarette fell out of her mouth and into the water.

I picked it up and said, "I don't care about all that other stuff, Mother. I just want to be like you."

Mother rubbed her eyes. She said, "At first your father called me his little drop of milk in his big bucket of tar."

Then she said, "And it's not like I ever became anything more than a drop of milk in the bucket of tar. I didn't spread out. I didn't evaporate. I just stayed a drop of milk and he just stayed a bucket."

Mother took a deep breath. I couldn't listen. I told her again that I wanted to be just like her, and she moaned, "Then be like me, Hannah."

⁓

The doorbell rang and it was the desk lady again. She said to tell Mother that there was a man around asking for her. She said she wasn't looking for no trouble, but facts were facts: someone had been sniffing around. Mother shouted from the bathroom, "Shut that damn door!" The desk

lady asked me how long it was we were planning on staying. I smiled graciously to get her to leave, and then she did leave.

We turned the TV set low. We could hear Mother splashing water in
the tub, saying, "It's not possible! How the hell could it be possible!" She
got out of the tub and started throwing all our clothes in a big pile near
the door.

⌣

The bell rang again, and this time we all looked out the window and saw
the pizza delivery guy. Mother opened the door and said, "I called you
hours ago! Do I need to make reservations a week in advance for a freaking pizza?"

The pizza guy said, "I got lost, that's all. No biggie." He placed a big
soggy box on the floor next to our pile and began to chew his nails. He
had streaked blond hair and legs with muscles. His shirt was open. He had
what *Wonderful Teen* would call "that unmistakable surfer air."

The guy was eyeing Mother as she was fishing for some dollar bills. He
asked her finally, "So what time do you knock off babysitting?" Mother
was searching for her pocketbook. She was only wearing a towel. Tess
moved over and started twirling her hair with her finger. She gave him a
big smile. She was only five.

He rubbed the back of his neck with his hand. I suddenly realized that
I was wearing feet pajamas, but I was praying he hadn't noticed. "And
when I am a full woman, I will wear baby dolls. And when I am a full
woman, I will wear baby dolls. Thank you, Father." Mother mumbled
something at him and handed over a ten-dollar bill. He grinned and bent
his head down to hers—did I mention that he was probably over six feet
tall in his stocking feet and had five-o'clock shadow? He asked Mother if
he could speak to her outside for a moment. "Why?" Mother asked, but
she was already going into the bathroom with a sundress from the pile.

I sauntered over to the pizza guy. I put my hands on my hips and
spread out my fingers wide so that it would look like something big and
good was there. And then he stared into my eyes for a whole sixty seconds.
They were as blue as Mother's new eye shadow. He put his warm hands on
my shoulders, which were pulsating a feeling up to him. I was almost as
tall as he was. I'd say he stared into my eyes for a good eighty seconds. I'd
say that there was definitely love there.

Standing with me there, he said, "*Baby*," and he said it so that I would have to follow his lips to really know the depth of his entire being. And I felt my whole essence get crushed and I knew that this had most certainly been a *Wonderful Teen* moment. I felt the beating of my rapid heart and all my favorite songs filling my head, like "Where Is My World." They were filling my soul. Baby. I wanted to sing. Heaven was really a place you could see before you died.

And then Mother came out of the bathroom with her yellow sundress on. The pizza guy pulled his hands away quickly and said, "That's a cute girl there. Where's her mother? I mean, I know you ain't their mother." Mother stopped a second, then she burst out laughing and said, "Of course they're mine, silly, I'm old enough." She pushed him gently out the door and followed, grinning gaily.

I went into the bathroom and turned on the water. The others were watching *Gentle Giant* and tearing off pieces of pizza from the box. I began scrubbing my face with cold water and the palms of my hands. Just water and hands. I looked up in the mirror over the sink after a minute and I thought I saw myself going, but when I blinked my eyes, I was all there.

Out the window, the moon came out in full and the air was cooling down. I used our family-size jar of Vaseline for grease and did my hair again. I couldn't get the five braids, but I did smooth my hair out more, even my girl sideburns. I got two braids down the back of my head, Indian warrior fashion.

Mother came into the room after fifteen minutes. "That boy!" she said, giggling. Her face was red, and the blobs on it were even redder. "What a crazy *boy*!" She knelt near the pizza box and tore out a slice and stuffed it in her mouth. She said, when everyone kept watching TV, "All he wanted to do was ask me out on a date! Now isn't that a crazy *boy*?" And she let out a string of giggles that sounded like they could've come from a cow. Todd said, "This pizza is too goddamn cold," but all Mother did was grab him and start hugging him. Her face was all lit up. She looked ugly. She didn't punish him for using the wrong language. Mother grabbed Tess and Lee and began hugging them too and kissing them and pretty soon they were all rolling on the floor, happy like puppies. They were all giggling in little lumps, like on a string, not laughing in one big laugh. Mother asked, "Where's Hannah?" but they were all too happy and giggling to answer. It was the first time in a long time.

Then Mother spread her arms out like wings around Tess and Todd and Lee and said, "My babies, you are all mine." And I could hear tears in her voice. It was the saddest time I ever knew. Mother rocked them like they were all back in the nest. I closed the door to the bathroom, where I was standing, looking, and I wondered if they would ever remember that I wasn't there, ever.

⁓

Before we went to bed, Mother called Dad again. She was still wearing her sundress and her new makeup. Dad picked up, saying it was pretty damn late to be calling and did she know she was facing possible kidnapping charges? Mother put Tess on the phone, then the boys. They all cried in no time. When you faced facts, they were all nothing but children, pure and simple. When I got on the phone, I told Dad, "I have everything under control. I'm not your baby." Then I said, "Yes. Yes, I miss you. I already told you that before." Then I said calmly, "*Why couldn't you have been something different?*" Someone here needed to get to the bottom of things. Mother smacked me hard on the back and told me to mind my own freaking business. She took the phone into her own hands.

⁓

Back in the bathroom, I put on Mother's eye shadow and lipstick and pink foundation. I put it on seriously. There was this article in the last issue of *Wonderful Teen* called "Dress But Don't Confess," which said that all wonderful teens had secrets in them that should only come out with the right man. Not just any man, the absolute right one. It said that lip gloss and eyeliner and a great tan were important, but the right man didn't need too much to see all the treasures that a wonderful teen possessed. I used to believe that. Only now I didn't know what to believe anymore. I studied my face in the mirror. From the side I could still pretend. From the side I knew for sure that I resembled Mother. That was a fact as plain as day, couldn't anyone deny it. But when I looked forward in the mirror, my face was homely and alone. I didn't know if I could fully believe *Wonderful Teen*. I realized, for example, that there were no treasures, not on the outside, not below.

When I looked straight in the mirror, all I could ask was "*Why couldn't it have been anything else?*" I sat down in the empty bathtub and cried and cried. Never again. Never again. Never again. Never again.

Milk tar. Mother knocked on the door of the bathroom and asked me if she could please give me a hug. "Never again!" I shouted, and nothing could change my mind, not even something to eat or drink, not even Mother's kisses, or her crying from the bed.

Dana Johnson

This story was a long time coming; hard to write because I resisted see-
ing what was to be seen. Many drafts later, I realized that the trouble I
was having getting this story down on the page had everything to do
with denial. There's pain and reconciliation in trying to reclaim one's
identity after years of not understanding its value, but the image of
greens kept coming to me. These greens ended up being the metaphori-
cal and literal connection between mother and daughter, the past, pres-
ent, and future. I mean to speak about Southern migration and how
important it is to African American culture and American culture. I
mean to speak about mothers and daughters, and how important these
relationships are to all our histories.

Markers

From Break Any Woman Down, a short-story collection

WHEN MY BIG BROTHER calls me up and tells me to do something, I do it. That's all. He couldn't drive mama to do her errand today because of his double-shift at the sprinkler factory, but somebody ought to, because it's one of the hottest days on California record, and our Mama ain't got no business standing around waiting for a bus on a day like this, and could I drive out and do it? he asked. Told.

Driving with my mother, I'm imagining all the things I will have to do when I get back home to Max, who will be there waiting to loudly tick off all the items I will have inevitably forgotten. All the tomatoes I've chosen that are too firm or too soft, asking me why did I buy the cheeses at the cheap local market, *disgusting*, when I should have gone to the gourmet market where, any idiot knows, they have the best cheeses, Avery, he'll say. And then he will start on how late I am, where have I *been*? What have I been *doing* all this time? All that time just to run an errand with my mother? But because he and my mother don't know each other so well, not even after four years, he will have no idea how these things can take so much time, how maddening it can be that my mother doesn't know where she is going.

She never knows, because in all her fifty-six years she's never learned how to drive. She relies on markers, like they used to when she lived in Arkansas, I guess. *When you see the tree stump down the road, turn right.* That kind of stuff. My visits with her turn into taking her here or there, around and around, looking for a place, only to end up where we left off, nowhere near where we need to be.

It's 102 degrees and my Jaguar has no air-conditioning. The car's old—1975—and hasn't got much else going for it, really, except several dents in the body and expensive engine problems. This car was one of those Max ideas that seemed like a good one at the time. He was tired of getting phone calls from me, broken down, whining to be saved from odd places at odd times. I couldn't afford a new car, so he bought me this one. One thing I could afford was to paint over the dull, peeling brown, so I did. Red. Because if I'm going to have a classy car, I want it to look good, at least.

"You need to keep it clean. That's what you need to do," my mother always says. "You got all kind of Wendy's and Burger King papers and whatnot, talking about painting it. You throwing bad money after bad!" she said after I told her about my paint job.

She doesn't get it, my mother. She thinks sparkling clean-on-the-inside makes the same statement as clean on the outside, the kind of thinking that's the most frustrating thing about her. She thinks either/or, and is always saying *why don't you just*.

"Why don't you just make a right here?" she says.

We've done that, turned right, turned here so many times that there's no number for it. Still, I turn right. We're driving the San Gabriel Valley, somewhere in parched Pomona. I'm anxious. I'm not comfortable in these broken-down neighborhoods. They bother me, like not being able to rest until you figure out a forgotten name, reminding me of when I was a little girl and lived in South Central L.A.

It's painfully hot in my car. The heat and the smog are too much. Something bad and unhealthy must be happening to me and to my mother. Because what is it in the air that makes our eyes water and burn so much? And yet, my mother doesn't say anything about the heat. I actually whimper, but she wipes her brow with a wrinkled tissue in silence.

The heat waves above the pavement make everything seem like I'm looking at it through an orange, smoggy film. For reasons that I haven't been able to afford to find out all summer, and because I won't overcome my stubbornness to ask Max for money to help me fix it, heat blows out of my car's vents, though the heater is off. As we pass the same Boy Market for the third time, I feel the irritating tickle of a bead of sweat traveling between my breasts.

I yell at my mother. "How could you not know where this place is, Mom? How many times have you been here? You always do this." I flip down the sun visor because it gives me something to do, like counting to ten before you say something or do something you'll be sorry for later. I drive hunched over the steering wheel, gripping it, as if somehow the intensity of these actions will help us find the food stamp office. I hear my words long after I've said them. Ten years ago, when I felt like I was the kid and she was the parent, my mother would have popped me. But at twenty-eight, I'm too old for that.

"The bus route is different from the way we came. I don't usually get a ride here," she says, and I look at her, expecting a face of accusation and instead her face is full of gratitude. "There," my mother says, pointing to a mini-mall on our right that looks like twelve others we've passed in an hour.

"We've *been* here," I say, "passed it about five times."

"Well," my mother says, getting her paperwork together, "sorry, Love, but this is it."

As I pull into the parking lot I'm almost sorry that we've found the place, though ten minutes ago all I wanted out of life was to be here. The mini-mall lot is crammed with people trying to get food stamps, checks cashed, bus passes, and junk from the ninety-nine-cent store. I can't take hot *and* people, not this kind of hot, not so many people, and all I can think of is how, on top of everything, this is going to make me even later than I already am to help Max with his dinner party.

"This is awful," I say. We crawl slowly through the lot in search of a spot. "How long do you think this is going to take?" Before my mother can answer, I cut her off.

"Bitch," I say, and give the finger to a young woman in a rusted-out Oldsmobile who has taken my parking space. When I was living in my parents' house, I could never swear, and I feel funny but don't apologize for it, because that doesn't seem right, either, as though I've passed the point of little-girl concessions. I end up parking next to the woman who has taken my spot, and when I get out I glare at her. She looks at me coolly and glassy-eyed. She takes her time walking to me, like she's bored with the fact that she's got to be bothered. She's inches from my face.

"Watch. Who. You. Mess. With." She states each word deliberately, each one digging a deep hole for me to get thrown into with the dirt packed tight. She's Tootsie Roll-colored, with dark brown irises surrounded by blue-white hair pulled back tightly in a bun, and except for her stubby height, looks just like me. But I'm afraid of her.

I glance at my mother, who has gotten out of the car but says nothing.

She looks at me with raised eyebrows. I know that she won't say anything to help me. It's not her way.

In the lifetime of two seconds it takes me to decide what to do, I back down.

"Let's go, Mom." I turn my back on the woman, and my mother and I find our way to the line moving post-office slow. The loudness of this hole-in-the-wall is unbearable—little kids running all over the place screaming and crawling across the floor, parents screaming at their kids just as loudly.

"Look at these little bad-ass kids." My mother shakes her head. "I would have wore you out, running around acting crazy."

I cough a quick laugh and my mother laughs with me. I realize it's been a long time since we've laughed together. It embarrasses me.

"Nicky!" a young woman calls out. "I'ma beat your ass if you don't get over here right now! I told you to stick close to me!"

"Look here." My mother taps my shoulder. "I need to go to that ninety-nine-cent store after we done here."

I stand on my toes a bit out of line to see how many people are ahead of us. Two, which could very well take two hours. "Why do you need to go there?" I ask, and before my mother can answer I say, "I may not have time because I'm having some people over tonight. Besides, the stuff in there is cheap, it's junk, Mom."

"Same reason I need to come here."

"What?" I've forgotten I even asked her a question and I'm distracted because as we approach the bullet-proof glass of the clerk I see it's the Oldsmobile woman. She looks through me.

"How you doing today?" my mother asks her, slipping her plastic food stamp card and identification under the window. The woman ignores my mother. "Hot today, ain't it?" my mother tries again. I want to say, *Mom, don't waste your time*, and that's another thing about her: being nice to people who treat her like crap. I want to pull her aside and tell her this in hushed tones, like mothers do to their kids when they're setting them straight.

"I like your nails," my mother says to the clerk. The nails are hideous orange fake claws, probably done at the nail salon three doors down.

"Where's your other green ID card?" the woman states flatly, as though she hasn't heard a word my mother has said.

My mother's mouth forms an O and her eyes widen. "Don't you know I left it at home. I can't believe I did that."

I take off my sunglasses to see better. I can't believe what I'm hearing. I've driven from Santa Monica, one hour, for nothing.

"Can you take information from my other card, anyway? It's kind of hard for me to get here," my mother says politely. It's agonizing, like she's begging. The woman shoves my mother's cards back at us. I'm realizing that if my mother can't get her food stamps now, we'll have to drive the half hour back to her house in West Covina and come back. I don't want to come back here.

"You'll have to come back," the clerk says as if programmed.

"But—"

"You'll have to come back. That's all to it. Next."

I panic. "My mother needs these stamps today. We can't come back."

The clerk leans toward the dull, silver-colored speaker hanging in the middle of the glass partition. "Miss Fancy Car," she says, real low. I can barely hear her. "I think you can wait another day for your food stamps, OK? Now collect your shit and move on before I go off on your ass." Her eyes are on my mother when she says this, and my mother looks shaken. I want her to fight the clerk, to let her know who she's talking to. But I know she won't.

I grab my mother's cards from underneath the glass and before I turn to leave I say, "My car and I have nothing to do with my mother."

I hurry to my car, leaving my mother behind. I can barely get my key in the door because I'm so impatient to get out of here and take my mother home so I can go home. I remember she wants to go to the store. "You still want to go to the store?" I ask, but the way I ask it, it sounds like *You better not want to go to the damn store.* My mother shakes her head.

"No. Take me home."

⌣

She's quiet on the way back to her house. A bad habit I learned from my father, who could hardly find the words to talk at any given time and place, who found it especially painful in the closed-in space of a car, is to turn on the radio immediately—turn it up and only turn it down if somebody is saying something to me, or me to them. I particularly don't like to talk much when I'm driving the freeway because I can't do both at the same time.

So the radio's playing an oldie by the Platters. "Only You." But my mother's quiet makes me uneasy, so I talk.

I ask her about her job search, which isn't going well. She thinks that she can't find work because of bad luck or because she isn't looking hard enough. She thinks simply working hard will get her somewhere, like when she was a girl and could just sew people's clothes to make a living. She's old-fashioned. I don't tell her what I know: that she's a fifty-six-year-old woman with an eighth-grade education, that all the hard work in the world won't change the fact that that's not enough anymore. This is difficult to know. So instead I say something easy, something that I halfway believe—"Mom, everything will turn out OK"—and drive on down the Pomona freeway.

When we first moved to the suburbs, my father of course had a job. He was a factory worker in L.A. commuting back and forth. But my mother had to work two jobs so that we could afford the house. Our new house had a lawn. There were no gunshots at night. We didn't even lock the doors. That summer before school started, before I started looking at myself with different eyes, these things were good enough.

In the motel rooms cleaned by my mother, I would stay out of her way and do homework in a corner. But I would sometimes leave slips of paper with her initials written on them, like a signature. Sometimes I left them under the beds or in between the folds of a towel hardened by the water and chemicals it was washed in. Sometimes I'd leave the paper under a lamp with gold-colored, peeling plastic.

One day, watching my mother clean is when I first got the idea of cards. I said, "Mama, I'm making you business cards."

"Do what now?" She had sprayed some ammonia on a window and turned her back to me. I watched her behind wiggle as she cleaned the window like she was rubbing a hole in it.

"I said I'm making you up some business cards so you can leave them around when you done."

"Girl, don't nobody want my business on a card," she said, turning to see what I was talking about. I had written a curly *R* and *A* for Ruby Arlington on my notebook paper in red ink. "Gone mess around and get me fired talking about some cards. This room is supposed to be *clean* when I leave it. When people pay for this room and come in, they see that it's clean. As clean a room as they ever gone get. That's my business card. Now keep your head in that book you brought and stop worrying me so I can finish and we can get home."

I had put the scraps away and started reading my American history book. But I was still thinking that my mother should get credit for her work. So I sometimes left scraps of paper, even though she told me not to. I thought she should be known and envisioned her becoming famous for her work, like maybe on the TV show "Real People."

When I started going to my new school in the sixth grade, I bragged that my mama was the best motel room cleaner there was because I knew they'd be impressed and then I'd make a lot of friends.

"So what? Your mother's a maid," said one kid who was always trying to spit on the other kids and getting in trouble for it.

Lisa, this girl whose blonde hair was always greasy, and who usually smelled like pee, thought it was kind of interesting. So did Melvin, who I secretly loved. All his clothes were studded like a superstar's. Nobody liked Lisa, even though she was always trying to buy people, because she was trashy. Nobody liked Melvin because he was new, and nobody liked me because I was black and new. But after a while, I wasn't new anymore, and eventually they tolerated my blackness.

I was only eleven, and when I think back, when I remember, I can't believe how good-hearted I was, how young. I can't believe my mother was so young, just in her thirties, when she seemed so old to me.

I steal glances at my mother as I'm driving. She looks somber, not peaceful like she usually does. Her expression triggers a memory: I'm leaving for college, USC, on scholarship. It's two years after Owen, my brother, has moved out and already started his own family, one year before my father leaves my mother, and we're still a family. I'm crying because I'm afraid to leave home. I'm only seventeen, but I know that the next time I see her I'll be even more of a stranger. She'll be the same and I'll be different, and home won't be home. I can't say all this to her. I just say, "Mama," and hug her good-bye. She holds my face in her hands and says, "Ain't no need of crying. You going now."

⌒

I can never leave my mother's house quickly. I'm always in a hurry, and she's always keeping me with small talk and questions. This time she's asking about my trip to Tuscany that Max paid for, even though I'm sure she doesn't know where Tuscany is. Max wanted me to meet his family, see where he came from, but it could have been to Tuscany, Iowa, it wouldn't have made any difference. And Max, I don't even like to talk about him to my mother, who doesn't like him but tries not to show it. And Max, he doesn't *dislike* my mother, but neither has he ever said that he really liked her.

The first time she met Max was at a family gathering, my Aunt Ruthie's sixtieth birthday, which nobody who was alive and around could miss and show their faces ever again. Max and I were late, so when we walked through my Aunt Ruthie's door everybody was already drinking and dancing to Eddie Cleanhead Vinson singing *Homeboy, homeboy, looks like you drunk again.* Playing spades at one table and dominoes at another, talking trash at both.

Owen put his cards down long enough to rise and say, "Hey." All my female relatives thought Max was handsome, gathered around him and told him, "You so fine," which made him turn red, and my mother was shy and polite and quiet. So Max stuck with my brother and Uncle Ra Ra, who shoved a glass of brandy in his hand and immediately nicknamed him "Mass" before Massimo got to tell him he could call him Max. Owen slapped Max on the back and told me between brags and talking trash at the card table that any dude who had money and treated me right was all right with him.

Still, I worried all night, about who was thinking what about whom. What did Max think of all my loud drunk relatives? What did they all think of me for bringing in this, this Mass? *You know proper-talking Avery would turn up with some white boy.* Later that night in bed with Max, in his own house, which would become mine in a matter of weeks, he said that my mother was nice but kind of boring. I was angry, at the time, that he would call my mother boring, but I allowed myself to believe he didn't know how to say best in English what he actually meant, because he was Italian.

And so, I can still to this day be angry at Max about calling my mother boring, but I can never stay in her house long myself. I'm always antsy to leave it. I don't know if it's because I'm bored or because every time I'm in my mother's house, the house I grew up in, everything in it is a reminder, like the swap-meet prints of Jesus hanging everywhere, which my father would have never allowed when he was living here. I'm always begging her to stop buying all these tacky things and spend her money on things that she needs.

"Why don't you just cut it out, Mom?" I've said it forty times.

She used to have a couple of pictures of my father around, but those seem to be gone. He left for another woman, and she's taken care of herself with little education while he started a new life. When my mother and father were together, they had terrible fights over money, other women, my mother's crazy, stubborn ways. There were loud voices, hitting, shoving. I wanted my mother to be quiet, to stop arguing. She would never back down, not until my father left the house to get away from the fighting. I always blamed her for chasing Daddy away—for never shutting up, just once. But now that she's more like the woman I thought I wanted her to be, just a tiny bit more weak, I've figured out there are many different ways to be weak.

"Mom," I used to say, "it's not too late to go back to school." But I don't say that anymore. What good, I often wonder, did a degree in art do for me? Make me completely unemployable. All those motel rooms so that I could "create," throw paint on canvases, and give her nothing in return.

Now we are sitting at the glass dining room table fanning ourselves and drinking water. Even though I really do have to be going, I ask her if she wants to go back to get her food stamps today. I only ask because I can see the tiredness on her face and I know she'll say no.

"No. I'm not messing around with them anymore today. Tomorrow, if it cools down, I'm a get over there then."

"OK, Mom," I say. "I should get going, then."

"Wait." My mother goes to her refrigerator and pulls out three bunches of mustard greens. "For your dinner." She smiles. "And let me give you this ham hock." She puts all of it in two plastic grocery bags and holds them out to me.

Greens are my favorite, and these are a rich, lush green, like a neon crayon. They don't go with what I'm serving, though: four courses of food with pronunciation that never rolls off my tongue like it does Max's. Italian food. I tell my mother this.

"What kind of dinner don't go with greens?" She frowns. "I never heard tell of that before. You must be having Max's friend's over. All them Euro-peeans."

"Mom," I say. "Please." But what she says is true.

I first met one of Max's best friends—Christian the Austrian, I call him—at a dinner party thick with Germans, Austrians, and Italians. Christian served roast duck for ten of us and told stories of his exploits in Naples. I'd never had duck before, and I thought it was greasy and fleshy. I preferred chicken.

"That's a bit south of Rome, Avery," he informed me about Naples parenthetically. I knew exactly where it was because I had been there.

"She knows where it is, you asshole," Max said. He drunkenly flicked ashes from his Dunhill on the white tablecloth. And later he yelled at me for not sticking up for myself. "I have seen you strong. When you want.

But you fall into yourself around these, these *jokers*. You become a mouse. They intimate you. Why Avie?"

"*Intimidate*," I said sullenly. Max was right, but how did I explain that sometimes I felt as though I was in grade school, but older and still not wiser? He was furiously mixing tumeric, cumin, and chili pepper for a paste. "That is what I said. *Intimate*. They already think I am only with you for your ass and you are with me for my wallet."

"What do you care what people think?" I had asked another time, one of the biggest fights we've ever had. When we first met, I considered being a cleaning woman for a short time, set my own hours, have some flexibility—until I could find another job. Max is well-off and older and free with his money. I wanted to be free with mine, too. But I had a degree in one pocket and no money in the other.

Max, lying beside me in bed, threw up his hands in frustration. "What will people think, Avie? I can take care of you."

"I want to take care of myself," I said.

"Have some respect for yourself. Don't clean people's toilets. You were educated at a university. You are smarter than all the idiots I know. It's stupid, this idea. Look." He pointed to the large oil painting I had done a few years ago, inspired by friends. There were three women's torsos, in different shades of brown, dancing. Max loved the painting and insisted we hang it, even though I wasn't sure about it myself. "See that, Avie? You did that. It's beautiful. I am so proud." He took my hands and massaged them. "These hands are for painting, not toilets. Definitely not for cooking. No." He grinned at me, and I smiled at him, even though we had been fighting like cobras just minutes before. "So." He punched a pillow and turned over on his side, his back to me. "I won't let you do it."

I never did do it. But I've always meant to argue the point of respect with Max, exactly the *point* of the job. Maybe I should stick up for myself more, but he doesn't give me the chance. The words are always out of his mouth first. And anyway, since then, Max and I have let each other down so many times that we've lost what we used to have. It's turned out that they were all right, about the ass and the wallet.

But here I am now, still, rushing away from my mother to run to Max. "Avery, I want you to have these greens," my mother says, holding them out to me.

"You should spend your money on you, Mom. You shouldn't be throwing it away like this."

"Money spent on you was never thrown away. Now, here," she says. "I ain't going to tell you again." So I take them and offer her some cash until she can get her food stamps.

"That's Max's money."

"Mom, does it matter?"

"That's Max's money," she says, her arms crossed. I put it away.

She walks me to the door and stands at the top of the driveway as I go to my car. "I sure wish you could spend more time," she says.

"Next time," I call out to her. I drive off and can see her waving, getting smaller and smaller in my rearview mirror. I know she won't go into the house until I'm out of sight. When I realize I don't deserve this, it fills me with sorrow.

⌒

"Farsumaura, polenta with Bolognese meat sauce, and a salad with radicchieto leaves . . ." Max ticks off the courses, all his fingers splayed except the pinky tucked into his palm. He jerks his head back to subdue a blue-black strand of hair that has fallen into his eyes. "What am I forgetting?"

"La Zuppa di Ceci del Corsi," I recite dutifully. Max's best friend, who he loves like a brother, Silvio Corsi, the man who taught him to cook in Rome, made up this soup of thick chickpeas, but we can never simply say, "Silvio's soup." I've tried. *Zuppa di!* . . . Max will prompt. *Di Ce-ci del Cor-si*, I'll finish in my most exaggerated Italian.

"Yes," Max says, grinning. "Good girl." He pats me on the ass, rubs it. When he's grinning like this, boyish and mischievous, touching me like he still wants only me, he seems kind. These moments remind me of all the times we've invested in each other, through deaths and the births of people in our families. I forget how mean and demanding he can be, but only lately so demanding because I don't feel like fighting. He likes to give orders, likes things to be done his way, insisted on dinner this evening when he knew I had to drive to the suburbs to help my mother, would maybe like to stay. But when he grins at me, the squint of his right eye still charms me, and I can almost forget that he's fucking the hostess at the restaurant he chefs at. Two shades darker than me, she is, which is sometimes all it takes to catch Max's eye.

"So you take the polenta and the salad." Max's sharp blue eyes scan the ceiling. "I can do the rest." He swats my ass for emphasis. "Is OK?"

I suppose. But either way, because Max isn't really expecting me to say no, I don't answer. He won't ever let me cook food he thinks is too complicated for me. Not in three years of living together. He even checks to see how I boil water.

"We don't have a vegetable," I say. I remember my mother's greens. I go to the refrigerator and pull them out. "We could cook these."

I'm picking a fight, that's all. Max planned the dinner a week ago and will not want to serve these with his other courses, I already know. Or maybe I'm not picking a fight. Maybe I'm giving him the chance to indulge me in the smallest thing, like when we first met and everything I said was endearing and every minute he told me I was beautiful.

"Avie, those don't go." He brushes past me and buries his head in the refrigerator. "There is spinaci," he says muffled, far away. He pulls his head out. Bottles clink and rattle when he slams the door. "A little olive oil and garlic. It will be fine."

"I think mustard greens will go just as well with polenta."

"Too heavy. Spinaci is better."

"You could let people decide, Massimo. We could cook *both*."

He stares at me with his hands on his waist. I don't even want the greens, not that badly. I just want the final words this time.

"You are whining like a kid."

"What's wrong with my mother's greens?" I still have them in my hands. I shake them at him.

"My head," Max mutters. "With them, nothing is wrong." He holds his head in his hands and massages his temples. "But you. You are another matter."

⌒

This dinner tonight will be a disaster, if not for Silvio. Pretty candles and nice presentation doesn't clear the air. Max's old friends and coworkers from his first restaurant—Lucky, Sanchez, and Sanchez's girlfriend—will come. "It has been too long," Max said when planning the dinner. Silvio will come, too, and I like him best of all Max's friends. He's warm. He's truly kind. He teases me, calls me Black Beauty.

"Black Beauty is a horse," I said, the first time he called me that.

"But, ah, Bellisima," he teased, "you are just as beautiful as the horse." He's the only one I want to talk to tonight.

Max is not speaking to me because I ruined the polenta. It should have been thick and firm enough to quiver when I shook it.

"What have you done to the polenta!" he yelled as if I had cut off his right arm. It was thin and runny as soup when I spooned it into one of our best serving bowls.

"Massimo," Silvio said gently, trying to smooth things. "It's only cornmeal. Right, Avery?" He kissed me on the forehead and I appreciated the scratchiness of his gray beard. He stuck his finger in the mess and tried not to make a face after he tasted it.

So we're getting by without it and Max looks at everyone but me. There are eight of us, and the rest are doing their best to pretend they're not uncomfortable because the hosts are not speaking to each other. It's the worst thing Max can do to me, ignore me, look through me. I'd rather he throw a plate across the room, which is what he usually does when he's most furious.

To cope, everyone's getting drunk from the several bottles of wine the guests have brought for the dinner. Max sulks and chain-smokes. I pour wine like water and think about how I don't like Sanchez's date, Cookie, beautiful and caramel colored, dressed like a hooker. Fishnet stockings. I don't know who wears those anymore. They brought a friend, Theresa, who seems distant and snotty, probably because she's one of the most beautiful women I've ever seen, with hair for days and eyes the color of emeralds. Max somehow met her and thought I'd like her because she reminded him of me, which is mind-boggling. Because Sanchez, who *is* handsome, only seems to be interested in catching his reflection in the window and watching Theresa's every move, I like Lucky and Silvio the best tonight. They fight good-naturedly and are a study in opposites, enormous Lucky, near 300 pounds, and lanky Silvio. They keep my mind off of Max.

While Leonard Cohen sings in monotone from the CD player, Theresa decides to tell a story that she heard earlier, she says, about a parrot who was fed laxatives at the last party she went to. "And so this bird, it shits all over *everything*. I was *dying*! It was quite funny," she says. We all laugh politely and keep drinking, and Leonard Cohen gets more and more on my nerves. Max loves him for some reason, but I hate him; to me he sings like he's at a funeral that never ends. Parties aren't supposed to be reminiscent of funerals. I think about the last time I really had fun at a gathering, four years ago when my family first met Max. At the end of the night, Uncle Ra Ra said he was tired of me watching everybody else dance. He dragged me out into his living room to dance with him to the Ohio Players, *Roller coaster! Of love, say what?* And then Max cut in on us and we danced close and slow, even though it was a fast song.

All day worrying and worrying about getting to where I needed to be and this is it. A dinner funeral.

"Jesus," Lucky says finally tired of sparring with Silvio. "What the fuck?" He motions toward the stereo. "What are you trying to do? Depress us?"

I look around at all the people in our house. In Max's house. I want to be somewhere else. "That story? About the uh, the uh, bird?" I stutter. Theresa looks at me expectantly. I turn up a wine bottle and drink from it. I think I'm getting sick drunk. I can't tell yet. "That is the stupidest shit I ever heard."

⌒

Silvio's brought me outside to look at the stars because he thinks I need some air. "Silvio, I'm not so drunk that I don't know you can't see stars in L.A." I lean on him, wrap my arms around him. He's so tall that my face rests just below his chest.

"Yes, you can see them," he says. "Just squint like this." He takes off his tiny round silver glasses that make him look like he belongs in the 1920s. His eyes, syrupy brown, aren't as enormous without them. "Do the face like this." He crunches up his face and chuckles after he makes sure I imitate him. I do, but I still can't see anything.

"Ah, is OK. You can keep trying," he says, resting his head on top of my cropped, fuzzy head. I like that Silvio lets me lean into him. I like how deep his voice vibrates through his chest into my ear. He's warm and I feel so cold.

I rub his back, and he even lets me pull the shirttail from his pants, but this may only be because he's surprised. He doesn't stop me until my hands touch the bare skin on the small of his back, underneath the waist of his khakis.

"Bella, you are drunk. And I am old enough to be your father." He pulls my hand from his pants and traps it between his own large hands. Silvio looks at me as if I'm an amusing but incorrigible child.

And then I'm startled by Max's voice behind us. "Those things, yes," he says from a place in the yard I can't see. "And the third thing is that you are like a fucking father to *me*."

⌒

In the house, everyone puts on their jackets in a hurry and Silvio tries to calm Max down, but Max refuses. Silvio tries to pry my arms from around his waist, but I won't let go. I might fall down. "Massimo," he says, "we are all very drunk and tired, that is all. Avie meant nothing, no harm."

"Why are you speaking for her!" Max shouts after snatching a cigarette from his lips. He's failed to light it three times now. "Let me hear what she has got to say about it all."

Nothing. I have nothing to say. It's all I can do to make it to the bathroom to vomit.

⌒

Not until everyone leaves the house does Max smash half the dishes in the house and call me twenty different kinds of whores—in English and Italian.

"But what about the whore at the restaurant!" I've been saving this bombshell for maximum strength. He didn't know that I knew until now.

"That is different!" Max shoots back after a moment of shock. "She is not family!"

I'm much too drunk and much too sad and tired to argue that point, unlike my mother years and years ago.

We leave everything broken and I imagine that tomorrow Max will say this just isn't working anymore. And if he does, what will I do? I haven't had a job in three years, not since living with Max. How easily I was had. A tiramisu, compliments of Massimo the chef, and soon I was in his bed and living in his house, both of us stricken by the foreignness of the other. And how easily I had let Max down, faking a strength to match his, strength that's harder and harder to find.

I try to sleep on the couch in the living room, fighting waves of nausea and listening for sounds of Max tossing and turning in bed. It's so sad, how much he used to love me in that bed. How he used to marvel at the contrast between our skin. We used to lie side by side on our backs, my dark arm against his nearly translucent one, reaching toward the ceiling.

"How beautiful, Avie," he would say. "How beautiful is the skin."

And I would laugh at his bad syntax that was so charming.

⌒

Everything's swervy and wavy and I just want to fall asleep. I barely know where I am. I might be dying. I truly think I might be dying. Mama help me, like when I was a child and you rubbed Vicks salve all over my body. Or when you rubbed away the cramps in my leg that hurt so badly I screamed myself to sleep.

If I weren't so ill, I'd get in my car and drive to you. Tomorrow? Maybe tomorrow. But if it were now, and if I knew where I was, I'd get on the 101 freeway, then take the 10 to the 60. I'd make a right and go down Montana, where my elementary, junior high, and high school are all in a row. At the four-way stop I'd make a left onto Arboles, where I used to play with Ashley in the seventh grade. I'd make another left on Verdugo, to your house, Mama, in the center of all the houses on the dead end. When I got to your house I'd ring the doorbell, even though I have a key. Maybe you'd be surprised to see me, stand in the doorway and forget to let me in. The happiness on your face would shame me. You'd say, "What?" Pull your nightgown tight across your chest. "Did you forget something? Is everything OK?"

"Mama," I'd say finally. "I'm lost."

Lisa Jones

"It's Racier in the Bahamas" was written in 1989 and published in
Bulletproof Diva *in 1994. Back then, writing personal essays felt brand
new, dangerous, and liberating, akin to hang gliding or playing with
matches in the Big House. Middle-class Black women writers wore gir-
dles and wrote about sit-ins in Mississippi, not their personal lives. I
wanted to be a race woman, but I wanted to wear a leather jacket and
write about politics in the bedroom, about when the lights go off and he
asks you to wear a blonde wig. Then hip-hop arrived, and writing
about sexual politics became less interesting. Sex was everywhere—both
signifying everything and nothing at all. I remain committed to autobiographical writing, though I find it more of a challenge at this stage
of life. How does one balance substance, elegance, and the bare-ass
truth? Or maybe, says the other voice in my ear, I should just settle
down and write fiction.*

It's Racier in the Bahamas

From *Bulletproof Diva: Tales of Race, Sex, and Hair,*
a collection of essays

WE FOUND OUT a long time ago that everyone masturbates and that everyone wants to be rich. The new truth is that everyone is consumed with the same racial mythologies that made this country so great:

Blondes have more fun if they're sleeping with black men; black women of all complexions prefer dark-skinned black men; white men love themselves exclusively, they invented masturbation; Puerto Rican women in Hartford have the hots for black men; women who love women want to make it with women of color; white men in leather want black men, also in leather; Asians of both countries want it bad with everyone; light-skinned black American women with money think they invented pussy; light-skinned Latin men, especially Colombians, love and marry dark-skinned women from all Latin countries; progressive black American men with money say color isn't an issue, yet are only seen in public with women with "good hair"; progressive dark-skinned black American women who get no play from color-struck brothers are experimenting with white men; the finest men in the world are all black and are usually from Zimbabwe, Atlanta, or Brooklyn; the finest women in the world are from Brazil, come in all colors, but usually have hair like Troy Beyer, Diahann Carroll's daughter on *Dynasty*. And if you think you don't fit into all this, you're lying.

Two things happened recently that convinced me these allegories are held to be self-evident:

One: Last year before it got too cold, two friends and I were drinking beer one Sunday at an outdoor café on Bleecker Street. Sucker for heated discussion, I suggested that instead of sexual fantasies, we trade race fantasies (which would lead us to class and sex anyway).

First on the chopping block was Idris, a Latina from the Bronx, who confessed that her race fantasy was to be rich, like Donald Trump, and to marry a man who was even richer, like Howard Hughes. Though it was not crucial that her husband be Howard Hughes—after all, he was dead—it was most important that he be white, and for all practical purposes, impotent. She would jet around the world giving her husband's money away to people of color fighting wars of national liberation. She would take lovers at every port. These lovers could be of either sex, but would always be of color.

Up second was Patrick, black and gay from East New York. Pat said his race fantasies involved that idea of uplift as well. He wanted to be very rich, like Rockefeller, and run a home for young black and Latino homosexuals. He would be an idol of desire, father figure, and priest to these young men, but take none as his lover, preferring to date rich white men exclusively.

I am a child of leftist bohemians, so my fantasy involved the American dream. I'd bury my racial impurities forever by marrying into an old black family of race men, mother five heirs to the mantle, live in a huge house in the suburbs of a thriving black metropolis, vacation in Sag Harbor, and solely by virtue of my virtue as a black woman, be involved in changing the world every moment of my life. Some who know me well say this scenario is not true, and others say it's true without a doubt; which I guess gives it credence as a fantasy.

Even funnier than our three-hour conversation was that during the course of it we each witnessed an ex-flame of ours actually pass by strutting his fantasy. (Pat, an intense middle-aged black man in a beret, was strolling close to a young blueblood.) Was Bleecker Street really the crossroads of the fantasy world or had we been in New York too long?

Two: I went to the Bahamas.

You know about the blue waters, as in gems, and the white sands, as in powdered platinum, and the trees that tower like dinosaurs and bear fruit. You know about the bright drinks with too much rum, and the Isles of Perpetual June, where you spend petite eternities on the beach, toasting your body and reaping your soul. You know about the music. "Hot, Hot,

Hot." You know peas and rice go with conch fritters, and that crawfish walk backward and taste best with lemon and butter. And that "Purple Haze" is not about an acid trip, but the way the sun sets in the Caribbean, clinging to the sky like a scorned lover. These things you know.

But consider this ad for a film released through United Artists in 1958: "'Island Women.' The Whole Ripped-Bare Story of the Beach Babes of the Caribbean! White-hot off the blazing beaches of the Carib sin-ports. . . . The story of excitement-mad 'nice' girls looking for 'kicks' in the luxury isles. Everything you've heard about them is TRUE!"

So it's been going on for a long time. And thirty years later, on the sin-port of Eleuthera—the Bahamas's Beauty Queen, as it's called; one hundred miles of exquisite scenery and beaches, rolling hills and farmlands, white cliffs and seventeenth-century villages, once home to the world's premiere pineapple plantations—it's in full swing.

I'm here for a wedding. My oldest friend, a white woman, gave up painting a couple of years back and went to live in the Bahamas. She is now to marry a local gentleman of reputable family who was educated in North America. They will tend bar together, he will build her a house on a majestic cliff overlooking the aquamarine abyss, and she will find reason to paint again.

The wedding party arriving from stateside includes my friend (I'll call her Sarah) and her three college chums: a Jewish woman from California, a black man from Massachusetts (accompanied by his fiancée, a white woman), a brown-skinned Cuban woman with "good hair" (accompanied by her fiancé, a light-skinned brother with an M.B.A.); along with Sarah's sister (married to a black man), her mother (once married to a black man), and me (looking for a black man). We will spend a week together, including Thanksgiving Day, and share many things, race fantasies not among them.

Traveling in foreign countries is the only time I truly feel like an American. I'm middle class, more or less, and Ivy League–educated, though I'm still ranked as a perpetual minority (read: underclass) by belonging to a caste of people who, worldwide, even in their own countries, are disenfranchised. What this means in my own country is that I am never quite a citizen; or I don't feel like one; or more often than not, I'm not treated like one. One reason I do feel like an American when I travel is that I carry a verification of my citizenship. Even so, I usually spend my entire trip lugging my American baggage—the Howard Beach "accident," the ghost of Eleanor Bumpurs. And just when I've set all this down—it's time to go home.

But this is not home. Here I am in the islands. The sky is blue. The sun is shining. And everyone who is an American—minority, majority, whatever—belongs to one class, the foreigner class. And it is through this identity that I happen upon the curious sensation of being under the skin of a white girl, or at least, under the skin of some stereotype; the one who voyages to Carib sin-ports, meets handsome men who look something like Calvin Lockhart or the young Belafonte, and is wined and dined (though she may often pick up the tab) and made to feel like the most desired woman on the face of this earth.

This is an experience you are not often privy to as a black American woman, even if you are light-skinned and heterosexual like me and have a certain amount of privilege in your own culture. There is always a woman who is lighter, brighter than you are, has longer hair, and lighter eyes than you do, and is willing to give up more to get that brother in the suit. Yes, despite *Elle* magazine–style affirmative action and rap nationalists talking good-brother talk on your radio, the most desired woman on the face of this earth is still a Breck Girl.

And for most of my trip to Eleuthera, I am reminded of this. Perhaps even more so because my beach-side reading material is the copy of *Invisible Man* that I bought at the LaGuardia Airport bookshop before the flight down. (They had an impressive selection of books by black authors. Though I have a copy at home, I chose *Invisible Man* to send a message to the buyers that sacred black texts sell at airports.) *Invisible Man*, even on the beach, even on this beach, which is silver and littered with weeping palms, puts me in a mood: dark, brooding, and very colored (or, should I say, very judgmental?).

Over and over I read the passage in which two crazy men, on a bus bound up North, discuss the fate of our young hero: "Most of the time he'll be working, and so, much of his freedom will have to be symbolic. And what will be his or any man's most easily accessible symbol of freedom? Why, a woman of course." Then I instant replay a couple of scenes in my head:

One: Drinking at a local bar plastered with photos of the foreigner class in various states of debauchery, I encounter a young Bahamian who greets me with lust in his eyes. When I don't respond, he moves immediately to the woman on my left, a full-bodied brunette with blonde ambition. She arranges herself, with a deep breath, to receive his look, her cup size expanding by two letters. The fantasy I assigned the scene: a queen lapping up the sweat of a slave. The way they saw themselves may have been a different story.

Two: Sarah's father, who owns a furniture business in Latin America, tells me at the bar one night that, not only is he giving his daughter to her husband, he is giving her to the entire island. It's an offering the white man's burden requires him to make.

The well-to-do ladies of Eleuthera—the most dizzying array of light-skinned black women in polyester ever assembled under a thatch roof—throw Sarah a bridal shower. The women of the American wedding party, myself included, arrive late and are ushered to a table in the middle of the room where we sit by ourselves surrounded by red and pink streamers. As we file by the local women shoot us with looks that could raise the dead. I know these looks well because I am usually not on the receiving end, but dishing them out.

I realize that this is the first time in the five days that I've been here that I have spent more than five minutes in the company of black women. On the beaches and in the bars, it's women of the foreigner class and island gigolos. Here I am relieved to be setting eyes on them finally, and they're looking at me like I've got honorary white status. And I'd get more scorn for that than the other Americans would get for being white. And what about the white Americans? How do they see me down here? While Sarah is opening her gifts, the Jewish woman from California whispers to me, "I'm so glad they did this for her. Sarah's busted her ass for *these* people," as if Sarah had spent ten years doing missionary work on the island.

One day we drive out to Savannah Sound, the poor Eleuthera. Goats and chickens cross the roads casually. The sun seems brighter on this part of the island, as in no rest for the weary. Here the trees really weep, the wind makes their branches bow to the ground. Sarah has taken some of the American wedding party to visit her husband's poor relatives. They live in a little rectangle of a house that looks like a train car, worn at the edges, yet tended with love.

In the back room sits a pretty young woman in glasses, brown-skinned and petite, surrounded by ten children, two of them infants. She tells me that with two kids of her own, she is too poor to work outside of the home, so she minds neighborhood kids instead. The white women rush to the children, who are mostly boys, all pretty and brown with holes in their clothes, and pet and coo over them as if they were small animals. These are children who in the States would be passed up for adoption, who as young men would be seen as angry and without options—and by routine feared. I turn away to avoid shooting looks at anyone I have to share a hotel room with later.

In bed that night I read about the other Bahamian islands in a guide-book called *Welcome Bahamas*. "San Salvador: This island is preening for its Big Moment, October 12, 1992, the 500th anniversary of the arrival of Christopher Columbus in the New World. . . . Cat Cay: Posh, yachts, mil-lionaires, and fishing tournaments . . . the Prime Minister has announced plans to increase per capita income to $10,000 annually. This is the pri-mary criterion for entering the First World, a goal sought for the Bahamas by the twenty-first century." I write in my journal: "The way Sarah walked through the shack her new relatives live in; how grand she must feel living among such humble, appreciative people who treat her like royalty, make much of her otherness, gladly step and fetch. What security that yields, what accomplishment, what an affirmation of her femininity, of her class position, of her self worth."

What about Sarah? In grade school we took modern dance from a vampire on the Bowery; at fourteen, we were groupies to a black rock band; at eighteen, we did Europe by backpack. What could a nice bohemian girl like her want with a Cinderella fantasy like this? And why did she have to travel to the Caribbean to find it? For one thing, she didn't have to dress up like an investment banker and work overtime; or beg, borrow, and steal, like Sherri Levine, for a loft in Tribeca. In America, these days, even a white woman has to work hard to get to that brother in the suit. Down here, all Sarah had to do was be. The natives took care of the rest. I am reminded of the woman at the bar with the expanding cleavage: Who can affirm a queen, but a slave?

⌒

The wedding is a grand opera of color. The road, jet black from last night's rain; the trees, fragrant and moss green. As our car approaches the church, wedding guests overtake the road, and we must drive behind them form-ing a slow, almost lazy procession. The healthy brown of their skin sparkles red in the noon light. And the clothes: pink satins, every imagina-ble blue, from busy royal to powder pure, hot orange coupled with lace,

reds that scream (as in hibiscus), and reds that moan (as in burgundy).
The church, pastel green trimmed with vanilla, sits on a hill, earth green,
and spread out below are fifty perfectly whitewashed steps. The grooms-
men, magnificent in a white even brighter than the steps, their bow ties
and cummerbunds scorching aqua; the groom himself, all in white, could
be off to his first communion. The gold piping on the bibles, the purple
stained-glass windows, the little chestnut-skinned flower girl whose hair
glistens as orange as flying fish eggs. The bride, like a pearl, her dress shimmering under the sun, tells me later that she was completely naked underneath. When the reverend reads the objection clause, the packed church
holds its breath. The groom's legs shake violently. I expect an old girlfriend
of his to come running into the church and lay a baby at the altar. No one
is safe in paradise, I think. Not even a white girl.

The reception is held at a country club facing the Atlantic Coast of the
island. It was built in the fifties and hasn't been used for years; its white-
painted verandas and gazebos blistering under the rays, its paths and gar-
dens in need of grooming, all adding to the old-world elegance of the
place. (Oh colonialism, such a style war.) After the toasts, the reception
turns into an island jump up. At the bar, men in tuxedos place colored
potions before me: Bahama Mama, Torpedo Sunsplash, Lone Wolf (crème
de menthe, vodka, amaretto, with a garnish of rhubarb), Castro Libre (a
Cuba Libre with 150 proof Bacardi). A drug kingpin, who now owns
hotels, a regal black man in a navy blue jacket and white colonial kickers,
asks to ride me back to New York in his six-seater. A customs officer I met
at the Nassau airport offers me a job as his mistress. To my right and left,
I hear lines like: "God bless America, she lookin' fine"; "This package
wrapped nice, mon"; and "Gimme a beautiful sister like you, I'll cut the
white girls loose tomorrow."

For the first time in the seven days I've been here I realize how black
women of the foreigner class fit in. It seems we have an even higher currency
in these parts. The experience we offer is like traveling to China and buying
a Coca-Cola T-shirt. And what does the experience offer us? If you had no
ambition other than to feel like an heiress on the run from Mommy and
Daddy, being ogled over by brown-skinned men with wide white smiles
and large hands (playing Shirley Temple to his Bill Robinson or Fredi
Washington to his Paul Robeson, however you see yourself, ladies, this is the
islands, no one is judging), you could have stopped the clock, stood right
there, with one eye on the ocean, the other on the subject at hand.

But me, I'm sightseeing. Just want to look. Yes, I'm just here for the sights. The breeze off the ocean, ninety degrees in the shade. Just a little look-see. "Nice girl travels to sin-port meets carefree island hunk. Everything you heard is true" is not my fantasy. My fantasy, the consummate race man, is only a reality. In fact, that's his problem. He's back in America, giving it to some undeserving babe and giving it to her good: He calls it freedom. Oh the horrors. The tide has turned; I'm indignant. Someone has the nerve to request "Hot, Hot, Hot" for the third time. Two beach blondes, burned golden and flaunting it in white minis, walk into the country club and are carried aloft, like figureheads on a ship's bow, by five Bahamians gyrating to an R&B ode to Casanovas. This is a freaking minstrel show. I'm calling Delta tomorrow, change my flight goddammit. No, I don't want another drink. Don't even think about putting your hand on my thigh. I'm a black American, goddammit, and I'm not impressed.

The only person who could get a rise out of me at this moment is Denzel Washington—the closest thing Hollywood has to offer to a young race man. And, sure enough, he walks in. Not really, but there's enough of a resemblance to prompt a full-body rush. He appears under a gazebo, materializing from thin air, like Denzel did when he played Steve Biko in *Cry Freedom*. When you see a man like this, you realize why white men had to convince themselves colonialism was a God-given right. Michelangelo's David ain't got a thing on this. This is God's idea of Development. If blue collar is your fantasy, you've got the wrong number. This is the lost Nubian prince hotline. Never mind the class wars, give us a king, but make him dark skinned. The sculpture of the head and always the dialectic: blackness of hair against brownness of skin. Every gesture, done as if to music, and the eyes, the brown eyes. Later for Cupid's bow, this boy is throwing javelins from across the ballroom, and they're aimed straight at the groin.

I went back for Christmas.

Helen Elaine Lee

Reading was a kind of religion in my family. So literature had always had this central role in my life, and I think I've taken my primary nourishment from the companion activities of reading and writing. I write fiction because it is the thing that makes me feel most alive, and because stories transform and enrich people. Stories can disturb the reader from complacency so that she examines and reconsiders personal and community choices and allegiances, and they can also bring healing. I hope to make readers say: That's about me, that says something to me about where I stand and how I might approach my life, about what matters.

Writing fiction is part mystery, part discipline. You have to be able to live with uncertainty and doubt, as these are parts of the territory of making art. And you must be in the world paying great attention, as a story can begin anywhere, with an image; a bit of overheard conversation; a family tale; a person observed or known; an object or place. Once snagged, I try to follow the seemingly small thing that compels me into the unknown, trusting that I will be led somewhere meaningful, and working hard for the words that will bring it to life. I sit down and try in a regular way, with the help of habit and ceremony, which varies from time to time and might involve the morning newspaper, journal writing, tending my plants, listening to my favorite music, even lighting candles on my altar. And I do this knowing that writing is a mysterious process where there are no external rewards or givens.

The excerpt included here is a chapter from my first novel, which grew out of a short story about the two characters, Ouida and Zella, inspired by my great-aunt and her lover of fifty years. In writing this, I was trying to recognize and honor the story of women loving each other as far back as the Twenties, and to talk about the silences people keep and impose which prevent them from being known, and which may compromise their integrity. Several people who read that short story, which captures them in old age and looks back at their life together, said it seemed like it wanted to be bigger than it was, and it became one of the narrative threads of the novel. Through those threads, which periodically intersect, the novel raises questions about risk-taking and renewal, about what the hero's journey entails and costs. Ouida makes such a journey, full of emotional risk and rich struggles for awareness, and she makes it with Zella at her side.

From *The Serpent's Gift*, a novel

Just as LaRue was getting to know Olive, Ouida was having her own summer of discovery. She was finding out about choosing, and about a woman she had never expected to know.

Her kisses were like nighttime secrets, and Ouida swore that her laugh, like the rain, made things grow. Zella Bridgeforth touched her somewhere timeless, held her, compelled her with her rhythms, and Ouida answered her call. She chose her, after all, but the path that led to Zella took her, first, through other choices.

The summer of 1926, the summer they had met, Ouida would later think of as her "swan song." She had swung her corset-cinched body along the streets of the city with long steady strides, smiling but never meeting the eyes of those who paused from whatever they were doing to partake of her radiance. Just divorced from Junior, she was finished, finally, with trying to will their union into rightness.

As soon as she had landed her manicurist job and rented her flat, she had surveyed the range of the possible from the vantage point of her manicurist's table, feeling, for the first time in her life, that she owned the choice. From the spin of options, she made assessments. And she did some choosing.

She chose Johnston Franklin, the middle-aged white man who stopped in the shop on his business trips from Louisville. He came in and stared at her while waiting for a chair, and she met his glance, her chin in the air, and kept working. While he sat for his haircut and shave, he asked Alton, one of the barbers, who she was. When Alton didn't answer, Johnston Franklin turned in the chair, his face half-covered with lather, and addressed Alton with a demanding look. Alton turned away and stirred his soap, assessing the cost of defiance. Finally, he said, "I think she's married, sir. Least that's what I've heard."

Johnston Franklin laughed and said, "Well, I'm not interested in her husband. What is her name?"

Alton stirred his soap some more and then answered, "Ouida Staples. Miss Ouida Staples."

Ouida had noticed the exchange and could see Johnston Franklin coming her way out of the corner of her eye, but she refused to look up. She sat at her table humming while she polished and arranged her instruments, the edge of his gold fob, a crisply creased pant leg, and the tip of an expensive shoe just within view. Finally, when he realized that she wasn't going to look up at him, he sat down and ordered a manicure. She took his hands and began her task.

"I understand your name is Ouida," he said, "and that's an unusual name." She lifted her eyes slowly, as if it was an effort, assessed his face in an instant, and returned to his hands. The barbers watched to see what she would do.

"And how *are* you today, Ouida?" Johnston Franklin tried again.

"Oh, I'm just fine," she answered with a hint of insolence as she lifted her eyes, "sir."

"Well . . . I don't recall seeing your lovely face in this establishment before . . ." Ouida kept filing, silently.

"I come in here every month or so . . . here on business, quite regularly, and I will certainly make it a habit to visit this establishment more often." She filed his nails silently, thinking how soft and pale his hands were.

"Well . . ." he ventured, "this town sure is different from my home . . . it's the city, all right, and I do like, now and again, seeing something besides trees . . . of course, this town doesn't compare to New York . . . now that's a different story, that's the real city. Have you ever been to New York, Ouida . . . Miss Ouida?"

She shook her head, and kept working on his nails. And receiving neither information nor interest, he jerked his hand away as she was finishing up, paid his bill, and left. He returned the next week, and the next, watching her from the barber chair, and when he was finished being shaved, he came up to her and leaned over her table until she met his eyes. Matter-of-factly, he said, "It would be my pleasure if we could spend some time together . . . tonight, perhaps."

She looked at him, her head tilted, and measured the choice. She saw a square pink face, not so different from many she had seen, well fed and well tended, and even though it wasn't a face that moved her much, she thought she could look into his restless moss green eyes for a little while. It was a face that held the promise of things she couldn't afford, and their delivery with a kind of homage.

She glanced over at the barbers, Alton and Regis, who watched the whole thing unfold and waited for her to resist sweetly, and their expectations bred defiance. The other barber, Flood, never looked her way.

"Not tonight," she answered as she stood up and went to tend to some other job, making him wait until she returned to tell him when.

It was a timeless play, the choreographed conquest of strange exotic prey, and Ouida was willing to play it for a time. It was a variation on a role she knew, and even though she was familiar with the script, she liked to think that it was she, in fact, who controlled the hunt, fooling the hunter into thinking things moved along by his design. She figured she could learn something about the rest of the world from Johnston Franklin, about the places he visited that she had never been. She liked the challenge. She liked the gifts he brought. And she liked his liking, too.

Their first night of sex, Johnston Franklin had undressed completely and was waiting for her in the bed when she came in from the bathroom, and she stood, fully dressed, and looked at him. "Well, you certainly are direct, Johnston Franklin. You get right to the point."

She found herself calling him by his full name, even in bed. And after they had sex he talked to her of his business trips, of meetings and sales and the shops and restaurants he had visited. It was as if just being around Ouida made something in him loosen and spill out, the things he held separate from the rest of his life. Eventually, he started discharging the details of his day, his aspirations and his self-doubts, as soon as he saw her, and he talked all the way through undressing, right up to their first embrace.

He was captivated by her beauty, and her knowledge of its power, and he had seen it in the way she made him wait that first day he saw her, and had wanted it for his own, sensing there was something, some kind of magic, that she knew. He wanted to know it too.

He wanted to know about the way she lived life up close. While he heard things and looked at colors and shapes from somewhere outside of himself, he could tell that when Ouida did something, she was right in the middle of it. He asked her to reveal to him her eye for things, and he asked her to give him the rich details she saw. "Tell me a texture," he would say, as they lay in the rich linen of his hotel, and she would begin to describe some fabric she had seen.

"Silky, like a river in sunlight, and purple, with flaws that aren't flaws, but just the way of the cloth. And it feels purple, Johnston Franklin. You know how purple feels? Rich, with a grain that's both kind to and hard on the fingertips. Now it is your turn," she said, lying back on the pillows. "Tell me about the trees you have at home."

"Okay . . . well . . . let's see," he said and then stopped. "I can't," he protested, but she continued to prod him. "Okay, okay. The trees in my front yard are oak trees. They are live oak trees."

"Live oaks," she said.

"Yes. Live oak."

"Well, that doesn't mean a whole lot to me, Johnston Franklin. Are they shaped like fat stodgy men, or lithe like young girls? Are they dark, and do other colors show through in spots? Are they sheltering, or does the rain get past the leaves? And what does the bark feel like to the touch . . . does it stand away or cling to the wood?"

He leaned back against the pillow and tried to imagine them. "They're shaped . . . like oak trees are shaped, I guess. I never noticed. And they're green . . . and brown, like I suppose most trees are."

"Well, how does the trunk feel?" Ouida asked.

"They are like . . . they're live oak, that's all. I don't know what else to say," he stammered, as she shook her head and argued. "I know what you call them, Johnston Franklin, but what are they like to you?"

"We had them put in a long time ago . . . they're what everyone has . . . and they're old . . . and big . . . and they have leaves, like all trees. I don't know what else to say. I don't know, that's all I see."

Ouida looked at him, propped on her elbow, and then slid down under the covers and went to sleep.

Johnston Franklin visited weekly for several months, but Ouida began to withdraw from him as she felt him trying to hold her closer and closer, like a butterfly in a Ball canning jar. Waxed paper stretched across the top. Breathing holes punched through.

The last time they met, on one of his regular forays from his wife and family, he held on to her as she got up to leave, and demanded to know where she was going. Ouida pulled her arm free and gave him a decimating look as she got her things to leave. When she glanced back to look at him for the last time, she saw a child whose fingers held traces of the black and orange dust of captured butterflies.

When it was just about finished with Johnston Franklin, Ouida chose the barber, Flood, who drew her with the economy of his attention, and looked at her from underneath his eyes. The other barbers flirted with her all the time, and played at asking her out. "You shore is one fine-lookin' woman," Alton would say, leaning on the arm of his chair as he waited for his first customer, shaking his head. "When, just when, are you gon' marry me?"

"After she marry me and I leave her," Regis answered, " 'cause you know a woman fine as she is don't mean nothin' but trouble. I prefer the ugly ones, truth be told, 'cause that way you're glad when they leave you."

She laughed at them playfully, and said, "You two are just no good. What about that devoted little lady of yours at home, Alton?"

"She would understand. She know I just married her 'cause I was waitin' on you."

Flood never joined in the joking, and he barely even smiled. Ouida didn't even know if he was married, and as she wasn't looking for a husband, she didn't care. He never looked her way when Johnston Franklin came to the shop, and he never shaved him or cut his hair. He prepared all of his own lotions and tools, neither accepting nor offering help. He traveled solo, with a hardness about him that she wanted to work soft.

When Ouida had passed between barber chairs one afternoon in search of towels, and brushed against his arm, he hadn't started, or looked at her, but she had seen the muscles in his forearm tense as he gripped his comb. After that she found reasons to go by his chair. Knowing that she would have to go after him, and thrilled by the pursuit, she brought him a cup of tea one morning and left it on the counter behind his chair. He let it sit all day, never thanking her and never drinking it. She did the same thing the next day, and the next, until, holding the cup with both hands, warming his palms, he lifted it to his mouth and drank. And as he lowered the cup, he looked at her with desire, and a trace of contempt.

The next evening, she waited until Alton and McGraw were gone, and she and Flood were left to lock up. Fiddling with his scissors and combs, he slowly cleaned up his chair and the floor around it, while she arranged and rearranged her manicurist tools, unable to speak. He went for his coat and hat and headed for the door. As he reached for the doorknob, she spoke.

"Flood?"

He stood with his hand on the knob and his back to her and then he turned, and she said nothing as he stood at the door waiting for her. They walked to her flat, and as soon as they got inside the door, they tore at each other's clothes, and took each other on the bare floor, as if it couldn't be helped, as if it had to be that way, the hard urgency a hurting they both wanted to feel. As soon as it was over, he dressed and left without saying good-bye, and Ouida didn't think of the risk she had taken until it was too late.

At the barbershop, things didn't change on the surface, and Ouida knew little more about Flood than before. What she did know was that the heat, the tension between them would make him return, and she waited for him to come to her again. At times she wondered if she had dreamed it, until a week later, she had stood watching him after Alton and McGraw had left, and he looked at her and grasped the back of his chair tight, until the leather squeaked. She knew he wanted her again; and again, he waited at the door.

In their fevered loving, Ouida saw Flood surrender, silently, to something in her. She wanted to be the one who reached him, against his will, the one whom he couldn't help but come back to, the one who excavated his pain, his need, and for a time, she was willing to exchange peace for the intensity of the fight. Again and again, she tugged on the one string that joined them and she reeled him in.

When this was no longer enough, Ouida had tried to push it further, to find out who he was, but the two of them were stuck in a moment in time, repeating again and again the same act, moving nowhere. By the time she heard Zella's call, she was letting go of what she had, and didn't have, with Flood, and she chose Zella, rain-voiced, in whom she met herself.

The first time she saw her, Zella was standing on the corner waiting for a streetcar as it began to shower, and Ouida watched her digging in her bag from the barbershop window for something to shield herself, cursing as her hair got wet. As soon as she had pulled out a newspaper to cover her head, she had tossed it down and stood there laughing as her head got soaked. Ouida glanced up and saw her as she was putting her instruments away, and moved to the window to watch as Zella lifted her arms and face to the rain and shook her head, opening her generous mouth to taste the falling water.

The next time she saw her, Zella had come into the shop for a haircut on the weekday allotted for colored customers, and Ouida had watched her enter and approach Alton's chair, struck by the way she moved with authority over space. She was tall and slender, and a few years older than Ouida, almost thirty. Her skin was copper-colored and her hair was a mass of dark ringlets, but it was her large flashing black eyes that were remarkable, one smaller than the other. When she walked over to Alton's chair and sat down, he came around to face her and declared, "Now you don't need a shave, and I know you not even thinkin' 'bout cuttin' off all that pretty hair, so just what are you doin' in my chair?"

Zella frowned and gave him a look that was a challenge. "You cut hair, don't you," she stated, rather than asked, and Alton nodded. "Well," she said, "I suspect you cut it like your customers ask you to, is that right?" and Alton nodded again. "Then I suggest you get busy with your scissors and crop mine just above my cheek. Right about here," she said, gesturing with her hand.

Alton argued with her a while, but he gave in when Zella said, "Why is it that colored folks feel every bit of our hair ought to be on our heads! If we were as concerned with what's in our heads as we are with what's on them, we'd be a lot further along."

At that, Alton had to laugh, and he took up his scissors. He shook his head as her hair fell to the floor, and exclaimed what a shame it was the entire time, and after Zella looked at the finished product in the mirror, she got up, paid him, and left, nodding to Ouida on the way out.

"Well," Alton said, as she was leaving, "Girl, bet' not mess with that one. I know her peoples, and she ain't quite right. What I mean to say is . . . she ain't normal."

When Ouida stared at him, wanting to know more but afraid to ask, he continued, "I know she'd like a sweet young thing like you all for own. Her kind, they like that."

"Now that's a lovely woman," Zella said to herself once she was outside. She turned back and caught Ouida's eye through the window, and there was between them a moment of recognition, whose power made them turn away.

Ouida went to the family house that evening and stayed the night, and Vesta sat on the edge of her bed working lotion into her face while Ouida was brushing and plaiting her hair. "Vesta, I met someone who's different," she ventured, unsure of herself.

"Different . . ." Vesta replied. "What does that mean?" And Ouida paused. "I don't know. Different, somehow. I don't know how to explain it."

"You gotta do better than that, Ouida," Vesta said. "It's late and I'm not up to reading minds tonight."

"Well . . . she gets her hair cut short, and at the shop," she began, to which Vesta raised her eyebrows. "I don't know, she's kind of not feminine, but she is feminine after all." Vesta just looked at her.

Ouida told Vesta what Alton had said and then she stopped brushing and asked, "What do you think, Vesta? You know anything about these things?"

Vesta didn't and so she shook her head. "I've heard of people like that, but no, I don't know at all about that sort of thing. I can say, for sure, though, that it sounds like trouble to me," and then she finished up with her face, turned her bed down, and curled up facing the wall. But she lay there in the darkness considering what Ouida had said, and it was a long time before she fell asleep.

The next time Ouida saw Zella, two weeks later, she had thought about what Alton and Vesta had said and she was ready for Zella's greeting, but not for the way she made her feel, like a dry part of her was being watered. "Rain," she whispered to herself, "Rain."

After her haircut, Zella sat down at Ouida's table and said, "I think I'm due for a manicure." In fact, she had never had a manicure, but something in Ouida's response to her glance had pulled her there, and she had to see what her voice sounded like.

"My name is Zella," she opened, and Ouida responded, "Ouida . . . Ouida is my name."

They smiled and Zella asked her what kind of name it was and where she got it. She said quietly, "It was passed down. Or so my mother said." As Ouida worked on Zella's hands, she noticed how strong and worn with experience they looked and felt, and she wanted to know where those hands had been.

Zella began to feel the need for a weekly haircut or a manicure, and she and Ouida found themselves sitting for hours talking while she surrendered her fingers to Ouida's, and felt something in her tear loose. Each time she left she told herself on the way home that she was risking her heart foolishly, that in the end, she would be destroyed. She knew, somehow, that Ouida had known only men, and she told herself that she could never have her and that she had to stop going. But she always found a reason to return.

She stayed one time until the barbershop closed, and the two of them kept on walking down the street toward Ouida's flat. They stopped to buy fruit and when they got to the flat, Ouida made tea and offered Zella one of her chipped cups, and then they sat in the nook she had made next to the kitchen with her cerulean blue chairs, telling about themselves until their hands, both reaching for the teapot, touched.

"Say yes," Zella whispered.

"Yes," Ouida answered. "Yes."

They sat in the last light of the day as it thickened and became gold, entering through the window, coming down to them, meeting them. Lowering itself into their laps, the golden light thick with all that the day had held. Light not merely for seeing, but for touch. For love.

⌣

It was almost dawn again. Almost light, but not yet, not yet. Zella rose from the bed and went to the icebox to get a pear. She sliced it into wedges and removed the seeds, and little beads of juice stood out on the cool inner surface of the fruit. She knelt beside the bed and said, quietly, "Close your eyes."

And she turned a wedge of the iced fruit, turned it, to Ouida, and the open cool innerness of the wedge met her lips. Ouida sank her mouth into it, giving in to it, and Zella fed her, after she was spent, but not really, not quite, not yet, as the fire rose in her again, mingling with the ice-hot wetness of the fruit, into an ache that had to be quenched even though it was getting light, pale light, pale and thin and tinged with blue, thin, but not yet, and it had to be now, even though there would be time for it all again and again and again across the years, it must be now and now and now.

Catherine E. McKinley

I started writing The Book of Sarahs *in a period of intense mourning that followed a year of overwhelming revelations: in 1997, after seven years of searching for my birth family, I reunited with my biological parents and several of a dozen siblings, including two sisters who shared my original birth name, Sarah. The story of the Sarahs revealed my birth parents' choices and huge inabilities (partly stemming from my birth mother's struggle with mental illness). At the same time, I began integrating my Jewish birth mother's heritage, and my African American and Choctaw father's heritage into my heretofore unspecified (because my adoption records were legally "closed") "biracial" Black life. All of this new knowledge forced me to reckon with perhaps the most uncomfortable truth: the extent of the protective skein of fantasies and the lies I'd told on myself since early childhood.*

I am a fiction writer, and my creative wrestlings with transracial adoption originally came to me as fiction, but very soon, the real narrative of my birth history eclipsed my imagination. A writer I admire, Philip Gourevitch, has remarked: "This is what fascinates me most in existence: the peculiar necessity of imagining what is in fact real." He is writing about genocide in Rwanda. It's a wonderful quote, perhaps inappropriately applied here to individual tragicomedy. Yet I am a child of a once projected "genocide." Growing up as one of just a few thousand Black and "biracial" children adopted into white homes in the 1960s and 1970s, when Black social workers were calling up the specter of the mass destruction of Black children as they organized to end such adoptions. I spent most of my young life in the realm of imagination—imagining, reimagining and remaking myself a thousand times into the Black woman I thought I would be if I had grown up with my biological family, bucking my adoptive parent's largely socially isolated life of wilderness-seeking. At the same time, I was being handed a heritage and a connection to other Black lives through literature. I had trouble talking; I was alone most of the time. Writing became a way to communicate and to place myself comfortably within community. *By the time I began my search, I knew that I wanted to try to write, in an exacting way, about the* inside *of transracial adoption and a facet of the post-1960s transracially adopted "mulatta" (trans-bi) social experience. Everyone was projecting the tragic; I wanted to expose the pain and reach for the comic, the unsentimental.*

Now, if, even at the end of searching, my biological family—and what I once hoped would be a pass to easy, "legitimate" membership in a race, a family—is still lost to me, I do have the community of the word and the power as a writer to insert trans-bi girls into the literary imagination.

Catherine E. McKinley
1 September 2002

July 1978

From *The Book of Sarahs: A Family in Parts,* a memoir

Scotland. This is where the whispering began.

⌣

I sat with my family in a pub in Edinburgh, anxious to warm away the sea's soak, caught in the thick sponge of my clothes. We had walked the stretch of rocky shore bordering the campus of St. Andrews, climbing to the great pier that juts out at its edge, marching to my mother's memories. She had led us out along its reach, to the point where the waves began to swallow it, wildly singing processional songs from her days as a student. My brother and I had walked behind her, pacing our steps like supplicants, our riffs on her songs rising into shouts that fell off in the booming tide. My father had lagged behind us, a tiny magnifying glass in his hand, stooping to examine what had pooled among the breakers.

Now we paused for a meal, a drink to say farewell to another point on our tour, a journey back through the McKinley narrative of Scotch-Irish and English migrations. We sat in a far corner of the pub, to the side of a table where two men drank and blew smoke rings in a kind of dramatic repose. The men both wore heavy glasses and well-oiled afros, combed up from the collars of Harris tweed jackets. One wore a trilogy of patterned wool straight down to the tops of platform shoes. I sat and watched their quiet faces, soaking up their languor, imagining I could smell their cologne and pomade in the encircling smoke.

Suddenly an eyebrow raised in one face. The other man sat up. And the whole room seemed to shift, as if on cue. I turned with them and watched an awesome reddish, curled wig and a head, tied with a green and red plaid wool scarf in a beautiful high arch, move above the crowd. The women's headpieces framed smooth, dark faces, penciled with heavy black brows drawn nearly to their temples. Their dark-lined, lipsticked mouths moved together, offering excited greetings as they settled at the table. I sat examining the waxy-sheened, bright print dresses they wore, which revealed sweaters at their wide embroidered and laced necklines. It was an odd way to wear a sweater—on the inside—I thought. But their dresses were so beautiful and the logic of it made simple, new sense to me. Their clothes and talk sent a raucous flash through a gray and green clothed room. They were so lovely to me, reweaving the dull, familiar textures of that world, of home, where the only sight of Africa was an occasional face floating behind the windshield of a passing car, always en route to some-where else. I had come all the way from Attleboro, Massachusetts, to get a good look at Black people.

This trip was a family return, and for me, a reprieve from turning eleven in the dulling heat and tensions of summer in Attleboro. But with every stake put down in the family's past and every new discovery, I was beginning to feel oddly cold. Sitting there, I felt weak, in the way we used it in middle school. Wussy. Soft. Suddenly self-conscious of my knit Skye cardigan and the kilt I wore, fastened at my knees with my grandmother's silver thistle-shaped pin, set with a heavy purple stone. Earlier that day, as my parents shopped for Isle sweaters in the rows of tiny boutiques in town, I had looked for the McKinley tartan among the plaids piled into the shelves. I had talked myself out of my fixation, out of the disappoint-ment of not finding our cloth or crest after the girls in one shop put a chart of old Scottish clans in front of me, pointing to it and laughing, so that I was no longer sure of their kindness. "Are you Scottish?" they asked, looking at my family and then scrutinizing my face, different from theirs, brown like the lighter edge of an iron burn.

"My family is Scotch-Irish," I said, my voice cracking.

I tried to console myself; it wasn't a beautiful tartan at all.

Now the woman's headscarf almost seemed to be taunting me, saying, *Hey, what is this plaid anyway?*

I felt the weakness spreading as I sat watching their table, and I got up and made for the bathroom. I washed the tight stain of salt air from my face and stood looking at myself in the mottled glass above the sink. My thick, curly eyebrows had begun to darken and spread across the bridge of my nose. Those brows, my nose—long and a bit wide and a little turned up at the same time, my brownness, and the two shoulder-length braids I'd worn since primary school had earned me the name "Pocahontas." Mysterious, exotic in those parts, the schoolyard curio. Pocahontas in Scotland, the mirror said. I took off my hat and combed out my hair with my hand. It was cut for the first time in a short afro. I'd taken the afro as my mother's defeat in the battle of caring for my thick, soft naps of hair. It was the end of Pocahontas. And it was my defeat as well—the only afro under the reign of hair spray and Farrah Fawcett flipped bangs at Willet Middle School.

My brother watched me return to the table and to watching them. He sat enjoying me from under a thick shock of white-blond bangs, angling, and then he kicked me under the table, his mouth hanging open in a moronic pose.

"Duuh! Don't stare. It's not polite, and you'll make them feel like they don't belong here."

My mother leaned toward us, whispering. "They're students at the university, I would guess. Africans. They must be Nigerians. There were some Nigerian students when I was there. And William's right—don't stare!"

But I stared so that I barely ate. I watched every shift and gesture they made, while I struggled through the questions that had been growing in me all year. When the Lutheran Church–sponsored Laotian refugee children arrived in our class, prejudice had become part of our lessons. There was talk of race riots in nearby Boston and a lot of relief expressed when it was certain that Attleboro was beyond the possible busing zones. There was the funny confusion I was experiencing of being talked about as "Afro-American" and "Black" and "colored" and "Negro" all at the same time and knowing those things had something to do with Africa, but what exactly? And when I was able to settle that confusion, someone was there to ask another question about being "adopted," or (different from my brother) being adopted "transracially," and having Black and white "biological parents," and being "mixed race," and that other list of things all at the same time. I felt tortured by my strange status and by my isolation and distance from so many things. I watched the table next to ours. Was this the world where I belonged in bigger parts?

I wanted to cross over to them and sit in the roar of their open laughter and the ease they inhabited. Would my confusion stop then?

I was still staring; my mother hissed her schoolteacher's warning at me.

At the sound, one of the men turned. He caught me deep in the eye and winked and smiled at me in a way that I thought offered so much understanding. He turned back to his friends but I kept watching him, hoping he would pull me back with that wink again.

My father paid the bill, and as we rose to leave, the man leaned out from his table and held out his hand to me.

"Dear Lady, what is your name?" he asked.

"Ah, then pleased to meet you, Madame Catherine," he said, drawing out his reply as he dropped his head in a long, elegant nod.

I giggled at his name—Wooly? Wally?—and hurried shyly to my mother's side. He turned back to his conversation and didn't notice me looking back at them on my way to the door until the crowd in the room sealed off my view.

As we walked back through town to the bed-and-breakfast where we'd been staying, I felt rocked with an ache, an old, unspecified kind of grief that would not leave my chest. I lay in bed for hours that night, pretending to read, watching the odd sunlight in the late night sky while William and my parents pored over maps, planning our route into the northern countryside.

⌐‿⌐

The next day we rose before dawn. As we drove further from the city, that ache continued to hold me. Scotland's melancholy began to drift over me. With each movement north, the desolate herds of highland cattle, the mournfulness of the often mist-covered land, the sheep marooned on the confounding pattern of hills, the collapse of peat underfoot as we stopped to stretch, walking the countryside, made me feel that I was losing my hold.

Our family travels always seemed intent on distancing ourselves from other people: packing into the Grand Teton mountains on horseback; canoeing or hiking or skiing for many days without company; weekends when we took off for the woods hoping for two days uninterrupted by the sight of other outdoorers. We traveled for several days now, stopping along the way to hike, or fish at the lakes, or walk along the stone-walled edges of people's farms.

One morning we stopped at a place in the road where we could park our car and began a climb up one of the giant "stacks," the mountainlike hills that dotted the countryside. As we began our hike, my mother and I fell into our rituals of silence, comfortable together in our own heads, letting William and my father blaze the trail ahead of us. We stopped when we guessed we were about halfway to the top, and as we rested, I began one of our scouting games. I loved these games—when we imagined we were pushing through impossible terrain, and getting past it depended on my helping to read the navigational signs. I was not good at the real work of map reading, the setting of equipment, or the gauging of time and elements that William and my parents loved, spending hours at times in an intensely fixed threesome. But together with my mother like this, with my eagle eye and strength and my special sixth sense, I could chart a world of pleasure and have her all to myself.

"Is that sky or mountain?" I began, pointing at the cloudy wall of the horizon.

"It's sky, silly." She moved behind me, one arm wrapping my waist, as she pressed her binoculars to my eyes. She braced my elbow as I tried to steady and focus the glass. I felt her breath hot against my cheek, and my nose was filled with the smells of whiskey and chocolate, familiar balms against the cool air. In just that moment, as I found my sight in the tiny lenses, the etching of clouds had moved, breaking the steep, jagged line of their ascent.

"Your mountain has become smoke," she said, laughing. Then she tried to swing me around the narrow ledge, groaning at my weight, so we could look out further eastward where the sky was uninterrupted by clouds.

"Can you see Cape Wrath? If we jump out wide from here we'll land at the very tip of Scotland!"

I looked down and saw the charcoal water breaking the countless rolls of brilliant green countryside below into a thin wrist of land stretching into the sea. But with the sight of that tip of earth, and the sound of my mother's triumph for reaching this place so far away from everyone, an intense coldness washed over me. She stood for a while, staring through the glasses, locked in a kind of ecstatic trance.

"Mummy, why did you adopt me? Why didn't I get adopted by an African—an Afro-American—family?" I asked, wanting to pull her back to me, surprised by my own question and at the anger trembling in my voice.

At first she didn't seem to hear me, but then she sighed very deeply and dropped the binoculars to her chest, closing her jacket over them. "Well, I guess we came first. You know, we really wanted a second child; we'd waited for a long time. There were very few healthy white infants available to couples who wanted to adopt, and we were asked to consider adopting a Black or mixed-race child. And how could we have refused you?"

It was not a new question. I had asked it in so many configurations that it was no longer the question that mattered. It had become a signal of some anxiety in me—and she had begun to answer me reflexively and to try to take care of the real need more quietly. But this time my question betrayed anger, and I had called out who else I might belong to. The anger I felt seemed lodged in what I knew her answer would be. I was beginning to feel there was something wrong in what she was saying, however much she was trying to speak to a complicated thing and still preserve our "truths" and the need for clarity.

"Come on, let's not waste time," she said, with a sudden gruffness. I immediately wanted to take away the feeling of something difficult erupting between us, to pull her back to our closeness and hold her there. But she had already moved from where we were standing and was lost in her powerful stride and her excitement about what lay further up the trail. I felt something else erupt in the moment she turned from me, and every step now felt labored by my rage.

As we neared the peak, the trail narrowed to little more than a stony goat path, with an eroding earthen wall and a precipice on either side. Waves of nausea and cold sweat began to roll over me, and it seemed that space was collapsing and then opening wild around me. My breath came in ragged waves and then seemed to halt completely. I stood facing the wall, gripping dry, hanging roots, trying to feel my breath moving in me. I could not move. It was as if I had never felt space and wind like this before; I was no longer the brave veteran of our family climbs. They had moved surefootedly beyond me, expecting the baby in the family to push her last bit of strength, proudly keeping up with them. But I was caught in the fist of my anger and breathlessness several shelves of the cliff track below.

I smelled the too-sweet stench of sweat and Lady Mum deodorant from the curve of my armpits and felt the warm liquid drop from their hollow to my waist. My body trembled, and I felt that I would lose myself without the weight of my backpack holding me at the center of gravity.

I looked up at my mother now, moving closer to where William and my father rested at the bald patch of earth at the mountain's very top. She was peering through her glass, looking out again toward the sea.

I wanted the safety of being close to them. But even in my fear, I felt some exhilaration at letting go. I felt myself wanting to test the lines between where I belonged and where I didn't; where I was safe and where I was out of bounds; where they could hold me and where they would let me go. I felt trapped inside an airless space where I was left sputtering, choked with rage. Scotland had brought on something like the emotions of an asthma attack—the kind of terrible struggle you feel when your body cannot take in the air that freely surrounds you, while the people you hope will save you look on from outside, perversely gulping it in. That feeling emerged there on the cliff, and it seemed to hold me for many years.

Itabari Njeri

Every Good-bye Ain't Gone *was my first book, and I was naive when I wrote it. Naive in that I didn't fully comprehend the impact on family, friends, and enemies of seeing representations of them published for posterity. Even though some of the book's most revealing chapters were published earlier as essays and magazine articles in major American newspapers, the disposable quality of broadsheet, a tabloid—the stuff used to line birdcages—mitigates, in the minds of some, the power of language to immortalize experience.*

A family member threatened to sue me over her representation in my memoir, even though she had approved the publication of the same information in the Los Angeles Times *several years earlier. "Well, that, that," she sputtered, "was just a newspaper. How many people read that?" Maybe about a million on Sunday, I told her at the time. "It's not the same thing," she railed. Yeah, it's not. If I'm lucky, I said, maybe a million people will have read* Every Good-bye Ain't Gone *by 2525. "That's just it. People can go to the library and pull out that, that, that thing you call a book forever."*

I was quite shaken that I had upset someone so dear to me, especially when I considered my portrait of her a loving one. I had no such qualms about the subject of the chapter included in this anthology.

I started off by saying I did not fully comprehend the lasting impact of portraying people in print. My background as a journalist accounted for that. The birdcage is dated newsroom imagery, but the fate of the carefully crafted, thirty-inch gem of a story one writes for the morning daily is usually the equivalent of a parakeet's dump site. So when men come up to me a dozen years after the publication of my memoir and say brothers around the country still bend forward and protectively cup their balls every time they read "What's Love Got to Do with It?" I take perverse satisfaction. This chapter was not written as an angry message to men but to a particular man; and when many brothers who know him called me to say they told him, "She got you good," my perverse satisfaction grew into a powerful recognition. I have the gift, the power, to nail anybody's ass to the cross for posterity if I choose. I promise, henceforth, however, to use my superpowers only for the good of humankind.

Itabari Njeri
May 5, 2002
Cambridge, MA

What's Love Got to Do with It?

From *Every Good-bye Ain't Gone*, a memoir

THE BEAUTIFUL WOMAN was half naked and running. She sped down Convent Avenue past a row of tenements on one side, City College on the other, her ponytail flying behind her, her spotless white panties and white bra hugging the most private parts of her cinnamon-colored body. Her feet were bare, her thighs were powerful, her legs were long, her knees came near the tips of her rocket breasts as she propelled herself over curbs, ignoring Don't Walk signs, escaping sure, but to me unseen, danger.

She disregarded Satchel Paige's timeless warning and looked over her shoulder in the next block, losing momentum. If someone was gaining on her, I couldn't make it out. She picked up speed and disappeared down the avenue while I stood on the corner biting a dill pickle, eating from a bag of barbecue potato chips, stupidly staring at her vanishing cloud of cinnamon dust. Why, I wondered, did the beautiful lady have no clothes on? Why was she running? Who could she be running from? It was summer. I was ten. It was all a mystery to me.

It is spring. I am twenty-eight. I have met Nick. Why the cinnamon lady vanished is less a mystery to me now.

◡

I got a present for my birthday. "You're pregnant," the doctor said. My face froze and then I laughed soundlessly. The doctor smiled.

"What about my blocked tubes?" I asked, knowing it was a stupid question now.

"Well, at least one of them is unblocked now," she told me, and said wasn't it "wonderful" to know I could get pregnant after all.

I was silent.

"You and the father should talk this over and make plans for the baby," she futilely encouraged. My face told her what my plans were.

Years before, I'd had a misdiagnosed case of pelvic inflammatory disease. By the time the doctors realized what it was, the infection had left masses of scar tissue in and around my fallopian tubes. The surgeon who operated on me thought it improbable that I'd ever have children. I stopped taking the pill and for years had relied on other forms of birth control successfully—the diaphragm, foams, jellies, and those few "safe" days each month. It was on a safe night, when the moon was full over Miami, that I got pregnant. Dumb.

But I wasn't about to compound my error. I wanted a child one day, but I didn't want one then and I didn't want one by Nicholas Wright. It was a full moon that made me do it and I was infatuated with another man, a thousand miles away.

"I am quite sure that I want an abortion," I told the doctor.

She stiffened. "If you decide to do that, I'll have to refer you to another physician. I don't do abortions," she said, "and I don't think you should have one."

I rolled my tongue around the front of my teeth and said, "Ah-huh." My paper gown crinkled as she put her arm across my shoulders.

"Talk it over with the baby's father," she said softly.

As I got dressed, I chose to focus all my rage on her. How dare she tell me not to have an abortion. But I'd seen all those bad movies about this situation and knew I should at least discuss my plans with Nicholas.

I went back to work. I felt sleepy. Everything nauseated me. I got up from my computer terminal in the newsroom and headed for the bathroom. I walked differently. My pelvis seemed to jut forward more, my thin hips felt loaded with sacks and swayed with the momentum of women I'd seen twice my size. I was almost twelve weeks pregnant and, despite the nausea, liked the feeling. I sat in the bathroom stall considering how great it was to carry the future within you. That I could have a baby after all did thrill me, and I worried if aborting this child would endanger my chances of having another.

I don't remember how many days passed before I told Nick. But when

I called him, he was at work, at one of the paper's satellite offices near my apartment.

"I need to talk to you."

"What's the matter?" he said.

"I just need to talk to you."

"Can't you tell me on the phone what's the matter? I'm real busy."

I held the phone from my ear and looked at the kitchen ceiling. Is this man going to be a total jerk? "I need to talk to you about this in person," I went on. Hadn't he seen the movies? Did I have to spell it out? See, he was going to be just the ass I expected. Why bother telling him? My better judgment had kept him at bay for over a year. I only succumbed under the power of a full moon, and when it's full, it's even fuller in Miami, often looking like a harvest moon, poised low on the horizon, skimming the surface of the Atlantic.

"Can you at least give me an indication of what this is about?" he asked, like a man who knows exactly what this is about.

"All right, Nicholas, whenever."

"Okay, okay, I'll be over as soon as I can."

I was sleepy; I was depressed. I was throwing up. I went back to bed and left the apartment door open. He walked through it less than half an hour after I'd hung up the phone.

I said something about the swiftness of his arrival while he looked at me warily. "Why is the door open?"

"So I wouldn't have to get up to let you in," I said sullenly. I was sitting up in the bed, my arms wrapped around my stomach. He walked around the bed and sat in a chair beside me.

I looked straight ahead instead of at him. "I am pregnant. You are the father." I waited half a beat for him to say something louselike here. He didn't. "I thought it only right to discuss with you what I'm going to do." I addressed him with the impersonal hostility of a prosecutor offering a plea bargain to a known crook. "Next Saturday, I am going to have an abortion. I would like you to pick me up that morning, take me to the hospital, wait for me then bring me home. Since I make more money than you, I will pay for any costs not covered by my insurance." I breathed in deeply then let it out with a shudder more internal than apparent.

I half turned to look at him. His hands were clasped and he nodded slightly. "You wanted to discuss this with me or just wanted to give me instructions?"

I tried to chuckle but it came out a faint snort. "Yeah, well, that's what I want you to do. Do you have any objections?" He shook his head. I got under the bed covers. "You reacted better than I thought," I mumbled, pressing the back of my head into the pillow and my backside into the mattress.

"You expected me to act like a jerk and just walk away?"

Why should he walk away? I had the no-fault plan all laid out. I was going to pay for it, too. All he had to do was drive the getaway car. If Nicholas knew someone else could and would take responsibility for everything, why should he make the effort to change anything? And I had made it easy.

Always Sir Charm, he became Prince Magnanimous now, too. "I wouldn't let you go through this alone."

He made me get up when he left. "Don't leave that door open again," he said.

⌣

"My husband doesn't know I'm here," a woman seated next to me said to another. She spoke with a Spanish accent and told the woman she had four children already. About a dozen of us sat in the hospital's abortion clinic anteroom. A slim redhead in her early twenties reassured an even younger-looking woman. "This is my third," she said. "It's nothing."

I got up and walked around the perimeter of the room. A door with a glass window separated us from waiting mothers, sisters, and various male liaisons. Nicholas sat with his head bent toward spread, bouncing knees. His arms rested on his thighs and his clasped hands periodically beat his forehead. I was surprised. I smiled.

They kept me at the hospital longer than usual, the nurses consoling me, a doctor holding my hand and talking to me for a very long time. I could not stop crying. I can think of few circumstances that would compel me to have an abortion again.

When I was home and comfortably in bed, Nicholas asked me if I had everything I needed. I lied and said yes. That I thought stoicism virtue and was emotionally incapable of saying I needed anyone may have been obvious to some, but it was not yet apparent to me. He left quickly. My bitterness imploded. It was cemented when I later learned the reason for his hurried exit: a plane flight, with the woman he'd been seeing regularly in Miami on it. While she was out of town, she had phoned to tell him she was pregnant too.

When this woman instigated a friendship with me—I knew I was being used but it gave me access to information about Nicholas—I discovered hers had been a hysterical pregnancy. By now, months had passed and Nicholas and I had formed a curious platonic friendship. It became evident that the abortion had been emotionally traumatic for both of us, and while he would not talk about it, it tied us to each other. Janice knew little about the history of our relationship, just that Nicholas and I were close. She'd been tapping all his friends lately for sympathy and information about Nick.

She called me in tears one Saturday, regurgitating Nicholas's latest emotional abuse. His continued womanizing had become intolerable, she said. After all, she had left another man for him—broken her engagement—after cheating on her fiancé with Nicholas for months, apparently.

I made my house call and sat in her living room nodding sympathetically at her travails. "Yes," I concurred, if Nicholas cocked his leg at a fire hydrant, I wouldn't be surprised. "And a bourgeois, emotional hustler," I added. "So what more do you want me to say, Janice? I can't tell you what to do. I know all of Nicholas's faults. That he and I are friends at all"—I paused—"well, it's a strange set of circumstances." She sniffed into a tissue and looked at me with wide, green, whatever-do-you-mean? eyes. I feigned a verbal fumble with a dismissive shake of my head and said nothing.

Then she dropped some pillow talk. Nicholas had told her about our sexual relationship—"he liked the strawberries and whipped cream" but he could take or leave the rest, she intimated. Then, to cement our camaraderie, she threw in that she knew the lack of sexual interest was mutual.

I smiled indulgently. "Nicholas," I said, "suffers from classic Don Juanism."

"I know he's immature," she said, and blew her nose. We were both older than Nick and she had several years on me. "With Larry," her former fiancé—she blinked several times, then tried to smooth a bent, pale-blond eyelash with her finger—"we were always entertaining interesting people with intellectual and artistic interests."

She and I knew Nicholas was no intellectual. But he was bright and quick-witted, and you don't need much more than that to be a competent journalist. Nicholas, however, had something extra—charisma. Lots of men liked him too. He burst through the newsroom doors each day like a satisfied gunslinger—his sexual conquests notched on the handle of his six-shooter and one hand swinging a lariat of well-hung flesh instead of a rope. At the time, I was glad few knew I'd been lassoed. But this Janice was dying to dig out the poop and I was glad for the opportunity to reciprocate her bitchiness. It would reveal my ties with Nick went beyond casual sex. I didn't count on it being replayed for a larger audience.

Nicholas came looking for me. "Where's little bigmouth?" he demanded, storming into my section of the newsroom. "She's not here," he claimed half a dozen people replied in unison.

He was seething when he found me. I think I was in the cafeteria. He whispered, "You said something to somebody that I don't think you should have said." Mr. No Sweat had a mad-on. I looked at him benignly.

"Janice confided her concerns to me and one thing led to another. It was my story to tell, too, if I chose. And I did."

"Did you choose to have her get drunk, stand outside my house at two A.M., and broadcast to the whole neighborhood: 'You got Itabari pregnant when I told you I was pregnant, too'?"

⌒

I don't remember how long Nicholas and I didn't speak to each other after that one. But within months, given the incestuous nature of journalism, I got involved with Janice's best friend, a television reporter with whom she worked. It soon became obvious that this was not going to work out and I suggested we end it. The man insisted he was willing to try anything to make it work. I went out of town on a story for several weeks and when I returned he was in a new relationship without having said a word. I was insulted but not particularly upset. Nicholas, of all people, was fuming. "I'm really pissed at the way this guy is treating Itabari," he admitted telling a mutual friend.

Then I started a wild affair with a man Nick thought dangerous. He warned me to be careful. I told him I would.

Nicholas had become the one to whom I told my secrets. And we laughed at each other's perversities.

He was seeing Debbie now, again, on and off. She was the one woman I believed he loved. I always thought they'd get married—when he was ready to get married, which I knew was a long way off. She was brainy, sensuous, and, at the same time, had a level of self-esteem several leagues beneath the sea. She worshiped Nick and seemed willing to endure whatever he did, albeit with the forlorn countenance of a wife shunned by her husband at every social event they attended. She was content to be the one he took home—most often.

Nicholas needed one woman on whom he could depend, someone who—after he'd outraged all the others—would give him unconditional love. And since we have social taboos regarding incest, he picked Debbie.

One night a group of us gave a good-bye party for a fellow journalist at a restaurant. The day before, it had been announced that I was leaving the paper for a year to accept a fellowship. After dinner, Nicholas got up from the opposite end of the table where he'd been sitting with Debbie and put a chair next to me. He sat. "So you're actually leaving," he said incredulously, and shook his head. I nodded, then turned to talk to the person beside me. "So," he repeated, sounding marginally intelligent, "Itabari's really leaving."

"Yes, but I'll be back."

"You know, I'm . . . I'm going to miss you . . . really."

I gave him an aw-shucks smile, then turned away. Debbie had ground down an eighth of an inch of teeth trying to ignore us. I did not want her to think I was one of Nicholas's current side events. Our party was milling around the table. As soon as I got the opportunity I said to her, "Why don't you take my seat and let me work your end of the table? You belong in this spot anyway."

My impending departure emotionally panicked Nicholas. He wanted to spend time with me. He wanted to come visit me while I was on my fellowship.

I had to talk this through with Dr. J., my shrink. It took several weeks of emergency sessions.

One night in a bar I looked at Nick and spoke very carefully. "I can only speak for myself. I don't want to suggest that you . . . Let me begin again. I don't know about you, but I'm afraid of getting involved with you. It's not like before and I'm afraid of what I feel."

"I am too," he said, and reached across the table for my hand.

We had known each other for three years.

Not long after that night in the bar he wanted to go for a drink after work. We were both going to be at the paper late so I said I would.

Debbie walked in, planted herself at his desk and decided to wait for him. He came up behind me while I was reading a memo on the newsroom bulletin board. "I see your wife is here," I said without looking at him, "so forget it." I went straight home.

My phone rang after midnight. He was calling from a phone booth. Could he come over? Could he spend the night? He needed to be with me.

I told him no. He knew my position on being a side event. I minimally required equal billing if not star status. "Please . . ." he began to beg. This was getting difficult; Nick was not a pleader. I felt my legs. I hadn't shaved them. "No," I said firmly, running my hand across the stubble. Besides, I have an early day tomorrow, I told myself. And it's far too late to get up and shave, I told myself. And the house was a mess. . . . How frightened was I of this man?

At my healthiest, I sought men as friends and emotional partners. At my most neurotic, I had no use for them outside of sex. The disastrous model of my parents' marriage had taught me the erroneous lesson that men were obstacles; they just got in the way of everything a woman wanted and needed to do for herself. On the health-neurosis scale, I'd not yet found my equilibrium when I knew Nick.

I'd been a musician more of my professional life than a journalist, and it's easy to avoid commitments when you're on the road or the person you're seeing is in town for one week and won't be back for another six. (Actually, I've had similar relationships with lots of journalists, so having and being a vagabond lover was habitual.) In short, my career choices bolstered the myriad defenses I had erected to protect myself from rejection.

I was groaning the pronoun "I . . . I . . . I . . ." as Dr. J. watched. "I . . . guess . . . maybe, I might . . . love him." By the time the session was over I stumbled out deciding I did.

Since I believed in confronting one's demons—an appropriate term, I thought, for Nick—I had to act on this revelation. I sent him a bunch of balloons with a note stating: ". . . and by the way . . . I love you." Then I hid.

The spheres of hot air were flying high over his desk in the newsroom when I walked in. A walled corridor kept me out of sight for several feet until it became a half-walled partition on the left. He was on the phone and didn't notice me when I passed. My department was a good distance from his desk. I sat down at the computer terminal—not mine. I picked one farther out of sight, became a hunchback, and started typing.

"What's the matter with you?" my friend Teresa, another reporter, asked. She eyed my lowered profile quizzically.

"I'm kind of hiding."

"I see." She sucked in her cheeks. "From anyone I know? I'm just inquiring so I can protect you from whomever it is."

"I'll tell you later."

"Nicholas was looking for you," she reported dryly. She didn't care for Nick. None of the sensible women I knew did. I looked around her to see the other side of the newsroom. Nicholas was off the phone. He got up. He got waylaid by an editor. I skulked off to the bathroom.

I tried to convince myself that I hadn't done anything so terrible—except to tell the cad of the decade what I really felt, just like all those other bimbettes. But it was done. I strode confidently out of the bathroom stall. I sat at my own desk. The phone rang.

"I got your balloons." He said nothing about the note.

"Ah-huh," I said. He invited me to dinner after work. I said, "Ah-huh." When he picked me up at my apartment, I let him in the door and said, "Hi, have a seat; I'll be right back," then rushed into the bedroom. When I came out, we rode down the elevator in silence. The doorman went to get Nick's car. Resembling a sad sack of potatoes, I dangerously sat on the dolly used for tenant's groceries.

"You don't look like you feel too well," he said.

"Hmmmm," I responded.

In the car I said less. Over dinner, little. At his apartment, he made love to me without saying he loved me. It all felt wrong.

Within weeks I heard Nicholas had been cheating on Debbie not only with me but with her former roommate too—both when the woman was her roommate and after.

⌣

The phone rang at my office desk. The voice was a hoarse whisper: "Itabari." I could hardly hear the person and I was on deadline.

"Who is this?" I demanded, my fingers pounding the computer keyboard.

"Itabari?"

"Yes," I answered gruffly.

"This is Nicholas. How much money do you have on you?"

"What's the matter with you? Where are you?" I looked at the clock.

He stopped whispering but mumbled as if his mouth was pressed hard against the receiver. "I'm at the police station."

"What did you do?" I inquired unsympathetically.

He had gone to the police station to examine some records for a news story. When he gave the officer his driver's license as identification, his name jumped out of the computer. He had hundreds of dollars in outstanding traffic tickets. They weren't going to let him leave the station until he paid up.

"Do you have a couple of hundred dollars?" he asked me.

"I haven't cashed my paycheck, I don't know what my balance is, and I don't have time to look now. And why do I get the royal honor of bailing you out? You've got a whole stable to choose from." The indignity of the ever-elegant Nicholas Wright being detained by police while playing ace reporter and dressed for a *GQ* cover was an image that fueled my writing speed. I beat my deadline just so I could hurry up and savor his humiliation at my leisure.

No one in the stable's inner circle bailed him out. He had to go to its periphery, a secretary at the paper.

I picked a fight and we stopped talking.

A month or more later, we made up.

In my apartment, the wall of bedroom windows overlooked Biscayne Bay. The moon was whole and low over the pitch-black water. He was already in bed, his naked back to me, as I entered the room. I stood at the door. Where the curve of his waist dipped in then rose toward his hip, the moonlight fell, illuminating a spot of deep brown perfection. He was tall and looked longer in repose. He was firm and seemed harder prone. I'd never witnessed him so still, so much a sculptor's dream, so completely present. I feared no one else could fill my bed again. In the morning, each curve of his found a resting place in mine. Slow and weak he said, "Lady . . . you . . . feel . . . good . . ."

Lady? Outraged, I told my shrink: "Is that his catchall name for everyone he beds?" Perhaps I was misinterpreting his sentiments, Dr. J. suggested.

It was hard for me to be rational. I was now beyond mere lunar influences with Nicholas. Whenever he approached me, he was surrounded by a blue haze. He stood over me one day while I sat at my desk and asked me something. But I couldn't hear him. The inside of my head felt stuffed with cotton batting as I tried to fathom the meaning of the blue aura. Interrupting him, I finally said, "I can't stand this."

"You can't stand what?"

"Every time I look at you now you've got this damn blue cloud of smoke around you."

"Don't worry about it." He smiled smugly. "It's good for you." He wanted to see me that night.

"No. I don't want to see you—ever."

His face dropped. "You don't mean that."

"That really kills me, you with a wounded look." A reporter passed us to get to his desk. "I'll talk to you later," I told him.

Later became a series of missives from me—he never wrote—and delayed, elliptical responses from him. "It takes me a while to answer you because you always . . . you dissect." He stopped. "Let's just say you're not shallow and I have to think it over before I can respond," he explained.

My letters advanced the virtues of the examined life. Nicholas conceded that he had thought about seeing a therapist. His compulsive womanizing had hurt a lot of people, and I wondered out loud to him if he really liked women at all. He never followed through on the therapy, to my knowledge, and always conveyed the attitude that the women caused all the problems by their excessive demands—fidelity the primary one, of course.

But Nicholas wasn't married, there was no reason why he shouldn't be with whomever he wanted, I told him. He just wanted to be with everyone and was cavalier about who got hurt in the end.

Yet for all his sexual bravado, there was something emotionally very feminine about Nick. I mean that there was—in that psychological balance of yin and yang—a "feminine" malleability of soul, a profound desire to yield that revealed itself when he submitted to his deeper nature. Maybe it was just the child in him, ever ready to love and be loved. He seemed to know intuitively, I think, what a woman desires and how she desires it. But it was an ability used mainly to manipulate them. I sensed he feared that emotional surrender to another meant a plummet without end, or a destined crash. All that anxiety may have compelled much of his macho posturing. When I looked into his eyes I saw the tiniest pair of sneakers, poised for the emotional getaway. And he confessed that I triggered, unlike anyone else, images of surrender at the rose-covered cottage. Personally, I wouldn't live in such a place. I told Nick all I wanted was consistency in our relationship. He thought that would inevitably lead to marriage. I thought it would give me the opportunity to see if he was marriageable.

He admitted my unpredictability unnerved him; his inability to control me made him want to "shake my brains loose," he said. "And I'm just not used to being with a woman who doesn't let me do what I want to do," he conceded. Then, with a shiver your grandma told you meant someone was walking on your grave, he told me, "I don't want to love anybody."

I, however, was into the sweetness of surrender now. And if Nicholas didn't want to take our relationship for an exclusive test run, I was ready to move on. I was leaving for the University of Michigan in a few weeks to start my fellowship. I had a whole year to explore new territory. But first, I made a side trip.

The National Association of Black Journalists was holding its annual convention in Atlanta that year. I drove there on my way to Michigan. I thought it best to avoid Nicholas. We'd parted on good terms in Miami and I was content to leave it that way.

"Where have you been?" he asked at a cocktail party a couple of days into the convention.

I shrugged. "Around."

That night more than a dozen of us went to a popular Atlanta restaurant for dinner. We lingered over drinks in the lounge for a long time waiting to be seated. I was talking to a young reporter from Miami named Alex. At the time, I thought he was far too young for me. "But I'll grow up," he told me one night at a similar gathering in Miami. Nicholas was there that night, too. Alex was charming, bright, and sensitive. Nicholas could tell we liked each other and butted into our conversation.

"I know you," he whispered in my ear. "What do the two of you have planned tonight?" When he left the table, Alex looked at me incredulously. "You two really like each other. I don't get it. I don't see what women see in him."

Nick butted in again now at the Atlanta restaurant and deposited himself next to me. When our party was called for dinner he put himself at the head of the table with me beside him. I spent the whole evening trying to prevent him from pulling my underwear off from under the table.

When the bunch of us returned to the hotel, Nicholas got off the elevator when I did. "Where are you going?" I asked.

He mumbled like a little boy. "Wit-chu." What the hell, I was going away for a year.

I was in the bathroom, standing in front of the mirror, taking off my jewelry, when he came up behind me, his pants all undone. He pressed against me, his hands reaching and rubbing my thighs till the hem of my silk dress hung at my hips. His breath was in my ears and in my eyes when he whispered, "I love you, too." I looked at our reflection in the mirror. My mouth was open. "Say something," he pleaded.

I groaned a sound of pain, surprise, and something like a baby dribbling. "I can't believe it," I mumbled.

"I've always loved you. I always thought you were the most wonderful, talented, exciting woman I ever met . . ."

In the night I said, "I need you."

In the dark he said, "You got me."

And then there was a long silence.

A month into the silence I called him. "You didn't mean it," I said.

"Don't tell me I didn't mean it. I meant it. I just have to think about what I'm going to do. I need a couple of weeks to think." That was in September of one year. I didn't see him until October of the next. But I did see his parents.

I had met his father in Miami but never his mother. I had a standing invitation to visit them whenever I was in Chicago and did, for a long weekend. Nicholas was an only child and his bedroom had been turned into a shrine—elementary school, high school, and college mementos everywhere. His father suggested the room be used as office space, but his mother kept it ready for Nick, just in case he wanted to move back home, she said.

Over breakfast, she told me, "Nicholas has been telling us about you for years. How wonderful you are. How . . ." In short, everything he had whispered to me that night in Atlanta.

And then I met a man he'd grown up with, went to college with, at a party while I was in Michigan. We'd been chatting for several minutes when he said, "Wait, you're here on a fellowship and you're from Miami? Is your name Itabari?" I told him it was and he proceeded to tell me my life history and everything about me but what size underwear I wore. But no word from Nick.

I had a great year and returned to Miami with two goals: finish a book and avoid Nicholas Wright.

It was useless to stay in a constant state of rage with Nick. I decided to be civil at all times but distant.

I'd been back a couple of months and the first complete sentence he spoke was "Could I borrow some money?" It was an insignificant amount and he said he'd give me a check and it would clear in a week and blah blah blah. I told him I was busy and to call me at home later. "What's your number?" he asked. I'd been back two months and he was asking me my number. That sealed it. I knew all this was a test to see if I was still on the emotional hook. I would have said no anyhow. But I did it with decorative venom when he called. "Go to a loan shark, motherfucker. With your repayment record, my prayers will be answered."

Every time I saw his head pop up in the newsroom, I felt my right eyelid twitch and my stomach knot. But I stored the venom. I couldn't let him distract me from my book.

He struck again about a month later. He wanted my opinion on a political matter and suggested a late lunch. It became an early dinner.

A master of the amnesiac's stare, he gazed at me from across the table, then gave me the *Gaslight* treatment. "What do you mean about the last time we were together? I thought the last time we were together everything was cool." I had dished up the past after he served the bullshit pretext for the dinner.

"You know, Nicholas," I began softly and with a smile, "nothing has changed. I still love you, unfortunately. I just don't respect you. I never did, really. You're a man for whom the past never happened, the present doesn't matter, and the future never comes." And then I vowed to myself: I'm going to teach him the meaning of the Word. The pen is mightier than the penis. But before I would get to that, there were scenes to be played.

The bill came and, mealymouthed, he said something about just having enough to pay his half of the bill. "I'm glad you do," I said quietly, and watched him count out twenty-two pennies.

On the way back to the paper, we passed the company parking lot. I glanced across the hedges at my Mustang. In its trunk, wrapped in a finger towel, was a knife with a lovely black handle. It was not an uncommon knife; you could find it among the better cutlery at any Kmart—in fact, I think that's where I bought mine. Meant simply for the mundane chores of paring, it was beautifully designed, sculpted to fit the pinky where the handle curved inward an inch from the end. From there it rose toward the center, where it arched to cushion the middle fingers, then dipped inward again to fit the index finger. It was perfect for skinning a peach, peeling a potato, or a quick, low-hand thrust to the groin.

I had put the knife in the trunk after Nicholas requested money and then my phone number so he could delineate his plea.

As we rode up the escalator, my mood seemed mellow, my face serene. I asked Nicholas if he was still seeing Debbie. "Just as a friend," he said quietly. He looked at me with big, apologetic eyes, one of the more obvious ploys in his arsenal of body language designed to avoid the commitment of words. The amnesiac's stare was now replaced by a soulful, liquid gaze, from which I was to surmise his regret and continued affection. I said nothing either. And if my gestures spoke resignation and goodwill while my mind plotted dismemberment and disposal, what deception could he think possible? For rather than seethe and strike without warning, hadn't I always been the snake that rattled, the one who verbalized and dissected his feelings and mine, his motivations and mine, ad infinitum? As we walked through the corridor, he looked sad. My angelic countenance radiated both love and the realization that some lovers are forever estranged. There was no reason to distrust me. Toward him, my word and deed had been one. For me to behave otherwise would have been, to him, unthinkable. I was into my soap opera mode now.

I'd been back in Miami—the most socially desolate outpost in America for black people, but a great news town because so much bad happens there—for four months. Between work at the paper and my own writing, I hadn't had much time to socialize. But when I put my manuscript aside and looked around, I was bored. When I'm bored, I manufacture my own entertainment if there's none to be found. *You write the script, you direct the play, and you star in the show*, Dr. J. had cautioned. Nicholas was going to be my entertainment.

Weeks passed and he made friendly overtures. "I really like the way you come in to work, all business—your own business—" He added pointedly, "Then go home."

I looked up from my computer. "I'm so glad you approve of my behavior."

"You know," he began a few weeks later, "I don't think I like the way you just come in to work, have nothing to say, then leave." So we talked.

One afternoon he came by my apartment. I assumed the attitude of a *Dynasty* bitch looking over her lover's shoulder and smiling villainously, strains of "What's Love Got to Do with It" playing in her head. Nothing he did would hurt as much if I played this out as high-camp soap.

"You look really tired," he told me, observing me in profile. I was sorting through a stack of records and I *was* tired. It takes a lot of psychic energy to maintain a mad-on. He was sitting on the sofa and leaned toward me on the floor. "Whenever you wanted to reach out to me," he said quickly, "I . . . I acted like a bastard. Whenever I wanted to reach out to you, you acted like a bitch." Well, that was half the truth. He started to say more but I got up and left the room.

I talked to my reflection in the bathroom mirror. "Too late. I'm not going for it." My nose was red and my eyes were puffy. I threw cold water on my face, then went back to the living room.

"Nicholas, why are you here, why are you doing this?" I stood staring at him.

"I don't know," he mumbled, then pulled me toward him, then down on the sofa, and then he kissed my face and neck gently. I pulled away and eased myself to the floor. I looked at an album cover for a long time while we both said nothing. "Don't do that," he said, and pulled me back on the couch. He wiped the wetness from my cheek with his hand then held me. "I don't want to, but I have to go," he said after the stillness had settled us. "I'd rather be with you than . . . but I have to go. I'm in this situation . . . but it's not going to last much longer . . ."

Whoever it was, whatever it was, it was going to be a replay. No words passed my lips, no expression played across my face. He went to the bathroom. When he opened the door to leave it, I blocked his path. History had taught me he was most vulnerable in the can. I wrapped my arms around him and kissed him hard; he had trouble walking to the front door. "Women don't have this problem," he half groaned, half spoke. He stood there a few minutes trying to straighten up. I smiled, then kissed him hard again. I opened the door and he walked out stiffly. About a minute later, I looked through the peephole and saw him still standing there, shaking his head like he'd been smacked upside it and blessed quite suddenly with total recall. He was going to have a lot more to remember.

We both had to be in New York on business the following week and planned to meet for dinner and go to the theater. He left for New York before I did, but I didn't remember if he was leaving town on Thursday or Friday. We'd seen each other at work, but not after hours, since the afternoon in my apartment. I called him Thursday night to say how much I was looking forward to seeing him in New York Saturday. A woman answered the phone.

Nicholas had not delineated the "situation" he was in, but it must have been unique. Nick had stay-overs, but not live-ins. This had serious implications. I'd been waiting for him to do something that would push me over the edge, and she was it. I was feverish—emotionally and clinically hot. I had the flu. I hung up the phone, the woman's bovine voice still resonating moolike in my head. "Hel-lo," she'd answered lazily.

I got up from my bed and, through the window, saw the full, giant moon skimming the Atlantic. I went to the kitchen, where I'd stored an empty champagne bottle, its neck perfectly suited to slip into the gas tank of a little red Alfa Romeo. I went down to my garage to get the beautiful black-handled knife from my trunk—a perfect implement for ripping the cloth top of a convertible.

In the kitchen, I filled the champagne bottle with sugar. The inside of the bottle was wet. I'd washed it out. The sugar stuck. I threw the bottle away. I took the whole canister of sugar and a plastic measuring cup and put them in a small peach-colored shopping bag with the name of one of Miami's better department stores, Jordan Marsh, printed on it. I wrapped the black-handled knife in a paper towel and placed it in the bag, too.

Then I got my clothes for the evening. It was winter in Miami—that meant 70 degrees at night. I pulled out a black ski mask, a black long-sleeved turtleneck, baggy black cotton slacks, black high-top sneakers, and short black wool gloves. It was nearly 11:00 P.M. I went to case his house.

I parked around the corner from his low-rise apartment building. His car was parked in a space directly in front of his living room window. Another car was parked behind it. I peeped in the window. She was full-bodied if not actually bovine and seated on the sofa watching the late news. I marched into the apartment lobby and stood outside his door, sans ski mask. I huffed up and I puffed up and then I though it wise not to pound the door down. I listened for a few seconds to the TV. Yeah, she was in there all right. I'd be back.

I drove home, took a few shots of Vicks Formula 44 for my cough, then set the alarm clock for 3:00 A.M. It would take twenty minutes to get to his apartment. I decided that the cow and the rest of the neighborhood would be in a deep REM phase of sleep between 3:30 and 4:00 in the morning on a weeknight.

At 3:35 A.M. I parked my car under a tree in an open, unpaved lot directly across from his building. As I opened my 1978 Mustang's door, the hinges *squeeeeeeeeaked* and the interior light illuminated my black-clad figure. Grimacing, I flicked off the light. I grabbed my chic peach satchel and eased the door open again. It squeaked even louder and I closed it as quickly as I could without slamming it. I rushed on sneakered feet to his car. His lot was illuminated by bright spotlights, one of them aimed directly at his car. I went to open the gas tank. It was locked. I'd forgotten. I pulled out the knife. The left side of his car faced the street but was hidden by another parked car. I went for the front left tire first. I stopped. I heard a car. But there was no car. I had never done anything like this before. I'd dismissed as childish and irrational all those women I'd ever heard of, seen, or read about who busted up the "other woman" in some smoky nightclub, pulverized her on her own living room floor à la Mrs. Lionel Ritchie, or done what that really bad sister had: turned Al Green to grits and made him get religion all over again. Unlike those women, I couldn't admit that I cared enough to enter the emotional fray. But here I was about to stab this man's car, which I actually imagined to be a red Alfa Romeo given to him by one of the older, generous women he once told me about. That it was actually a Honda Civic hatchback made no difference. With his wrecked finances the damage would be just as painful. I raised the knife and plunged it in. *Poowwwwwwwwww!* I ran with my mouth open and eyes bulging back to my car. I'd never heard a stabbed tire explode. Sounded like a Beirut car bomb on the late news. "Whewwww," I whispered to myself.

You write the script, you direct the play, you star in the show.

"Hmmmmmm." I envisioned a Miami cop catching me in the act and arresting me. The *Herald* would send its ace cop reporter, the famous Edna Buchanan, to write a story about one of their own getting busted for a romantically motivated deed of banal vengeance. Edna would get that it was a reciprocal act of trust betrayed. Maybe. I decided the script called for me to go now.

I was ten minutes from the crime scene when I stopped my car on a side street. I was coughing so hard I thought I'd choke. When I finally stopped, I leaned on the steering wheel trying to catch my breath. "You got up out of bed to put a hole in one tire?" My ten-year-old self was sitting beside me in the front seat. She looked at me dumbly as she had at the vanishing dust of the half-naked cinnamon lady, then bit off a piece of pickle. Her toe kicked a clump of knitted black wool on the car floor. I had thrown the ski mask there. Cellophane crackled as she dug into a bag of barbecue potato chips. She crunched one. "How come you had this hot thing on your head?" she asked, toeing the ski mask. I started coughing again and could not stop for half a minute or more. My eyes were watery, my face was red, and a veil of perspiration hung around my forehead and temples. "You look bad," she said as she chewed a chip.

I sucked my teeth. "Girl, shut up. You ain't never loved a man." Then I drove back and stabbed all the other tires.

⌣

To this day, Nicholas doesn't know for certain that I was the tire slasher in the night, so along with this book, I'm sending him four Goodyear radials.

As for all those women who have been his, read this, suck their teeth, then say: "Shhh, he didn't tell her anything he didn't tell me," all I have to say is: *MAY*-be, but *my* version gets immortalized 'cause I can write it so good.

ZZ Packer

I'd always thought that the Washington Post's *Summer Reading Issue featured lighthearted essays about summer—that summer romance, that perfect beach—that sort of thing. When I realized I wanted to write about a near abduction—mine—during one of the most frightening periods in black Atlanta's recent history—those years from 1979 to 1981 known as the years of the Atlanta Child Murders—I worried that I would disrupt the delicate balance of the Summer Reading Issue and, what's more, that I wouldn't do justice to the climate of absolute fear which then ruled Atlanta.*

The Post's *magazine editor gave me the go-ahead, but by then I'd been so flooded with memories, half-buried emotions, and two-decades-too-late realizations that I didn't need any go-ahead; I'd already written three-quarters of the essay in a single, caffeine-fueled spurt.*

It did not surprise me that I got emotional writing the piece; the primary thought that played through my mind while writing "The Stranger" was "If I hadn't run away from him, I'd be dead now." I wasn't, however, prepared for the many, seemingly incongruous memo-

ries surrounding the incident: how learning all the latest dances amounted to a veritable rite of passage; how we read and reread books in the hope of unlocking the great mysteries of the world; how, as children, we loved life without pretense or forethought.

At first these all seemed superfluous details and sentimental tangents, but as the essay began to unfold, I saw these bits and pieces as parts of the mosaic that was black childhood in Atlanta at that time and, by extension, black Atlanta itself. My parents—and parents like them—felt about Atlanta the way immigrants coming to the States feel about America: wary, but hopeful. Atlanta was the Black Mecca, and though we still heard some of those old, backward, misguided dictums—"Don't go in the sun or you'll get black," "Don't go in the pool or your hair will nap up"—most of our parents had come to Atlanta to escape such backwardness and take advantage of the economic and cultural opportunities of living in a prosperous, majority-black city.

It was simply beyond our parents' belief that the purported killer of twenty-nine black children could be a black man. Our parents loved us, but we were suddenly at the age when we began to suspect that the rest of the world did not share their view, and the Atlanta Child Murders seemed to confirm our suspicions. In writing "The Stranger" I discovered that our loss of childhood innocence was compounded by our parents' disillusionment. I hope that "The Stranger" serves as a prism, reflecting and refracting both the loss of innocence and disillusionment, that world of black girlhood in a place where anything and everything—including the dangerous and deadly—was possible.

The Stranger, a personal essay

"REWA'S GONNA be there, and so are Norka and April and Stephanie," my friend Arnethia told me over the phone. Summer had begun, but summer vacation hadn't—we still had two more weeks of school left when she called me, trying to persuade me to go to summer day camp with her at Moseley Park. Moseley Park was barely a park at all, more like a little swatch of green lawn so close to Atlanta's Martin Luther King Jr. Drive that car exhaust and the steady traffic prevented anyone from picnicking there. Yet somehow Arnethia was convinced Moseley Park was the place to be. We were third-graders, obsessed with candy, reading Judy Blume books, and learning the latest dance craze.

Arnethia's particular fascination that summer was with a dance called "The Smurf," named after the blue elfin cartoon creatures. The dance required us to stick out our butts while rubbing our chests like an ER defibrillator. After that we'd make a neat little turn that ended in a series of convulsions. "Man," Arnethia said, "we'll have 'The Smurf' *down pat* by the end of the summer."

This was in 1981, during the height of the Atlanta child murders; by this time 25 or more black children and teenagers had turned up dead. Every school in the city had geared up with safety programs to warn us about the "dangers of strangers." Just a month earlier, I'd sat with Arnethia and my schoolmates in our classroom while the principal repeated the mantra we'd heard a thousand times before: "Don't talk to strangers . . . Hold your parent's hand . . . Always tell a friend where you're going . . ."

I was afraid of the principal, a light-skinned woman who probably could have passed for white—though I didn't know what passing meant back then. She had a dark blond pageboy streaked with white. But being afraid of the principal didn't stop me from getting bored by hearing the same warnings about strangers over and over again, so I turned my attention to the cinder-block walls of the classroom, painted a chirpy yellow to mask how ugly they really were. Bulletin boards trimmed in crenelated cardboard featured black leaders we'd drawn with colored pencils: Martin Luther King, Malcolm X, Harriet Tubman, and Sojourner Truth. Benjamin E. Mays, George Washington Carver, and Frederick Douglass. Looking at those pictures, I just couldn't believe a black man could have been responsible for the murders.

Perhaps I'd heard my mother and father too often: "Not black folks," my mother said when she read in the paper that the police suspected the killer was a black male. If there was a serial killer on the loose somewhere, my mother would shake her head and say, "White folks."

I'd learned long ago that my parents divided the world into two camps: white folks and black folks. My mother adopted a different attitude with whites than with blacks; she enunciated her words more clearly and dispensed with the musical Southern lilt of her voice—especially when the white in question was a bill collector over the phone. My father also had his way of talking to whites, though he usually avoided talking to them at all; he'd grown up in Mississippi, where entrance signs to certain counties read: "Run Nigger Run! And If You Can't Read, Run Anyway!"

As I sat in the classroom, watching the principal lead a terrified boy up to the front of the room to demonstrate how a stranger might snatch a child away, I heard my mother's voice:

I just can't believe it was black folks who killed those poor children.

The principal droned on: ". . . Better yet, don't go anywhere so that you don't have to tell your friend where you're going . . . Memorize your phone number . . . Yell if an unfamiliar adult walks up to you . . . Don't talk to strangers. DO NOT TALK TO STRANGERS."

A few days before school let out, we had yet another assembly. This time Arnethia and I sat in the carpeted auditorium while a boy named Dickenson pulled Rewa's ponytail, surely out of lust. After our teacher rapped Dickenson on the knuckles, we listened as the police lectured us. We all looked up at the cops with wide eyes as they told us horror stories: ". . . And the man snapped the little boy's neck—CRACK! Just like that." The police officer wrenched his white hands around an imaginary boy's neck, simulating—with a bit too much glee—the torque required for such a maneuver.

But then school ended and the summer began, and the kiddie grapevine embodied itself in the sentinel of my best friend, Arnethia, to bring me the lowdown: The place to be that summer was Moseley Park day camp.

"I'll ask my mama," I said, trying not to sound too desperate. I knew even then that the more you wanted something, the more you had to appear not to want it. When I was off the phone, though, I was shameless about trying to fit into the cast of our third-grade soap opera. Best friends were made and dumped over the course of a lunch hour. And every day our rumor mill started up anew. One day it might announce that Natasha was going out with Demetrius, another day it would be that Angelika sent a "Yes? No? Maybe? Circle One" origami note to Anthony. It was high drama, and though I was not the most important cast member, I was enough of one to want a better, more flamboyant role. Moseley Park summer day camp was my chance.

Like all parents during the Atlanta child murders, my mother was apprehensive about letting me out of her sight, but then again, she'd need summer day care for me and my younger sister: She'd started working again to help my father pay for the massive mortgage on our new five-bedroom house, and as Arnethia regaled me with her predictions of what would go down at Moseley Park, I was busy devising the appropriate histrionics to make my mother succumb to my will. I begged and pleaded with her, and by the time she signed me up, I knew the "dangers of strangers" drill by heart, but as with most things kids memorize, I soon forgot why I had to know the stuff in the first place.

⌒

Arnethia had lied. Or at least, she was not in full possession of the truth. It turned out that Rewa wasn't going to be at Moseley Park; the caramel-skinned, doe-eyed creature was too busy with her child-modeling career. But April and Norka were there, and though Stephanie wasn't, a girl of the same height and Amazonian stature—5 feet 8 inches tall—was there. I remember that this girl had asked me if I had gotten my period like she had, and I'd lied, saying, "Yes. But only a little bit."

We knew about menstruation because we'd read *Are You There God? It's Me, Margaret* by Judy Blume, though I obviously didn't know enough to know you couldn't get your period "a little bit." We knew about wet dreams because we'd read Blume's *Then Again, Maybe I Won't*. Whenever we went to the library to check out Blume's *Forever*—the raciest book any of us had read—the book immediately fell open to the sex scene, the sex-scene page so worn from use and deciphering that it had come undone from the glue of its binding, fluttering into our hands as though it knew we'd been searching for it all along.

But we didn't really know about sex; we just knew that we should be interested in it, and keep our eyes and ears open for anything that smacked of it. We didn't understand what it meant when we'd heard on the news that Wayne Williams had been arrested in connection with the murders, and that most people suspected that he'd "molested" his victims. I remember looking up "molested" in the dictionary, only to find out that it meant "to bother." I usually asked my mother what unfamiliar words meant—even after I looked them up (she wouldn't tell me if I didn't make a good faith effort to find out for myself)—but I distinctly remember not asking her: Everything about the case "molested" her. The Atlanta police seemed to care more about the slaying of two white people by black men than about the missing black children who'd turned up dead soon after-ward. Then there was the fact that the arrested suspect was black, even though black Atlantans couldn't believe a black could be a serial killer.

Perhaps I didn't bother to ask her about the word "molest" because I was busy learning "The Smurf," wearing out Michael Jackson's "Off the Wall" and Pat Benatar's "Hit Me With Your Best Shot." Though the coun-selors at Moseley Park were trying to placate our parents' upper-middle-class aspirations by teaching us ballet and gymnastics, Arnethia, April, Norka, and I were busy learning a new dance called "The White Girl." It was pretty simple, and we did it mostly for fun and mockery, imitating what we believed to be the quintessential white girl by holding our noses by the thumb and forefinger—to simulate the skinny noses of white folks—and waving our other hand about in a downward, drowning motion. We did this on the parquet floor of the Moseley Park gym when the counselors took their smoke break, pushing away boys who tried to play basketball, because we were taller, and we could.

Despite the ballet and gymnastics lessons, Moseley Park was pretty much a dump. The gym floor was not one of those shiny peanut-colored expanses we'd seen when visiting Southwest Middle School, the school we'd go to after the fifth grade. This gym floor was marred by black streaks, probably from the imitation tap shoes of our counselor Paulette, who kept trying to get us to tap our hearts out like Gregory Hines. The main building was a concrete bunker with fallout shelter signs all over the place, and the main office was encased in bulletproof glass with a little round, microphoned window that you were supposed to speak into though the mike usually didn't work. Every day we received our lunches in flimsy cardboard boxes; inside were sandwiches in sealed bags, ballooned with air that we'd pop open, only to find limp luncheon meat on near-white lettuce. Since ketchup was considered a vegetable, we always found a packet of Heinz wedged between the sandwich and the invariably wormy-looking apple. The juice came in a box as tiny as those that held engagement rings.

There was, however, a pool. A beautiful, Smurf-colored, chlorine-blue pool that most of us girls couldn't enter because the water would "revert" our straightening-comb-pressed tresses. My mother wasn't like the other mothers; she didn't care if I got my hair wet, didn't care if it expanded to its full-size, post-Supremes Diana Ross 'fro. In fact, she preferred it. I'd spend days in the pool while my friends watched from the sidelines, fretting over "turning black" in the Georgia sun, though they were, of course, already black. I couldn't swim, but I could doggie-paddle, holding my head aloft so as not to ruin the limousine blackness of my long twin ponytails—my one "asset" in the hierarchy that ranked girls by the lightness of their skin and the length of their hair.

The problem with the pool, however, was the bathrooms: Our teen counselors took their lifeguard smoke breaks inside them, hiding out from the program directors. If kids tried to shower or pee while they were in there, they'd dump us in the deep end after they'd snubbed out their Newports.

One day when I was swimming, the restroom was crowded and I needed to go—*bad*. So I walked up the hill, toward the Moseley Park "make-out" gazebo, where the park bathrooms were. They were scary, filled with spiders. Beer cans and trash littered the floors, but the prospect of peeing in peace was too good to pass up.

I trudged up the hill, and that's when the man approached me. All I remember is that he was light-skinned, with a pock-marked face, and a small bush of hair that was longer than the then-popular "fade" most men wore, but not quite the full-blown Afro style my parents sported in pictures with me as a newborn.

"Your mother," he said, voice steady and calm, "told me to pick you up from school today."

School? School had ended nearly a month ago.

"No she didn't," I said.

I looked at him, too dumb, too stupefied, to think *take a mental picture* or *yell!* or, even, *run!* I looked at him, trying, I suppose, to figure out why he'd lie to me, why he'd lie at all. A thousand whys, and the whole time I stood there.

"Yes, she did," he said, this time with a smile, as though I might have forgotten something; like he was a teacher helping me with my multiplication tables.

"No she didn't," I said; my mother had always picked me up. Our routine was so unvarying that I'd almost hated her for it: She'd pick me up at camp, then pick my sister up from day care. Then we'd all take the Hightower MARTA to downtown, go to the library, get a soft-serve ice cream cone at McDonald's, then take the Vine Street bus so that we could spend interminable hours at my father's liquor store. Sometimes my father would dispense scientific non-truths to us to pass the time: "There's no moon," he'd once said, "it's only the Earth's reflection." Usually my mother gave me a look that said, "Don't believe it," and my father would catch the look, and they'd get into a huge fight until the next customer came in. I spent most of my time seated on the tall Naugahyde stool, finishing my homework, then rolling pennies into cylindrical sausage-shaped wrappers, or plotting ways to swipe Baby Ruth bars from his candy racks.

"She said she's sick, and that I'm gonna take you home—all right?"

That did it. I don't know why it took me so long, why I hadn't yelled like I'd been taught, why I hadn't run away, but something told me that as unthreatening as he seemed, this simply wasn't right, and now I ran.

I must have told the counselors at Moseley Park, and they must have called my mother, but all I can remember is my mother picking me up, then picking up my sister, and taking us straight home. She called the police, then put me on the phone. The police asked me questions: What did he look like? Was he white or black? Was he wearing a cap? What did his nose look like—like a white person's nose or a black person's?

My mother asked me, Was I certain it was a black man? Yes, I was certain this man was black—light-skinned, but black. He didn't look like the photographs I'd seen of Wayne Williams, but that made sense because he was already in custody.

That was the end of Moseley Park. For me at least. I don't remember missing it much, which seems strange, given how badly I'd wanted to go. I spent the rest of that summer with my mother's friend Mrs. Agbabune and her daughter, Etete, playing with Etete in her treehouse.

I think I remember my mother telling Mrs. Agbabune about what had happened, and Mrs. Agbabune shaking her head, then looking at me for a long time, perhaps to get a sense whether I knew what a close call I'd had. I don't remember how I arranged my face in reply; what I know now is that I had only the vaguest understanding of what could have happened. But all of that was moot. *Nothing* had happened to me.

I was fine.

⌒

It was still summer, but as is the norm for Southern states, we had already started school.

"Your haircut looks cute," someone said, and just when I was feeling the warm flush from the compliment, she countered, "but it'll take a long time to grow back."

Just before the first day of school, I had to get my hair cut in order to wear the latest style—the Jheri Curl. Though I swore up and down to the hairdresser that I only doggie-paddled in the pool, she said I'd have to cut off all the "chlorinated hair" and start from scratch. It was the end of the world. I sobbed in the bathroom, cursing my mother for letting the hairdresser cut off all my hair. It was as though I was shedding tears that had been dammed up since I ran from the man in Moseley Park.

It was by accident that the story of my almost-kidnapping got out. It was still the first day of fourth grade, and a teacher had finally pried me out of the bathroom and sent me to play with everyone else for recess. We were outside the school, on the runway of pavement near the semicircular driveway where parents dropped kids off and picked them up. Everyone recounted what had happened that past summer, and the kids who'd gone to Moseley Park told me about their exploits in dance class with Paulette, the cool counselors who smoked, and the cute boys. I'd piped up in agreement about how fun Moseley Park was when Arnethia set the record straight.

"She had to leave Moseley Park," she said.

Embarrassed on having missed out, I began to protest, wanting to explain, but Norka interrupted me.

"Man, Wayne Williams tried to kidnap her," Norka said.

"*Kill* her," Norka's twin, April, corrected.

Suddenly, girls who'd been casually milling around in their own sets and subsets surrounded me, even though the bell was calling us back inside for our first-day assembly. They hurled questions at me about "the kidnapping" and I answered them, adding details and flourishes.

"Did he push you into the car?" one of them said.

"No. But he grabbed me by the wrist—like this," I lied, grabbing my own wrist and straining my face.

"Well, how'd you get away?" another said.

"I screamed like I was hurt," I said, hunching my shoulders. "And he let me go."

"Was it *him*?" someone asked, meaning Wayne Williams.

"No. This dude was completely different. I mean, he was light-complexioned and all, but he just—I don't know—he looked different," I said. Lying was hurtful and deceitful, a thing you did to get yourself out of trouble or to get someone else into it. But this was different. This was storytelling; it was like truth, somehow, even if it didn't happen. "No. It wasn't him," I said. "It wasn't Wayne Williams."

Stephanie bugged out her eyes in mock horror. "He's *still* out there!" she said.

It should have been funny; everyone usually laughed at whatever Stephanie said, but this time no one did. For a brief moment, what I'd said had eclipsed whatever bons mots Stephanie might have to offer. I would—for a short time, and in a small circle—be known as "the girl who got away." I might be in the cafeteria line or in our library group when one of the girls—Stephanie or Rewa or Norka—might nudge me to tell the "kidnapping" story again. Eventually everyone forgot about it, but that first day of fourth grade at recess, it seemed as if no one could match me.

"Girrrl," Stephanie said, echoing Arnethia, "you were real lucky."

"Yeah," I said that day, "I was."

Phyllis Alesia Perry

When I was young and locked into a world of my own imagination, my mother never asked me to explain myself. She still doesn't, thank God. When you are a child, it's easier to create for its own sake. It's only when you grow up that other grown-ups demand reasons for what you do. Never having to explain yourself is a luxury. I feel nostalgic for that time every time someone asks me why or how I write. What motivates me. Who influenced me. I always come up with a response, but never an answer. Frankly, I hate having to think about the why, because it sucks some of the joy out of the whole process. Because I don't really know why. If I dwell on my ignorance about how and why it happens, I'll worry myself into an early grave. Are the ancestors talking? Am I reliving some past life? Am I a genius or a psycho? So I just give in. That's what writing ends up being for me. Nonresistance. And what a powerful thing passivity turns out to be.

April 1974—Johnson Creek

From *Stigmata*, a novel

I FEEL OLDER than old. Ancient and restless and wandering. I will myself to lie there, on my Aunt Eva's couch, and not get up and go out into the heavy darkness that surrounds, that protects, Johnson Creek, Alabama.

There is a funeral the next day and I do not sleep. I lie there drunk with a sadness with news of Aunt Mary Nell's death four days ago, a sadness that settled in the backseat beside me that morning as Daddy backed out of our driveway in Tuskegee to start the thirty-mile journey south.

Now melancholy keeps me company as I listen to past conversations moving through the house on thick summer air. I hear them, even over the sound of my father's snore in another part of the house. I hear them even over Aunt Eva's moaning hum from the kitchen, where I know she has spiked her tea with Jim Beam. She can't sleep either. I have never seen Aunt Eva without her sister Mary Nell, and what is left of Mary Nell rides the ivory pillow in a super-deluxe casket at Danvers Funeral Home, waiting for that last journey.

You know how sometimes when you're just about to fall asleep and sounds grow around you and maybe, just maybe, you hear your name floating by? Every time my eyes close, I feel an exhale of hot air brush my cheek and my lids fly open and I wonder about Aunt Mary Nell's last words.

She was my great-aunt really, my grandmother's sister. In the death room is a hazy, dream-like photograph of the three of them—Eva, Mary Nell, and my grandmother, Grace—standing on the front porch of a house. They were young then, teenagers in love with the camera, looking vibrant even in that fading old picture, an image from the other end of time. They wear identical high-pile hairdos with hats, dazzling white dresses, and black lace-up boots. They hold their white-gloved hands in various la-de-da poses ("Oh, yes," said Aunt Eva once. "It was Easter. First new clothes we'd had in three or four years. Store-bought, too. And we worked for days on that hair. A tornado couldn't move it.")

Grace, my mother Sarah's mother, is on the right, one hand on her hip, the other placed languidly against her long neck. But there is nothing posed about the way she holds up her chin and looks into the camera, eyes straight ahead and challenging.

Grace packed a trunk and left Johnson Creek in 1940 and was never seen alive by her family again. Forty years old, settled, from an old family. And then she hopped a train and was gone. To the folk of Johnson Creek, she will always be the church matron who just up and walked away from her husband and three children. A respectable woman disgraced is enough to provide juicy talk for decades. So by the time Grace died in 1958, before I was born, her legend was already well established. She never came back, but the trunk did—in 1945—accompanied by a mysterious letter to Mary Nell.

I never stop pestering Aunt Mary Nell about that letter and that trunk.

When I was younger, the end of the school year in Tuskegee would find my cousin Ruth Evans and I being packed up and shipped out to Johnson Creek to be deposited at Eva and Mary Nell's house. Mary Nell was Ruth's paternal grandmother.

Ruth and I often sat in the hall of the house at Johnson Creek long after we were supposed to be in bed, listening to Eva and Mary Nell talk, and Grace's funeral was one of their favorite subjects. There were folks who still believed the rumor that Grace had run away with some jackleg preacher man who caught her eye, but Mary Nell and Eva apparently knew better. They always rolled their eyes and shook their heads whenever that story surfaced.

They told the story the same way every time: First came the telegram from some man they didn't know and then the body to Union Springs. When the hearse arrived in Johnson Creek, everybody turned out to see the infamous woman who had abandoned her husband, George, and their children to run away "up the country somewhere."

"Grace sho' gave 'em a show," Aunt Eva would say, smiling. "They couldn't believe that fancy casket and all. And the singing and music she ordered . . . ! They still whispering round here 'bout how she made her money up north. And how she bought that land down here and set George and the children up real fine . . . oh, they was just green . . ."

"Poor George," Mary Nell would say. "He didn't know whether to play the grieving widower, the outraged husband, or the lord of the manor."

Then she would laugh until she snorted.

Speculating on the contents of the trunk was a never-ending game. Ruth and I invented elaborate stories about things we'd never seen, things that probably didn't exist. We didn't even know where the key was. The aunts often found us in Mary Nell's room fiddling with the trunk's old-fashioned, slightly rusting padlock. I think we hoped the thing would just fall apart in our hands and finally the contents of the magic box would be there before us. We were sure it held undreamed-of treasures.

Mary Nell would come into the room and look at us with wistful sadness before telling us to leave it alone. Their reticence about the trunk was strange to me because the two of them usually greeted almost every other thing we did—every exuberant prank and escapade—with loud laughter. But when I asked about the trunk, I was told: "You too young for that. You not ready yet."

"I am ready," I would say. When I was smaller, I always said this to a tummy or chest and Eva or Mary Nell would just hug me real hard and give me some chore to do. Lately, I'd been locking them both dead in the eyes. "I am ready," I said only a month ago while visiting with my mother, Sarah. I had straightened my back and, trying to project all the maturity of my fourteen years, locked onto Mary Nell's soft gaze and said, "Grandmama is dead. Why can't I read the letter? Why can't I look in the trunk?"

Mary Nell just shook her head and muttered, "Getting tall as Grace."

⌒

I never did get to sleep.

I stand blinking in the sun at Mary Nell's graveside, not far from where Grace is buried. I try to imagine the two of them giggling together now, though Mary Nell's boom of a laugh had become little more than a wistful smile by the time last year's stroke got through with her. She always seemed to expect another one after that.

"Seventy-two years is enough time for anyone, I suppose," she told me during that last visit. She was out on the porch slowly scooping dirt into clay pots for her geraniums. I resisted the urge to offer my help and just watched her loosely held trowel sink inch by inch into the tin bucket of soil. Most of the dirt ended up on the rough-planked boards of the porch, some of it slipping through the cracks; I could see Eva's gray cat sitting underneath the porch watching it pile up with growing fascination. Used to be, an excruciatingly neat Mary Nell would have swept up the mess right away. But that was last year, and she no longer had time to stop going about her business.

"Aunt Mary Nell," I said that day, flashing my sunniest smile. "You'll be out here kicking up a fuss when you're a hundred."

"No. I ready, I 'spect, to get on with it," she answered, holding up a geranium plant and shaking the roots. "Can't remember what color this blooms. Deep pink, I think. Just the color for summer."

A month later she died just as she was waking to a late-spring dawn. Massive stroke. Aunt Eva went into her room and found her there, sleepy-eyed and looking off in the distance at something no one else could see.

"She had been dreaming," Eva said later, without elaboration.

After the funeral is finished and Aunt Mary Nell laid down and the sticky red dirt smoothed over, after the steady parade of kinfolk and just-like-kinfolk have cried and giggled into their fried chicken, potato salad, and chocolate cake and then slowly drifted out, Aunt Eva's neighbor Son Jackson brings a large leather trunk out to the porch.

Ruth and her mother, Beatrice, come out of the house behind him, and Mother, who's standing there in the front yard leaning her short frame against my father's tall one, stops dabbing at her damp eyes to straighten and stare.

"Is that . . . ?" She looks at Aunt Eva, who nods and says, "Grace's."

Mother has already taken a step towards the trunk when Aunt Eva says, looking at Mother, but speaking to me, "Mary Nell was keeping it for you, Lizzie. She told me before she passed that she thought you were the right age for this." She turns away from my mother's stricken face and hands me a rusty key and a crumpled, aging letter. Dated 1945.

"She . . ." Mother pulls at the brim of her black, lace-draped hat, her lips knotted into a frown, her eyes still puffy from crying at the gravesite. "Why . . . ? Mama died before Lizzie was even born."

"Can't really answer that, baby," says Aunt Eva softly. "But she says in the letter to give it to her granddaughter."

Mother lowers her chin; the hat hides her eyes. I see Daddy come up behind her and wrap his large hand around hers.

He puts Grace's trunk in the back of the Buick and we go home to Tuskegee. All the way, I watch the back of Mother's head atop her ramrod-rigid spine. I know she has never seen the inside of the trunk. I know she is thinking about Grace's letter. I ask her if she's OK and she just mumbles at me.

After we get back and Daddy dumps Grace's trunk on the living room floor, he retreats to his study and Mother and I stand on either side of it. I don't know what to say to her, and for a few heartbeats she doesn't move at all. Then she says, her voice so tight that the words barely make it past her lips, "I'm so tired; we'll deal with it in the morning."

I try, really try to wait. I'm in bed an hour or so later when I hear my parents in their bedroom talking. Soon their voices fade and there is, it seems, just me and the night.

The darkness nestles in; it lies close to my face and perches on my young bones as I turn over and over against the sheets in the high iron bed. Might as well be back on Aunt Eva's couch.

No sleep. And that is the start of things. Because if you don't sleep, you think and have conversations with yourself that, in the morning, are startling.

In the quiet night, the trunk is all I think about. Ruth and I had talked about that unopened trunk for years. How was I going to wait until morning? I turn on the lamp and reach under my pillow, where I'd stuck my grandmother's letter. It is postmarked Detroit. The elegant handwriting is familiar.

Dearest Mary Nell,

The strangeness has dogged me north and I know to learn all I can about past days.

I took Mama's papers with me as you said I should, hope they would help me sort things out and they have. It pains me that I missed Mama's funeral but I had a sickness on me at that time that would not let me travel. I send the papers back to you with the other things. Things that belong with the family. I also have sent that quilt I was working on when I left. It's finished and Ayo's whole story is set on it. I feel better now it's through. No telling where I might end up so it be safer with you.

Now Mary please do not show these to my baby girl Sarah. Well I reckon she aint such a baby no more. She will ask questions that you cannot answer that I'm sure I can answer. And I could never burden her with the thought that her mother is crazy. I could not curse her with these things that are happening to me. I thought getting all that down on the quilt in front of me would get rid of it somehow. I don't know about that. But I know I can't pass it on to her this craziness. So save it but not for Sarah. Maybe Sarah will be safe.

I feel that others after us will need to know. Our grands maybe will need to get these things. Please leave these for my granddaughter. I know she aint here yet. But I have faith that you and Eva will know when the time is right and when it is she will be waiting.

Please don't worry. I am well. Somehow it is all easier to bear without being around the pity of your loved ones but it is harder too. My poor George would have done something about it. I am glad I saved him the trouble.

Kiss Eva and Sarah and my twin boys for me.

Your sister,
Grace

I slide the letter under the pillow, flick off the light. The trunk sits in the dark, and my conversation with myself searches for all the reasons one has to wait until morning for everything. But there is no reason, and I throw the covers off to search for my robe.

Tiptoeing down the dim hall, I stumble into the living room. The trunk is squarely where Daddy left it, in the center of the floor. I go on to the kitchen, to the drawer where there is a large flashlight. Mystery, I think, as I flicker it on. I like this. Maybe I've read too much Nancy Drew. I think there is one called *The Secret of the Old Trunk* or something. Only in a bona fide Nancy Drew Mystery, Nancy would find the trunk in a creepy, dusty basement, not at the end of a funeral. Nobody dies in Nancy Drew.

It is mere leather bound by wood, cracking in places, but I kneel before the trunk as if before an altar. The metal loops holding the lock have rusted and there, just under my beam of light, I see that a spider has made her dream home.

I've left the key in the lock and I turn it, opening the lid; an old smell, a sigh, a breath escapes from the past. But when I stick my light in, I see no treasure, just a stack of papers. None of Grace's imagined riches redis-covered. Paper.

A sheaf of it clings together, tied with ancient string. As I try to slide the string off, bits of paper crumble, becoming dust as I watch. I bite my lower lip and put the papers aside. There are other, official-looking papers in there too and, underneath, two shoe boxes and something that looks like cloth.

Inside one of the boxes there is jewelry—necklaces and brooches—as well as gloves and handkerchiefs edged with crocheted lace. Now this is more like it. Treasures. Old treasures, from the looks of things.

I lift one glove to my face and inhale: dust and, very briefly, lavender. Sneezing, I put it back and open the other box, which contains two well-worn leather pouches. One of these holds two stones and a very old bit of blue cloth. In the other, there is a small doll made of grass and sticks.

The doll falls apart in my hands, so I quickly put it back in the pouch, which, in turn, goes back into the shoe box.

I shine the flashlight on the sheaf of papers. The writing seems centuries old. I hold the light as close as I can to the surface of the yellow paper, trying to read without removing the string that ties it together. I don't understand any of it. Something about eternity.

> *We are forever. Here at the bottom of heaven we live in the circle. We back and gone and back again.*
> *I am Ayo. Joy. I choose to remember.*
> *This is for those whose bones lie in the heart of mother ocean for those who tomorrows I never knew who groaned and died in the damp dark beside me. You rite this daughter for me and for them.*

I hear a click, the shuffle of feet. Daddy, probably, on the way to the toilet. Off with the flashlight, the paper stuffed back into the trunk, the lid snapped down and shut. I go and crouch behind the sofa.

Small feet pad down the hall and I see a silhouette in the living room doorway. Not Daddy, though.

Mother comes in rather tentatively and I hold my breath. She puts her arms out in front of her, groping. I see their shadows in the weak light from the hall, stretching towards the dining room. When she goes into the kitchen I'll sneak back to bed.

But she stops and all I hear is her soft breathing. I shift my body so that I can see more of the room from my hiding place, and there she kneels, in much the same attitude as I had a few moments before, in front of the trunk.

Of course. From the moment Daddy slung it into the car, I'd thought of that trunk as mine. I'd wanted that treasure for so long, I'd forgotten that those objects had belonged to *her* mother, a woman she barely knew. Those bits of the past really belong to her, I guess. So, again, I wonder why it is now mine. Grace said in the letter that her granddaughter would "be waiting." I wasn't Grace's only grandchild, not even her only granddaughter, but Eva and Mary Nell had placed their sister's past into my hands without hesitation.

I can't see what Mother is doing, but I hear the crackle of paper and, thinking of the fragile bundle I had held in my hands, I jump from behind the sofa, click on the flashlight and yelp, "Wait! You'll tear it!"

"My God!" she says, putting up a hand to ward off the burst of light. "You scared me, girl!" She sits there with the trunk open and a half-drowsy, half-frightened expression on her face. I watch while it all dissolves into embarrassment.

"I was just on my way for a drink," she says, closing the lid. "And I . . . I don't know . . . I . . . um . . . got curious, I guess."

"I guess," I say. "Yeah."

"I mean, I know she left it to you, but . . . I've wondered for so long."

"Yeah, OK. Me too. I was looking before you came in."

She licks her lips and nods. I wonder why she looks scared.

"I haven't found much in there yet, but it looks interesting," I say, feeling around for the table lamp, turning it on and flicking off the flashlight. "I was afraid of waking you, but Daddy . . . well you know how deep he sleeps."

Mother already has the lid open again and holds the sheaf of papers. She looks at me inquiringly.

"A diary, I think. Somebody named Joy," I say.

My mother's eyes light up. "Joy! My grandmother. These must be really old." She works at the string and finally releases the knot. She closes the trunk lid again and spreads the papers on top.

" 'Mama don't move around much these days. She sits and pieces quilts,' " Mother reads. " 'Christmas . . . fine. Frank ate a lot and Sam was here with his wife and young uns and Mama make a big fuss over them but after they went home on down the road she sat for a long time lookin after them out the window.' " Mother stops and stares. We crouch side by side in that little pool of light coming from the lamp. "Frank . . . that's Granddaddy. I remember him, he was an Indian. He did seem to be eating all the time or thinking about eating all the time, but he never got fat."

I laugh. "Do we have pictures of him?"

"I've got one somewhere. It's not a good one, though. This must be Grandmama's. Joy's journal. I didn't know it existed. Wow." She looks at me and I find her obvious excitement fascinating. She isn't sing-out-loud excited, that wouldn't be her. But she brims with something that is part joy and part fear. I've never seen her look that way, not the completely composed Mrs. Dr. DuBose. I open my mouth to say—I'm not sure what—but she's already rebundling the papers and slipping them back inside the trunk.

"We've got church in the morning, Lizzie," she says. "We can spend all afternoon looking through this stuff, OK? You'd better go back to bed."

She puts her hand on the lid, but hesitates.

"Don't you want to see it?" I ask then, softly.

"What?" She frowns, her eyes still scanning the contents of the trunk. I can't even begin to guess why she pretends that it means little to her. She isn't good at it.

"Grandmama's letter. She mentions you in it."

Her body stiffens, so much so that I could see the knot of flesh form between her shoulder blades through her whisper of a nightgown.

"And . . . what did she have to say about me? Couldn't have been much . . . I was so small when she last saw me . . ." Mother thumps her palm against the leather lid as she closes it.

"Wait . . . I'll show you. Maybe you'll understand it."

I run to my bedroom to get the letter and run back, stopping for a moment in the living room doorway to watch her, still kneeling there, stroking the trunk idly, while her mind seems to be away somewhere else. Or sometime else.

"She just wanted you to be safe," I say, coming into the room again.

"Safe from what? From having a mother?" A tiny bitterness uglies her voice. But her expression remains blanc.

"I don't know, Mother. Here." I hand the yellowing letter to her and watch her read, watch her lips move over the words *I could not curse her with these things.*

"Crazy. Yes, that would explain some things." Mother sighs, folding the paper and starting to unfold her legs. "Although I think most of Johnson Creek had already figured that out about her."

"But what did she mean, 'Maybe Sarah will be safe?' What was she keeping you safe from? And why would she give me these things? How did she even know she'd have a granddaughter?"

"Why wouldn't she have one? Surely, she'd expect at least one of her children to have a daughter."

"But Aunt Eva gave it to me. Why did she give it to me? I'm not Grace's only granddaughter." The questions fall out of my mouth in a steady stream that I can't seem to stop.

"I don't know," my mother said wearily, getting to her feet. "Maybe because you're the most convenient. I just know she didn't leave it to me." She picks up the flashlight and takes it back into the kitchen. She comes out and turns out the living room light, her hand pressed into the small of my back, pushing me back to bed.

"You're asking me to get into the mind of a crazy country woman who died more than twenty years ago," she says. She bows her head and I see her pass a hand over her eyes. Is she crying? She won't lift her head. "I'm the last person you should be asking. The answer to all of your questions is I don't know. I'll probably never know. All the answers are in the grave with her."

She opens my palm and puts the letter in it.

"Go to bed," she says.

I stand in the doorway of my bedroom watching her pad down the hall, sure that this is not the end of it. No, it's just the beginning.

⌣

It gets even more interesting the next day.

Mother spreads Grace's quilt on the living room floor and sits at its edge, like a small animal beached on the shore of a great ocean. She wears white pumps and her peach-colored silk dress with the white collar, and still holds in one hand the funeral-home fan that she inadvertently took from church. Daddy, leaning his six-foot-four-inches against the doorway to the dining room, dabs at a coffee stain on his white shirt and then considers the quilt from behind his steaming cup.

I balance myself on the arm of the sofa, clutching Grace's letter and watching the shapes and colors dance. Daddy had insisted that we take everything out of the trunk and this was what was underneath the papers and stuff. Now-faded pictures skim its surface, people run lightly across, time moves, and there is, everywhere, water.

It is obviously the quilt Grace referred to in her letter, the one that she hoped would help her solve her problem, whatever that had been.

Mother's eyes have glazed over a bit. Trance-like, she touches an appliqué of a child. "I used to have a dress that color," she murmurs.

Daddy comes into the living room and squats down to look. "So, what was the big secret?" he asks, casually sipping. I hope he doesn't spill coffee on it. "It's all really interesting. But no reason to hide it away, is there? All that mystery, all that talk about giving it at the right time to the right person." He rolls his eyes. "That trunk should be your property, shouldn't it, Sarah?"

"The letter says quiet clearly that Mama wanted it to go to a granddaughter. I guess Eva thought Lizzie should be the granddaughter and that now was the time," says Mother, breathing deep and fanning herself. She still stares at the quilt. "What kind of quilt is that anyway? Just some pictures stuck to a background. No rhyme or reason. She wrote about it like it was supposed to mean something." She looks over at me, sitting on the sofa.

Of course the pictures mean something. I follow two figures walking down a road with baskets on their heads. A woman and a child. Their footprints stride behind side-by-side and then the smaller prints—the child's—branch off and end at the edge of a large body of water.

It's a story. My skin tingles just below the surface. My arms ache and I massage one and then the other, gently.

"Looks like it ended up with the right person, though," says Mother. "Just mysterious enough and quirky enough for Lizzie, don't you think, John?" She smiles at me, but there is no light in her eyes. I feel as if I'm hurting her and I don't know what to do to make it stop. Mother can just have the whole thing, if she wants. But she doesn't seem to. Despite her obvious curiosity, she keeps referring to it as "Lizzie's trunk. Lizzie's quilt."

I hold her eyes for a moment, but she looks away and stares at the living room wall. I follow her eyes and meet the long-ago gaze of Grace Mobley Lancaster, who seems to take in the whole room from that flat, faded photograph that hangs there among other dead family members. *What were you thinking?* I ask her silently.

Daddy begins folding the quilt and Mother gets up with a little shake of her head and begins helping him.

"Yeah," says Daddy. "This all fits you, Lizzie. Strange letters, quilts, and old dusty bits of the past. I think your Grandma Grace must have had some kind of premonition about you."

"Why don't you take it, Mother?" I say, watching my mother's downturned face. "It really is yours, don't you think?"

"No, it's not mine." She puts the quilt back in the bottom of the trunk and begins piling things on top. Daddy disappears into the kitchen for what I know will be cup number two.

"Besides," she says, shrugging. "My mother's been gone for a long time. What good is some old quilt to me?" Something lingers on the other side of her words. Sadness, maybe. Something that tugs at my heart and won't let go.

⌒

On nights like this, dreams come soft.

I lie half-fading into sleep, and a brown woman marches across the bed, wading through the moonlight. She is wrapped in color, a woman-child beside her. She adds her footprints to others on the road to the market, on the threads laid on the surface of my bed.

The quilt engulfs the twin bed, and I have folded it in half. I am safe underneath the story of my life; the brown woman is safe underneath my palm. On her way to the market.

It is hot, but I pull the quilt up to my chin. As always when the moon is full, I have drawn the curtain back to drink in the night. The room is bright as day, but the twilight world of dreams has arrived.

My mother has her hand on my head. I know it is my mother, though her face is unfamiliar.

"We have a long way. We must start," she says in a strange language. It isn't the weary voice of Mrs. Dr. Sarah Lancaster DuBose speaking her college-bred English; music falls from the lips of a full-brown woman. She gives me a small basket to carry, her eyes smiling, her mouth stern.

"Take this," she says. I don't know why I understand, and I don't stop to look in the basket; I know it's full of cloth. I balance it on my head and she hoists her own basket. We are going to market together.

The road stretches in an empty line. A rock stings me, and I pause to see the dirt gathered around my bare toes and wonder. Mother never lets me go barefoot. But as the thought flashes, my mother is a dozen steps ahead; her somewhat narrow body moves her loose wrapper this and that way as she walks. And when I run to catch her, she smiles at me inquiringly, but it isn't Mrs. Dr. DuBose; it is the full-brown woman, her head caressed by bright cloth. I smile back. I love going to the market, because my mother is a master dyer. My father sings songs about her, his first wife, his only wife, by the fire at night while I drink in the night.

When I wake to bright Alabama day, there is dust about my feet.

Patricia Powell

When I was three months old, I was sent away to be raised by my great-aunt. Perhaps my preoccupation with origin began there. Growing up in Jamaica, I was always curious about the Chinese families who lived in my neighborhood, and their children, with whom I went to school. What were the circumstances that drove them away from China and brought them to the Caribbean to live? I wondered then. Many, many years later and still my intrigue never waned. Though their contributions to Jamaican culture and society have often been minimized, the Chinese have lived in Jamaica since the 19th century. What were their experiences like, leaving their country and their families so far away and coming over as laborers stacked up inside those ships? And if they survived the turbulent crossing, what were the working conditions like on those sugar plantations, where just a few years earlier African slavery was in full bloom? What did it feel like to inhabit a body that now had to speak a new language, and live in a landscape so utterly unfamiliar, and be caught up in the middle of the country's racial and political preoccupations? How did they decide who could be trusted, who could be a friend, so they could create community? How did they man-age in this foreign territory as they reinvented themselves in order to fit in, sometimes literally, as in the case of Lowe, my main character, who cross-dressed and passed as a male shopkeeper in order to survive, in order to establish a sense of belonging?

From *The Pagoda*, a novel

Before daybreak, and with just a tip of his wide-brimmed hat to Miss Sylvie, who watched from the back door with eyes that seemed to be begging him not to go, not to leave her there alone and so soon, he climbed onto the saddled mule and was rumbling over winding, endless muddy dirt roads with the night at his shoulders and the cool morning air in his nostrils. He could not help her now; his own cauldron of grief was too deep; he had to look for help, look outside himself. Lowe rode quickly, keeping to the shadow of huts and lean-tos lining the hillside, slowing at bridges, mindful of rotting planks as he crossed beds of rivers and creeks, now dry and empty but notorious for rising up, overflowing nearby roads and washing away huts strewn along low-lying areas. He passed district after district, the markets like skeletons without the shouting, quarreling people, only rats and stray dogs and cats prowling through the garbage. He passed churches standing solemn and solitary without the singing, roaring congregation that would descend in less than three hours. It was Sunday, and the short steady clips of the mule's shoes were the only sounds that woke the quiet.

He rode past the bolted doors of unpainted, box-shaped concrete houses with corrugated zinc roofs, his trousers wet with the beast's sweat, until the sky started turning a shimmering rosy hue, and then the world took on life. He passed people, their donkeys laden with buckets of water, who nodded hello or called out "Mr. Chin." He began to smell coffee, pick out fingers of smoke from the pointed roofs of kitchens, smell frying, hear muttering voices. He passed naked children playing in the fine red dirt; thin white lines of smoke that rose from burning rubbish dumps; fat black carrion crows circling overhead; mule-drawn carts; listless donkeys; people drinking coffee from enamel mugs in the blackened doorways of houses and dunking in hardened pieces of bread.

He rode past yellowing pieces of white clothes hooked up on wire lines, and others spread out on jutting rocks to bleach. Now he rode past herds of cows; vegetable plots knee-deep with weeds; hills browned by drought; grass blackened by bush fires; endless fields with tall wire fences, empty now on a Sunday but on any other day flooded with workers. Amid all this, For Sale signs littered the countryside as deserted estate houses and factory buildings lay broken down in financial disaster, turning back to bush, in the wake of Emancipation. A pack of crotchety and emaciated dogs with powerful drooling jaws rushed at the mule, following it for a while, grew bored, then disappeared.

Up and down, up and down, the road ribboning through wild and untamed hillside, he replayed again and again in his head how they must've done it, the gang of them, stumbling round the foundation under the cover of night, sprinkling the ground with kerosene. He saw the sea of brown faces he'd seen every night since he'd had the shop huddled in a corner, talking softly and plotting. He knew that like the church hall, protest groups were founded right there on the piazza of his rum bar in the dead of night and in hushed tones. That the labor unrest sweeping through the countryside and the workers' rebellion strikes against landholders paying them little to nothing and overwhelming them with work had started up right there with the glassful of rum cocked in their hands and the heads close together.

But he never thought they'd turn on him, though it was common accord for them to burn down the Chinese people's shops. Common accord for them to loot. The more militant types intending to clear his people out of the country. Still, he never thought they'd turn on him. But they must not have known Cecil was inside. Poor Cecil. Or maybe they knew! Poor Cecil. With his eyes wide open like that. He must've leapt awake to the oil drums exploding, his heart giving out immediately. He must've jerked awake to columns of smoke, blazing bars of fire, his heart giving out at once. For there were no bruises, according to the coroner, who inspected him carefully before filling out the certificate. Still, it was strange, his gray eyes wide open like that, wide open and surprised and staring out as if bemused by the turn of events.

Indeed it was a strange turn. Cecil had brought him there, had given him the shop, and now both Cecil and the shop were gone. Strangely enough he was relieved. Though he was flooded with conflicted feelings and earnestly wished that all could've been settled with the daughter before his passing. But he didn't miss Cecil. He felt clean and unburdened from the chop and from Cecil's plans. Yes, he missed the rust of routine that had protected him all these years, for now he just felt naked and empty and listless. But somewhere deep in him he knew that for the first time he could sort out what it was he wanted to do with his life. That fate now, in the middle of all this tragedy, was handing him the reins to his own life. He could rethink again those reasons that had brought him to the island and try to live out some of his dreams. He longed to unburden himself. He longed to walk free, without hampers saddling his shoulders, thwarting his pace. But he wasn't sure how. There was still the daughter to contend with, his marriage to Miss Sylvie, and the fabulous masquerade that was his life.

The mule slowed as they entered a stretch of idle lands, and he thought briefly of investments, then shoved it aside. The savings, and there wasn't much now, was for the daughter. Plus the idea of employing farmhands frightened him. It was hard enough asking a woman as old as Dulcie to boil him a pot of tea, hard enough waking and asking Omar, his age-mate, to feed and saddle the mule. He was always envious of how commands steamed effortlessly from Miss Sylvie's velvet lips, but he knew they came with the authority of near-alabaster porcelain skin. The coppery mass of hair that fell to her waist. With him it was a different story. He was the outsider. The foreigner. The newcomer. He had the burned-down shop there to show, to remind him of his place there on the island.

At this his eyes filled up, and he dug his boots deeper into the animal's gut. He had to see Kywing and the others. He yearned for the music of their frenzied dialects, the euphony of clicking tiles as they played games, and his mouth watered in anticipation of stews Kywing would prepare, embryonic chickens with tender bones in peppered soup, pressed duck and tiny bottomless cups of tea. He longed for vestiges of his family mirrored in the men who came, in their gesticulations and corroded faces, in the Morse code of their languages, which he didn't even understand anymore, but anything to remind him that he wasn't alone there on that wretched island. And then he longed just to see Kywing and his family, with whom he had grown close over the years.

Lowe rode on through the light of haze and heart, stopping now and again to water the mule, keeping away from the centers of town, eating the lunch Dulcie had prepared, as he traveled endless winding roads that led to new districts, his face darkening under the onslaught of sun strokes.

All over the countryside church bells tolled, summoning sinners to worship. He heard feverish preaching and incredible pandemonium as hymns broke out and the possessed shrieked into the tin roofs. He passed the cluster of buildings sprawling along the hillside that made up Good Hope Estate, with its mills and its boiling and curing houses, and not too far off the thatched-roof barracks where the Negro people had once lived, and still farther off, the hundreds of acres of caneland, deserted now on a Sunday, just dry cane stalks and husks stretching to fill the horizon. Had it been yesterday, the yellowing stalks would've been peppered with glistening bodies: free Negroes; indentured Indian and Chinese laborers pouring in daily by the boatloads; Irishmen fleeing famine—hoeing, plowing, weeding, shielding themselves underneath wide-brimmed hats.

But though it was Sunday and no one was there, Lowe could still hear voices rise and fall to a tune that tiny trembling streams of wind had carried from afar, a song sung in an attempt to ignore assault from the never-ending backbreaking labor; singing to relieve pain in their twisted limbs, stomachs tormented from hunger, skins baking under a fiery sun; anger seething like trapped steam from lips. Sometimes breezes brought the whistling whip on its way to bite and cut and to dig away at the burned and desecrated flesh. But those sounds were no longer common, as there would be fights, murders, torchings carried out at night, households charred, heads wiped off by machetes and lined up by the gate for shiny, metallic flies to attack in the morning.

Lowe rode on, not a hut in sight, just a long, hopeless stretch of thorny acacia trees, an endless range of green hills then gray hills fading into the spacious white of the sky. Drowsy from the heat and from fatigue, he dozed to the steady lackadaisical clips of the mule's shoes, until braids of smell—musty charcoal from wood fires, pungent coconut oil, pickled pigs' feet—shimmered by his nostrils, lulled him to life, and he knew it would be only a matter of minutes and Kywing would be at the iron gate of the stucco house he had built behind the bakery.

He dismounted and let the mule loose in the pen across the road, where one of Kywing's boys would attend to it. He approached the house slowly, his head bowed, his heart broken, his shirt soaked with sweat, his hat in his hand. Sharmilla, Kywing's wife, was waiting. Her majestic arms, swaddled with silver bangles and some gold ones, jangled as she hugged him, the great cascades of her flesh and her sweet-smelling essences hemming him. "Man, we not safe here at all. Not safe at all." Her eyes, rimmed with black, glistened with tears, and Lowe grunted, his face a network of grimaces that meant nothing and everything.

He nodded and shook his head at intervals, not quite ready yet to stir up his grief. Though he wanted nothing more than to have lain there basking in her embrace, nothing more than to have her stroke his head and behind his ears and smother him with sweet tenderlings murmured in his chest. His suffering was so deep. His brokenness so complete. His confusion so enormous. Plus her embrace was never like Sylvie's; it wasn't full up with the same kind of yearning, as if some grave thing had been taken away, so that now she had to walk round with her arms outstretched and aching, and anything she touched she had to hold close, almost to the point of strangulation, just to make sure it didn't disappear.

But still he extracted himself neatly from Sharmilla's embrace and stepped back to admire the florid embroidery on the collar and pockets of her sleeveless cotton frock, and she broke down in laughter, showing the brown roots of her molars, and he laughed with her, wanting only to forget and to distract her curling eyes from lolling along the arches of his limbs, from reading him, a smooth-spined text.

For it was as if she knew exactly what lay behind the costume, though it was nothing she said, nothing she intimated, it was only in the rhythm of her eyelids, tugging at the brush of false hair that trembled above his lips, bursting the buttons of his striped short-sleeve shirt, stripping down his shorts, and so he could never linger long in the snugness of her embrace, never engage her for any length of time. It was always there between them, the overwhelming self-consciousness, the palpable silence, the charged glances. Once, for a brief and furtive moment, he thought perhaps she desired him, but he found the idea so worrisome, so marked with frustration and distress, that he wiped it completely from the shelves of his mind.

From his bag Lowe brought out the little surprises he had carried for the waiting children, twelve in all, who had turned out to greet him, stiff and shy in their starched and bristling Sunday shirts, the stunning frocks, their hair marbled and glistening from scented pomade. He handed out the colored bottles to match the assorted glass of their eyes, pairs of rubber catapults, and gifts from one of Miss Sylvie's husband's old trunks, wet with mildew and rotting in the buttery: three bloated copies of *Pilgrim's Progress*, with passages underlined in ink; a miniature birdcage, rusty and empty and with the gate missing; a magnifying glass with a jagged crack; an atlas with the pictures faded and the names of countries inked in Latin.

Behind them on the veranda, Kywing watched with a long gloomy face and a wide shaggy nose, and shook his head slowly, khaki trousers shimmering in the afternoon glare. Lowe climbed the short flight of concrete steps up to the shade of the veranda. He rested his wide-brimmed felt hat on the floor by his feet and sat down on the Morris chair with arms peeling. Around them, the insects hummed, wild with the heat. Sharmilla bellowed, and one of the boys appeared with a piping-hot glass full of jasmine tea on a tin tray enameled with bright-red apples. Then she disappeared into the maze and clutter of the house, her slippers dragging on linoleum floors, and Lowe knew she wasn't far.

"Burn down flat, flat, Lowe! Nothing!" They dipped cheeks, then lapsed into island speech. Lowe's Hakka and his Cantonese had long since atrophied, from both lack of use and mindful forgetting, as his only company had been the villagers those early years and he'd so badly wanted to start over. Kywing's face was stern, and he wore a mustache much like Lowe's, a thick black brush of bristles, but unlike Lowe, who never touched his at all, except now and again to check if it was still there and to readjust it by winding the sharp edges thoughtfully, Kywing fingered his at all times, plucking and twining and smoothing as he paced the length and breadth of the veranda.

Lowe shook his head, eyes bright, remembering his neighbors dousing the building in the dense dark of the morning.

"And Cecil, gone too!" Kywing's hands, pale and bony, sprang off his face and clapped at invisible mosquitoes and flies, and he yelled at one of the girls to bring the bottle. The girl came and she had one of the books underneath her arm and she smiled at Lowe and Kywing slapped a handful of the juice on his neck and throat and the smell made Lowe's eyes slowly leak. "They going to turn us mad in this place with they hate, Lowe, seriously." He stopped his pacing to drink from a glass of white rum and light a cigarette from a half-empty pack that lay on the flaky arms of the other chair. Then his voice grew softer, and his meandering and fondling started up again. "Sorry bout Cecil, man, I know he mean much to you. I know."

Lowe didn't say anything. He wondered what Kywing really knew. He had never told anyone about the hell he lived on that ship after he was caught; how Cecil locked him up inside that cabin that barely had air, barely had light for weeks and months.

Kywing's voice changed and it grew confidential. He wasn't much older than Lowe, but the mustache, which dropped alongside the edges of his face and covered his fine lips and broken teeth, gave him an ancient look. "How much you need to start over, Lowe? We have something wrap up inside. How much?"

Lowe looked up. Suddenly he was alarmed. He hadn't even been thinking of another shop.

"Well, maybe you shouldn't start so big again, Lowe. I mean they might burn it down again. And then you just lose everything again. And with the business so little, they don't want insure us. Look what happen to Woo Lee. Look Wong T'in. They asleep in the back. They set them on fire. And the fellows they catch get off light, light. You think maybe you housekeeper, what her name, Dulcie, have something to do with it? Or her son, the young boy there. You can't trust nobody. Not even people inside you own house."

And at that Lowe started, for just the idea that the fingers of death trembled so close to his throat was unbearable. He shoved away the thought and brought again to mind the voice of the caller, and he wondered why now, why after thirty years, and not before, when he had just arrived there, when he didn't know them yet and was so much more vulnerable to their onslaughts. Why now, after he had turned godfather to so many of their children, had trusted goods to so many of them so they wouldn't starve.

"Well, if you want start big again, maybe you should move. Come down this way. More of us here."

Still Lowe said nothing, and Kywing grew desperate. Then he reached over and grabbed Lowe's knees. "I know, man, it hard as hell. And on top of that with Cecil gone. And still nothing yet from the police." He paused and together they said nothing. Together they coughed timid ahems to clear their lungs. Together they took deep breaths that swelled the caves of their stomachs. Then Kywing started up again. "You must have something save up? I mean all these years you working. What bout the wife, Miss Sylvie? She must have something."

"I need to think a little, Kywing." Lowe's voice erupted sharper than he intended.

"Man, you crazy!" Kywing clapped at more invisible mosquitoes and wiped his face over and over with the soiled white towel at his shoulder. "You have to just open up another shop, quick. You have to pretend things not so bad. You can't show them we weak. You have to just accept it as bad luck. Man, you can't stop to think. They going to murder we in this place."

But Lowe didn't hear him; he was thinking of how the Chinese killed themselves over the shops, all so they could send money home, return rich like the dreams that had brought them. They slept back there underneath the counters on top of long-grain-rice and unbleached-flour bags. They didn't buy shoes, didn't buy new clothes, they had the shop open from daybreak till the last customer emptied the bottle of white rum and stumbled out into the darkness. They had everything stored underneath the counters and could marry goods when things were scarce. A cup of butter with one pound of salt fish. One box of detergent with one ball of blue. And how the ungrateful people heaped abuses on them.

"Mr. Chin, big gill of coconut oil."

It didn't matter, his name.

And when their lives hit rock bottom, they came waving their fists. "Chinee, you shortchange me again! You sell me the rotting meat again!"

"Chinee, you thief me again!"

As if a little manipulation wasn't often the nature of trade.

Sometimes a woman would come hollering with a red rag tying up her head, two half-naked thin-limbed children locked onto her hips, their stomachs bloated out with arrowroot, the arms and legs white and spotted with disease. "Chin, I don't eat since Tuesday gone." By then it was Friday. From underneath the counter he handed over half a pound of dried cod and two pounds of rice, for somehow they had become his people too; these women who cursed and haggled him one day and the next laid out their woes, begging for advice on their wayward husbands and lovers. Yet now the shop was there burned flat to the ground. Everything gone!

Lowe broke out into a hard dry sob, and just as abruptly, he stopped. For during those fleeting seconds he allowed himself to rise up from the dregs of his despair; he could see that it was indeed a blessing, this massive destruction. That indeed he could try out another kind of life altogether. Not one that his father or Cecil had routed out for him, but one he could weed out for himself. And then it came to him. And then he knew. "Look, Kywing," he cried out into the blazing heat, his eyes suddenly bright and bursting, "what about a school?"

Kywing didn't say anything at first. He wasn't an attractive man. He also wasn't a sharp thinker. And his mouth turned disappointed and hostile. "A school, Lowe." He said this quietly, slowing down to look closely at Lowe, whose mind had erupted into a torrent of fantastical ideas and schemes. He would rebuild the shop into a school! A school for the Chinese children born on the island. A school and meetinghouse where they could hold weddings and celebrate festivals. All over the country a multitude of schools had sprung up. Mico Teachers Training, Munro, Mannings. Down by his way alone, five more missionary schools, two trade centers, and a teacher training college. Why not one for the Chinese so they could learn Commerce and Geography, Elements of Astrology?

"But that won't bring in any money, Lowe."

"Well, maybe not right away, Kywing." He tried to keep his voice even. It was his first dream. He saw it withering away. He thought of his father and all his bottled up fantasies. He thought of Cecil and of the mangled bodies in his dreams. He thought of all those years he had so successfully and piece by piece erased himself. He didn't even have language!

"Well, that is damn nonsense, then, Lowe. I mean we not learners here, man. We didn't come to turn learners." Kywing lowered himself next to Lowe on the bench and began to separate, into small neat bunches, the hair on his face. "We just come here to catch we hands, sell a few things, catch we hands." He softened his voice. "Some of us going back home, as soon as the contract finish. Even my big boy there, talking this nonsense bout law, bout sacred and universal history! And the bakery there!"

"But, Kywing, maybe I could teach." He didn't like the whine of his voice, and so he coughed to clear his throat.

"But, Lowe"—he laughed out loud, and Lowe's face burned—"you not a teacher man, you not a scholar. How you wanting to teach?" He clapped Lowe on the shoulder. "You always ambitious, that's what I like about you. Ambitious."

"Well, maybe Wong Yan-sau." He'd been a schoolteacher in Kwantung Province and now ran a bakery not far from Kywing.

Kywing hissed. He leapt up from his seat next to Lowe and started pacing again. "Look, Lowe, just take my advice and start again with fifty. All right, Lowe. A Chinese school and meetinghouse, man. They would really chop we up on this place."

In the background, Kywing's wife scolded one of the children, then they heard a cuff, followed by shouts and a loud wailing, and Lowe knew, as if by intuition, in just that slap she had delivered, that Sharmilla had endorsed his plan. Kywing got up and yelled for one of the children to bring more drinks, signaling an end to the conversation. But Lowe's flurry of designs had just sprung to life. Every day now, boatloads of Chinese came. Maybe interested members could pool together what little money they had saved up and offer out loans, give out scholarships encouraging the next generation to take up law and medicine, public speaking and drama, and liberate themselves from shopkeeping. And just so the children would remember, maybe somebody could teach them Cantonese and Mandarin, so they could read literature. If they were still interested in business, then maybe they could form their own wholesale association, and then members could promote business and protect rights.

Further in the future, he saw this club, this benevolent society writing its own newspaper, reporting on events affecting Chinese both here and abroad. There would even be an obituary section and another announcing weddings and births, and still another reporting on those murdered in cold blood by the warmongering people, on those whose shops they looted and burned down, on those opening up new businesses. He would call it . . . And he thought for some time, until he arrived at the title of one of his father's short stories. The Pagoda. Later he would add on one or two extra buildings, a home for the aged, maybe even a kind of sanitarium for the ones maimed on the estates, those who couldn't work, too poor to pay the passage home. Maybe even a cemetery, where Chinese people could visit their ancestors, instead of those public plots where the government dumped poor people. Kywing handed him a tumbler of carrot juice, and Lowe turned it to his head, drinking with both feet stretched out ahead, as the future loomed bright with promises.

Nelly Rosario

I was raised by traditional Dominican parents whose favorite phrase echoed throughout our Brooklyn household on the regular: Hay una diferencia entre la libertad y el libertinaje. In the mid-1980s, my sister and I were too busy wanting to follow Seventeen *magazine's advice on dating to care what "those old-fashioned fogies" meant by the difference between "being liberated" and "being a libertine." All we knew was that the specter of illicit sex always hovered above those words; we had been warned: American women age before their time because they live worldly lives.*

Worldly woman that I am now (traveled and educated, writer and mother), I can better appreciate the nuances of my parents' litany. Though I may sometimes be unrestrained by convention, I don't believe that a search for the meaning of freedom necessarily leads to the "dissolute life of a libertine."

In the novel Song of the Water Saints, *Graciela is so consumed by wanderlust that she flees home life in the Dominican Republic on an aimless quest—all against the backdrop of a brutal turn-of-the-century national history. Her wanderlust forces her to look beyond what's in front of her, to aspire to the unknown—bring what it may. Her condition manifests as that inexplicable itch, literally and figuratively. Ultimately, this "libertine's" journey towards freedom ends up right back where she started: at Home. And Graciela's spirit encodes that circular journey into the genes of her subsequent progeny, particularly in her great-granddaughter, Leila.*

I grew up feeling that the price exacted for a woman's desire for freedom was some kind of sexual punishment, though I knew that that same freedom could lead to lots of delicious experiences. The chapter excerpted here, "Leila, 1998," speaks to this quandary, her unconscious repetition of Graciela's wandering. This time, however, close to the millennium and living in New York City, the bright 14-year-old has more opportunities (economic, educational, etc.) than Graciela did. Leila, too, ends up boomeranging Home and learning that liberating the mind along with the capacity for love of family can be the "free-est" of freedoms.

Leila, 1998

From *Song of the Water Saints*, a novel

"Leila Pimentel."

"Present."

Leila sat in biology class, very much present. It was the only class that put an A on her report card and earned her new clothes. The rest of her classes could bust as far as she was concerned, she had told Ms. Valenza in a parent-teacher conference, minus parents. In general, she maintained, she was an epistemophiliac whose lust for knowledge had nothing to do with grades.

Today they were studying the circulatory system, following a month-long tour of the human body. Leila smiled when Ms. Valenza said that the heart was about the size of a fist. When Ms. Valenza asked the students to check each other's pulses, Leila's study partner thought he had mis-counted.

"Nah, I'm just horny," she said only to watch the blood rise in his face.

Ventricles, the venae cavas, the valves, and aortas. She liked the *v*'s and *a*'s in her mouth, and repeated the words to keep from thinking about Him. Miguel Ulloa Hernández: the bastard who was straining the muscle that was supposed to beat seventy-two times a minute for the rest of her life.

⌣

Privacy was luxury. Leila's bed was in the living room, and Mercedes and Andrés slept in the bedroom. In a corner between the sofa and the arm-chair was a spot where on most afternoons the sun made a rhombus on the linoleum.

Leila was still angry at Them for not letting her go out with Mirangeli and Elsa. Mercedes and Andrés were good to her, but as Leila got older, the generation gap caused them to shout across canyons at each other. Her grandparents, no matter how strong and lucid they seemed, were in their eighties, getting ready to step away from life, while Leila was just beginning to get her feet wet. Her Uncle Ismael came over often to listen to Mercedes and Andrés' complaints, as well as to boss Leila around and give her an ear pull if need be. Always trying to act like the father he ain't. Then he would go right back to his life of money and women. Even the home attendant who cared for Mercedes and Andrés during the day was starting to get preachy with Leila. At times like this, Leila wished her mother would not have stayed behind in DR like a coward, and that her father would have not been such an asshole.

⌒

Leila sat with Mercedes to write Amalfi a letter.

Querida Amalfi . . .

How difficult for Leila to turn Mercedes' ramblings into neatly scripted letters. Mercedes dictated to Leila as if Amalfi sat right next to them in the bedroom.

—This goes to greet you in union with your family, that you may be in good health . . .

— . . . and Amalfi, my love, I keep telling that home attendant to stop buying me more panties . . . up to my neck in them.

The Spanish trudged through Leila's weak short-term memory and slow hands; a script full of fat spaces and balled dots. In the beginning she faithfully included Mercedes' every "humph" and her occasional laughter (written as "ja ja ja" in comic-strip bubbles). The process: take in the words tumbling out of Mercedes, remember them, translate them into English for meaning in her own mind, then translate them into Spanish, and, finally, write them neatly and correctly on the page—all the while listening for the next barrage.

"Damn, slow down, 'Buela! What was that again?"

Mercedes craned her neck to listen, and responded in her usual delay.

—¿What do you go to school for? ¿Now how do I start that story up again?

Mercedes snorted, then picked up the fringes of gossip for Amalfi: more robberies in the building, a dream of lots of little rabbits, the fish special at Key Foods, your daughter who can't even write a decent letter.

" 'Buela, I said slow the hell down!"

—. . . tell Amalfi also that I send a champú with Isma to make her hair good and twenty dollars, not for any boyfriends to gobble it up . . .

Mercedes pointed to the loose-leaf notebook in Leila's lap.

. . . *for you only and not for whoever cunnilinguses you, Ma,* Leila wrote.

—I pray you're well, Amalfi. ¿How's the foot?

Ma, when the fuck are you fucking coming to see me?

—¿What are you writing there? Mercedes said, peering at the change in the pen's rhythm.

—Should've gotten the home attendant for this, Mercedes said and picked at her housedress.

" 'Buela, Ma doesn't care about us. This is a waste of time," Leila whined.

But Mercedes had been sending letters to Amalfi for ten years, despite Andrés and Leila's frustration, despite arthritis and bad eyesight. When Mercedes had arrived in New York City, she made it her duty to understand the business of sending letters. Though Amalfi occasionally sent them white frying cheese or luxuriant hair conditioners with acquaintances traveling to New York, everyone knew she would never join them.

Leila bounced back on Mercedes' bed with a cramped hand.

—¡Get those tennies off my bed, little girl!

Leila laughed at her alarm and kicked off the sneakers. She shot the balled-up letter across the room to the mirror. Mercedes narrowed her eyes and slowly shook her head.

—The things you do . . . she said, then removed her dentures and put them into a jar on the bureau.

Leila crossed her arms, then uncrossed them, to rip threads from the curtains.

—If you don't want to do me favors, then go, Mercedes said with a wave of her hands.—And they killed the goat on you, look at those circles under your eyes, Mercedes blurted out.

"What?" Leila stopped unthreading the embroidered hummingbirds and ran to the bureau mirror.

—I know you have the menses, Mercedes said.

" 'Buela, how do you know?"

—I know more than you think, little girl.

Mercedes elbowed Leila out of the way and began opening the bureau drawers and unwrapping tissue paper. Occasionally she made scratchy noises with her throat. From one drawer she pulled out a ball of tissue. Then she slid onto the bed, where Leila now sat, to undo the ball with her veined hands. An amber crucifix lay in the wad like honey candy anchored in gold. Mercedes held it to the lamplight for Leila to see the delicate mite limbs trapped in resin.

—From Puerto Plata, I think. Mamá gave it to me before she died, when I was around your age. But in those times we never really knew our ages, because our parents would sometimes wait years before they officially declared your existence to the government offices. Yes, I must've been like you, maybe thicker, because I was thick, you know, like a woman even before my menses . . . had the sharpest mind . . . had all the menfolk coming to me, but I settled for Andrés because if there's one thing I know is to marry smart, get one who you know will never double-cross you. Early on, make sure to keep the kitchen knives hidden, so that he is the one who has to ask you for their use. You have to be smart, my sweet girl, you have to be smart in life.

Mercedes' eyes had grown milky and her lips without the dentures looked drawstringed. Leila hated when Mercedes got lost in her own memories.

"I am smart. Ms. Valenza tells me I should think more about a medical career 'cause I like biology. Can't I just be good at it?" Leila spoke even though her grandmother could not understand her English.

But Mercedes continued as if Leila had not spoken.

—Be smart, little girl. Here in this country, you can't be having too many kids, with no village around to help you raise them. Over there, anyone—the grocer, the butcher—had every right to box your ears if they saw you on the wrong path. But here, you're on your own. Everything you do alone in this country. That's why people get crazy here, forget the Lord. Remember, Leila, the Lord's eyes are big enough to see everything you do.

"Anyway, who gave Mamá Graciela the crucifix?" Leila had to ask twice, as Mercedes dug a fingernail into her own ear.

—A nun or a priest gave it to her, something like that. Mamá, I must say in this old age, was as smart as me to have had only me, so she could pick up and go at will—¿and did I tell you she had me with a fine man of the purest breed? Amalfi must have that picture . . .

A hollow noise came from Mercedes' throat as she inserted a hairpin to get at the inside of her ear.

" 'Buela, you're gonna destroy the stereocilia in your ear!" Leila said as she fingered the crucifix. It was perfect to wear over a messed-up heart. She wanted to pop the cross in her mouth.

"Wow. Looks like vitamin E."

—Real amber, sweet girl. It floats in the sea.

They were quiet for a while, admiring the tiny window in their hands. Mercedes told Leila how Graciela had admitted to almost eating the cross as well.

—Always remember the things I tell you.

"Nah, 'Buela, I live for the now. Everyone's either telling me to remember stuff I never lived, or to prepare for some who-knows future."

Mercedes yawned.

To Leila, those who carried the past carried the dead, and those who chased the future died of cardiac arrest.

—¿Can I wear the crucifix? she asked Mercedes carefully in Spanish.

—It's already yours, sweet girl.

⌐

—Late bloomers last longer, Andrés told Leila.

"But I wanna bloom now, man," she said under her breath.

Leila and Miguel were in the basement, hidden in the labyrinth of thick walls. He squeezed her flesh, searching for roundness that was not there. She moaned, afraid and excited that the superintendent of the building would catch them and trot upstairs to tell her grandparents. She imagined them racing down with her Uncle Ismael to beat up Miguel and then beat her with the belt, and Mercedes would then have the home attendant write a long I-told-you-so letter to Amalfi.

Leila felt a delicious rain of needles. Miguel's fingers were now drawing circles in her tightness. She was wet and swollen and full of water while sucking on his earlobe. He seemed nice, she thought, liking and wincing at the easy way his hand claimed the newest hairs down there. She tried to hide her smile when his other hand reached under her tank top and pinched her nipples, as if he were handling the married woman who had borne him three children. A rain of needles. Studying him through the peephole every morning as he left the building for work, she had initially thought he'd be more mysterious. But here, against the wall, his mystique reduced to his mouth smothering hers. They grappled against the wall until the creak of the elevator doors separated them.

A woman sang to her son on her way to the laundry room behind their wall. An echo of giggles. Leila was relieved, too flustered to continue. She really did not know what to do next. They could not do It in the basement. Once she had kissed a boy with soft hands named Danny at the YMCA summer camp, and one childhood summer in DR, she and her third cousin Alex had felt each other up under Mamá Graciela's cashew tree. Leila had decided she did not like to kiss, and, to her amazement, had in fact read in a book that people like her were called philematophobes. This man here did not seem to be curing her. But while smoothing down her hair and snapping her bra back into place, Miguel told her she was pretty—Mercedes' pigeon soup must be fattening her up so that it even made a man want to cheat on wifey. Miguel was flesh, more flesh than the Dannys and Alexes of her recycled fantasies. Next time, Leila would make him take her somewhere else. Not on the wall. She was about to ask him for his phone number, and he put his index finger to her lips. Shshsh. And before she slipped off ahead of him to ride the elevator back to reality, Miguel gave Leila his crisp business card.

⌣⁀

Two years of Leila's life were missing from family albums; after her twelfth birthday, it seemed she disappeared. From then on she wanted no more birthday pictures. She saved her grandparents' public-assistance money by refusing to sit for annual school portraits, and shutterbug friends called her a vampire for her absence in their photos. When she saw herself in pictures, it was as if she were looking at someone else, not the person she remembers being at the time of the photo. But, as Elsa said, Leila's problem was that she was too "self-conscientious—just stand there and smile, stupid."

On the morning of her fourteenth birthday, Leila looked through the albums. She peeled off the snapshots of her birthdays and lined them up on the floor to see how she had grown into the beanstalk she was now—despite platefuls of rice and beans, heaps of pasta, giant triangles of pizza. Her medical factoid book confirmed that she was planistethic, her chest flat as a board.

—Pigeon soup and malt extract should fatten you up good, Li'l

Greedy Gal, Mercedes said if a tank top highlighted the tiny knobs at Leila's chest.

Each successive snapshot captured Leila in front of the same cupboard and smiling to the world. She gathered the snapshots, the cheeky one-year-old in bright pink at the bottom of the pile, and, at the top, the twelve-year-old fatale with puffy bangs. Her fingers flipped through the twelve slices of her life. Back then, her stronger sense of self had allowed her to look straight into the camera. A toddler smiled in the opening frame where she reached toward a jeweled cake. Frame by frame, Leila stretched past Felíz Cumpleaños streamers (which become Happy Birthday by the sixth frame). With each frame, faces filled out, hairstyles flattened, and Mercedes and Andrés wrinkled, while the china cupboard behind them remained unchanged throughout Leila's growth and fading smiles. Each year, the cake was transformed into a doll, rabbit, heart.

The rhombus of sunlight had long disappeared. Mercedes and Andrés went to bed early, as usual. They slept snug and confident that their grand-daughter was up late studying hard for her future medical career.

Leila curled up by the television, the volume on mute. Her thumb was poised on the remote's Off button, her ears cocked for the sound of creaking floor behind the bedroom door. She had wound and rewound the videotape Mirangeli lent her to That Part. That Part, where a multitude of naked bodies wriggled in oil like a pit of ravenous snakes. A woman with melon breasts slid under a man with a face like Miguel's and the butt of a horse. Leila had munched her nails down to tender skin.

Finally, after fast-forwarding through monotonous fellatio scenes, the videotape stopped. Her heart pounded like a fist in her chest. Three floors above, Miguel was probably in bed with his wife, his three children sleeping soundly.

A child answered the phone.

—Good evening, ¿may I please speak to Mr. Miguel Hernández? Leila asked. She heard a cough, then the tiny voice yell out for Papi.

—¿Aló?

His phone voice was hoarser than she had expected. Leila pictured Miguel standing with a hand on his hip, maybe bare-chested and in boxer shorts.

—Meet me in the basement. Ten minutes.

Leila hung up the phone. Her tongue searched for her fingernail, then settled on the cuticle.

As she stuffed her bedsheets with sofa cushions, Leila shook her head at the cliché. With rough strokes, she brushed her teeth and combed around the hairline of her ponytail. Lights in the living room went out. She muffled the noisy padlock with her arm and then the bright hallway stung her eyes.

Leila waited. Each time the elevator door opened in the basement, her heart rattled. After a while, the heat inside her began to fizz. She stood against the wall where they had last heaved, right where the gray paint had been chipped off by a vandal.

—¿How'd you get my home number?

Miguel wore red checkered boxers and a V-neck undershirt.

—I have my ways, she said with a breath of surprise.

—I'm supposed to be throwing out the garbage, he said, then hooked his finger around the waist of her jeans.

His hips pinned her to the wall. His tongue was fatter than Leila remembered. His boxer shorts pointed forward against her belly.

—Suck it.

His hand pushed down on her shoulders. Suck it, she did. Close her eyes, she did. Enjoyed it, until she started to drown. No easy business.

Their eyes never met while Miguel wiped the corners of Leila's mouth with the heel of his hand.

—Don't call my house again, he said, I'll call you, ¿okay?

Leila nodded. Most of the heat had fizzled in her belly, but embers still glowed. A peck on her cheek, and with a swish of his house slippers, Miguel was gone as easily as he had appeared. Leila waited for the sound of the closing elevator doors, then bounded up the stairs to prepare for her biology exam.

Danzy Senna

I write fiction because I understand the world through stories. As a kid, this was how I put a distance between myself and reality: when something painful or even funny happened to me, I'd sometimes think about it later as a third-person story, thinking of myself as She rather than I. This was a sign either that I was a schizophrenic or that I was a fiction writer. Luckily, so far, only the latter has turned out to be true.

What interests me most is not my own life but a kind of parallel life—what might have happened—that little gray area between my own life and my imagination. It's there that I am hoping to surprise, entertain, engage myself—and, if I'm lucky, somebody else.

In terms of genre, novels have always been my first love. They are big and messy, and at their best they can force you to see the world through a perspective totally separate from your own. They can disorient you in an exciting way. I want to disorient people. I hope I did that a little bit with Caucasia.

The Body of Luce Rivera

From *Caucasia*, a novel

I LEARNED THE ART of changing at Nkrumah, a skill that would later become second nature to me. Maybe I was always good at it. Maybe it was a skill I had inherited from my mother, or my father, or my aunt Dot, or my Nana, the way some people inherit a talent for music or art or mathematics. Even before Nkrumah, Cole and I had gotten a thrill out of changing—spending our days dressed in old costumes, pretending to be queens of our make-believe nation. But only at Nkrumah did it become more than a game. There I learned how to do it for real—how to become someone else, how to erase the person I was before.

Cole had already done it. Changed. It had started with the Jergen's lotion, then with her hair, and before I knew it she was one of the more popular girls at the school. She still carried a book wherever she went, but now she was wearing lipstick, talking about boys as she tried to pull me along behind her. I knew I had to make more of an effort to blend in or I would lose her for good.

I started wearing my hair in a tight braid to mask its texture. I had my ears pierced and convinced my mother to buy me a pair of gold hoops like the other girls at school wore. My father was usually scornful of frivolous spending, but he must have sensed some serious desperation when I pleaded with him to buy me new clothes. On one weekend shopping spree at Tello's, with my sister shouting orders to me, I bought a pair of Sergio Valente jeans, a pink vest, a jean jacket with sparkles on the collar, and spanking-white Nike sneakers.

I stood many nights in front of the bathroom mirror, practicing how to say "nigger" the way the kids at school did it, dropping the "er" so that it became not a slur, but a term of endearment: *nigga.*

It took a while, but sometime late that fall at Nkrumah, my work paid off. A smell of burning wafted in the cool autumn air, and mounds of dead leaves were neatly piled on street corners like enormous fallen birds' nests. I had been sitting on the pavement during recess, tugging at my shoelace, when I felt myself being watched. I looked up to see Maria, the afternoon sunlight hitting her from behind, turning her into a gold-spangled silhouette. Her hair was now in braids, with multicolored ribbons woven throughout, and they fluttered in the breeze. Like most of the kids in the school, she wore all ironed and matching clothes. Today she wore black Jordache jeans and a bright-yellow sweater that brought out her reddish undertones. I had been chewing the ends of my hair, and now it hung damp around my face.

Finally, Maria spoke. "So, you black?"

I nodded slowly, as if unsure of it myself.

She sat down beside me and smiled almost wistfully. "I got a brother just like you. We're Cape Verdean."

I didn't know if that was black or white, or something else altogether.

I also wasn't sure whether she was playing another prank on me, so I decided to stay silent.

She pointed across the playground. "See that boy over there in the red sweater? Ali Parkman. He wants to go with you. At least that's what Cherise says. Anyway, I'm goin' out with his best friend, Ronald, so if you go out with him, you can be in the club."

"What club?"

"The Brown Sugars," she said matter-of-factly. "For girls that already got boyfriends. Cherise is in it. Maleka used to be in it, before Michael started going out with Cathy instead. The twins, Carol and Diana, are in it too."

I stared at the boy—Ali. He was the same one who had thrown a spitball at me my first day of school. *What you doin' in this school? You white?* Those were the words he had spoken. He was skinny and brown-skinned and all I knew of him was that he loved to draw spaceships and that his father was my father's friend Ronnie, the one from Dot's party.

Maria blurted, "So you want to go with him, or not? I need an answer by this afternoon. Otherwise, he's gonna ask Marcia instead."

"I guess so," was my weak reply.

So it was official. Ali Parkman and I were going steady, "talking," as the kids in school called it. It didn't mean much—we both were shy around each other. He would smile and wave at me in the hallway and sometimes pull my braid, but that was as close as touching got.

And with my new boyfriend came privileges. Soon Maria, Cherise, Cathy, and I were a clique. A new boyfriend had catapulted me into the world of the freshest girls in the school. Now that I had been knighted black by Maria, and pretty by Ali, the rest of the school saw me in a new light. But I never lost the anxiety, a gnawing in my bowels, a fear that at any moment I would be told it was all a big joke.

Maria and I spent our free time in the girls' room, combing each other's hair, talking about boys we liked and girls we didn't. Cole was glad, I could tell, to see I had some friends besides her. We still spent time together on the weekends. My mother wouldn't let me go out without her, so I would trail along after her to the roller-skating rink, where we would whiz around in circles to disco beats, or hunch over video games at a downtown arcade. In the Brown Sugars clique, we each had nicknames. Maria was "Roxy." Cathy was "Baby Curl." I was "Le Chic."

My mother, who was in a neighborhood women's consciousness-raising group, noticed the changes in Cole and me. She came into our attic after dinner one night and found us smearing our faces with her makeup in front of the big mirror. She rarely wore it anymore, but kept it in the back of a dresser drawer, rotting, some evidence of her old self. Cole had rubbed kohl liner on her eyes so she looked Asian. I had taken the same pencil to make a beauty mark over my lip. My mother watched us for a moment at the door, her arms crossed and an expression of fierce disgust on her face. She came and stood over us, her looming form casting a gigantic shadow.

"You girls are turning into little tarts before my eyes. This is the end, you realize."

"The end of what, Mum?" I said, putting on some bright magenta lipstick so that it went outside the edges of my lips.

"The end of freedom," she said, grabbing the lipstick out of my hand and putting it in her shirt pocket.

Whenever Jane or Linda came over, she would talk in a loud, disapproving voice about us. "Look at my daughters," she'd tell them, a cigarette dangling from her lips, a beer tucked between her thighs. "All they think about is how they look. It's revolting."

Cole and I ignored her. There was no way I was going back to the never-never land of my old self—scraggly hair, dirty knees, and a tomboy's swaggering gait. But I did feel different—more conscious of my body as a toy, and of the ways I could use it to disappear into the world around me.

One Friday night, when the trees were just skeletons and Boston hung frozen in a perpetual gray light, I went to Mattapan to spend the night at Maria's house. We left school together that afternoon, catching the 52 bus at the corner. I felt a thrill of urban adventure as I dropped my change into the slot and followed Maria to the back of the bus. Without my mother's and Cole's eyes on me, I felt that anything could happen. I stared at the faces of the bus riders, all various shades of brown, and tried to mimic their bored, exhausted expressions. Beside me, Maria sang softly to herself, off-key, Roberta Flack's "Feel Like Makin' Love," and I listened, staring out the window as we rolled past Franklin Park.

A girl my age had disappeared there a month earlier—and three weeks later her body had been found violated and dead, crumpled in the shadows of the pudding stone near where she had been lost in the first place, as if in some macabre "return to sender" trick. Her name was Luce Rivera, and her picture had been all over the news that month—a photograph of her smiling in her Catholic-school uniform, looking unsuspecting and utterly pure, the way photographs of the recently murdered often do. It was my mother who first pointed out that she looked a little like me. Then Cole noticed it, then the kids at school, who teased me, saying I was the ghost of Luce Rivera come back to seek revenge. The night they found Luce Rivera's body, my mother came into Cole's and my room in the attic. I was curled over my homework, while Cole lay stretched out on the floor, reading a magazine. My mother wiped her tears and announced to us that the police had recovered "Luce's torn and violated body" and that the search had finally ended. She stood silently by the half-moon window, looking out onto the street for a moment, then turned around rather violently. She came to me and squeezed me to her, so that I couldn't breathe. Then, as quickly as she had grabbed me, she pushed me away, held me at a distance, and stroked the hair out of my face. She hissed, spraying me with spittle, "Don't ever go into Franklin Park alone. You hear me, Bird? You be careful in Roxbury. Don't talk to anyone except your school friends. You understand? There are perverts, crazies, dirty old men, and they want little girls like you."

One of the peculiarities about my mother was that after a passionate diatribe, she could return to normal within seconds, as if nothing had been said or done. As soon as she finished her outburst, she went to our mirror and fussed with our pre-teen beauty products. She picked up Cole's black plastic pick and turned it over thoughtfully in her hands. She ran it through her thin hair, staring at herself in the mirror as she did so, with a sad smile. It struck me as odd that my mother hadn't warned Cole not to go to the park, just me. "There are perverts, crazies, dirty old men, and they want little girls like you."

Girls like you.

When she was gone, Cole looked up from her *Jet* magazine and watched me from behind her braids, which hung like bars across her face, dividing her features into sections.

⌒

Maria and I arrived in Mattapan. Her house sat on a block of twenty identical tract houses with endlessly shuttered windows and garbage-spackled lawns. There were teenage boys sitting on the stoop of the house next to hers, and they waved to her. She blushed, and yelled, "Hey, Darnell!" Then she whispered in my direction, "He's so cute. He said when I grow up he wants to go out. My brother used to hang with him."

As Maria opened the door to her house, a gust of heated air enveloped us. We stepped inside, and it took me a moment to adjust to the darkness. A piquant smell of sweet-and-sour sauce clung to the air.

Enraged and hysterical voices floated from behind a closed door at the end of the hall. Someone screamed, "You bitch! You'll never steal him from me!"

But as I listened closer, I could hear it was just the television. A soap opera.

Maria turned to me, shy suddenly. "You can just throw your stuff on the floor."

I took a minute to simply soak up the most exquisite home I had ever laid eyes on. The pink-and-purple-flower theme was omnipresent. Faux yucca trees sprung from black vases in the corners, and a fruit bowl with wooden apples and pears sat on the coffee table. The back wall was decorated with a velvet painting of two naked and afroed silhouettes—one curvaceous and female, the other muscular and male—intertwined in a lovemaking ritual with a backdrop of a bright magenta-and-pink horizon. I wanted to go and touch the painting, trace the bodies with my fin-

ger, but held back. The rest of the room's walls, I could see, were mirrored, and a crystalline chandelier hung over the shimmering mahogany
dining room set.

I breathed, "Your house is so beautiful."

Maria scoffed. "You think so? It's all right."

But I could tell she was proud. She went over to the wide-screen television set. "My daddy got this for us last Christmas. It's like a movie screen,
almost." She whispered, "He works in a TV warehouse and he took it
when no one was looking."

I thought about my mother. She sometimes took things when nobody
was looking. She would slip candy and barrettes into her pocket when we
went to Kmart. But she had never taken anything this big. "Where's your
father?"

"Oh, he lives in New York, but he comes up to see us every year. And
that's my brother, James. He's in the Army," she told me, pointing to a picture of a grinning, uniformed boy with hazel eyes and skin the color of my
own. "He's much older than me."

"Where's your mother now?"

"She's at work. She's a nurse at the hospital. She gets home real late
tonight. Like past midnight."

We spent the afternoon slumped in front of her television set with the
stereo booming behind us, the heat and lights on full blast. We gorged
ourselves and watched her favorite sitcoms—"Chico and the Man" and
"What's Happening"—in a green glowing silence.

By six o'clock we were restless and hungry and wandered into the
kitchen. Maria's mother had left spare ribs and potato salad in Tupperware
in the refrigerator. Maria threw the ribs in the oven and turned it on high.
My mother never cooked red meat. I felt I was being let into a secret world
I had been denied for so long, and I tried to hide the giddy feeling bub-
bling away in my stomach as Maria revealed one small luxury after
another.

Maria had more clothes than I could even imagine. She played the
clock radio beside her bed and sang along—knowing all of the words—as
she tossed clothes on the bed.

"This one—this one looks real cute on you," she said, holding up a
purple angora sweater with sparkles in the shape of a unicorn on the front.
"And we're gonna have to do something about your hair. Do you want me
to trim it and curl it?"

The next thing I knew, I was seated on the squishy toilet cushion and Maria was snipping away at my hair. "Just let me even out these split ends," she had said, but by the time it was over, my hair was a full inch and a half shorter.

She saw the look on my face. "It looks fine! Don't worry. I'm not done. It still needs to be curled."

She heated up the curling iron and sprayed my newly shorn hair with Queen Helene hairspray till it was wet. Each time she put the curling iron to a lock of my hairspray-soaked head, it let out a hiss and steam emerged. But I assumed she knew what she was doing, and stayed quiet.

When she was finished, my straight hair was curly. I stared at myself in the fogged mirror, amid the rows of beauty potions, and breathed in the sweet-and-sour spare-rib air of the apartment. The curls Maria had given me softened out my pointed features. As I admired my new look, I imagined myself to be just a girl who lived and had always lived in this splendid pink-and-purple palace where all the furniture matched, a girl whose mother worked late nights as a nurse and whose big brother was in the Army. I imagined my name was not Birdie or Jesse or even Patrice, but Yolanda, and that Maria was one of my many cousins. I imagined myself Cape Verdean.

Maria's voice broke into my thoughts. "Birdie, how do I look?"

I turned to see her standing in the door of the bathroom. She was transformed as well. She wore her mother's lipstick—Revlon's Toast of New York—and matching eye shadow. She had on skintight Jordache jeans over a burgundy leotard that clung to her body.

She leaned in close to me. I could smell the bubble gum on her breath as she fluffed my hair one more time, with an approving wink at her creation.

We spent the rest of the evening eating—soda, popcorn, hot wings— from Maria's endlessly stocked kitchen, watching TV, and listening to music. We gossiped about the other kids from school, and I felt she was accepting me into that bond of "best friend." Cathy was falling out of her favor, and I knew I needed to act right then if I wanted to replace her. At one point she brought me into her mother's room, which had a water bed, and the two of us lay on the sloshing mattress, looking up at ourselves in the smoked-mirror ceiling, singing along to the radio. The tint of the ceiling mirror darkened me, and with my newfound curls, I found that if I pouted my lips and squinted to blur my vision in just the right way, my face transformed into something resembling Cole's. Maria and I lay there for more than an hour, talking about our mutual love for Diana Ross, how we both hoped to marry Billy Dee Williams, and what we wanted to be when we grew up. She wanted to be an airline stewardess; I wanted to be a veterinarian. I asked her endless questions about her family—what her mother looked like, whom she dated, when her parents broke up, how her parents had met. I savored each detail and made a secret promise to myself that I would live in a house like this when I grew up and be just like Maria's mother, who I imagined looked like Marilyn McCoo. We lost track of time, lying side by side on the water bed, speaking to our mirror images that hovered above us like guardian angles.

Before going to bed, we took a bubble bath together using a concoction made from all of her mother's bath products that lined the edge of the tub. I studied Maria's nude body while we undressed in the reeking, steaming bathroom. She had small perfectly shaped nipples like Hershey's Kisses. I hugged myself and shivered, waiting to step in, as she swished the water with her hand to test the temperature.

We sat together in the tub for a long time, until our fingertips were ridged and prunelike and the water around us had turned lukewarm. It had begun to rain outside, softly, and Maria, on her knees behind me, washed my hair, seemingly fascinated by its limp consistency. I had wanted to leave the curls in, but she promised she'd redo them in the morning. She lathered my scalp, telling me what she would do if she had straight hair. I told her I wanted her hair, which she had carefully covered in a shower cap so as not to get it wet.

She asked me if I liked Ali. I crinkled my nose. "He's nice and all, but he's so young. You know, he's still just a child," I said, repeating something I had heard Cole say once about a boy.

We got out of the bath after it became too cold, and dried ourselves in fluffy pink towels. Maria chattered about Darnell, the older boy next door, and I looked out of the corner of my eye at the soft brown slope of her body. I felt ashamed for looking, and hid my face in the wet tangle of my hair.

I lay awake late into the night, listening to the dramatic beeps and yells on the streets outside, pretending that my mother worked the late shift and my daddy stole TVs.

Martha Southgate

People always tend to assume that fiction is directly related to the facts of an author's life, which drives me a little nuts. What I love about fiction is the freedom to make up a life, to make up people who aren't me, were never me, aren't even thinly disguised versions of me. Of course in those made-up people lie some of the deepest truths about what interests or obsesses me. Thus it is with both my first novel, Another Way to Dance, *and my second,* The Fall of Rome, *which is excerpted here. There are things in both that are related to my own experience: I did go to a prep school (but not a boarding school), like Rashid, and like Vicki in* Another Way to Dance, *I was an obsessed ballet student. I was not, however, all that talented as a dancer. I like to think I'm better off having become a novelist. Heaven knows I enjoy it enough. I hope my readers do too.*

Martha Southgate
Brooklyn, New York
July 2, 2002

The Wall of Pain

From *The Fall of Rome*, a novel

RASHID HAD NOT been able to sleep through the night since Kofi's death. Almost every morning around three A.M. he would find himself awake, feeling as though he had been shoved by a cold, flat hand. His eyes popped open as though someone had called his name, and he lay there staring at the ceiling, his heart pounding. When he was at home, most times he could get out of bed and go sit in the living room, staring out the window and waiting for the gray dawn to gather, or watching an infomercial to distract himself. Sometimes he'd get to the doorway of his bedroom and find that one of his parents was already up, sitting in his place at the window. Then he made his way back to his room, to lie stiffly on his bed till his alarm went off. His thoughts were usually memories of Kofi or questions about him—Kofi laughing, Kofi bloody in the street, what Kofi's last words might have been, the look on his face as the bullet pierced bone. During the day, Rashid found he could cope—Kofi's death always hovered there, a dark space in the corner of his mind, but he could push it away when he needed to. But at night it was unavoidable, burning his eyes and searing his throat.

Not much seemed to bother Gerald. He slept the sleep of a man who knew his place in the world, his breath soft and even, his sheets rustling occasionally. Sometimes Rashid wished he could talk to him, tell him what it was like not to be even able to fucking sleep. To be so tired all the time. So tired that his head felt full of cotton batting. Sometimes he wished he could tell him about the blood on the street, about the funeral, about how he wished he could talk to Kofi about school. But he couldn't.

Chelsea gave the boys very little free time during the school week, keeping them loaded with activities and schoolwork. But in the middle of each semester there came a short respite, separate from the traditional holidays like Thanksgiving and Christmas. Gerald invited Rashid home with him—"On me," he said—for the fall break, and Rashid, feeling awkward about the free ride but unable to afford a trip home, accepted.

"This boy said he'd pay your way for a visit?" said his father when Rashid called to tell them his plans.

"Yeah, Dad. It's okay. It was his idea. Him and his parents."

"And he's black?"

"Yes, Dad."

There was a long pause. "I guess it's all right, then. It seems a little funny, but if they can do it . . . Don't want you sitting up at school all by yourself while all your friends go off." His father's voice grew gruff. "And we can't afford to rent a car again just now. So you go on and have a good time."

"Thanks, Dad." As Rashid hung up, he realized that for the first time in months, his father had wished him well.

⌒

Gerald's dad, a lawyer, picked them up at the airport. Their car was nice, but not more than Rashid had expected. Mr. Davis was a bluff, friendly sort, obviously crazy about his son and willing to like anyone he brought home as a friend. Rashid felt an odd twist in his heart at the long, manly hug Gerald and his father exchanged at the gate. But he swallowed twice and busied himself with his luggage, not wanting to look weird.

But then the house. Rashid had never had a friend who lived like this—a separate bedroom for each child and a lawn and so new, so new and quiet. No roach would dare live there.

Gerald, chatting to his father, didn't seem to notice Rashid's sudden discomfort as they walked into the house. Every room had thick, soft carpet, and everywhere Rashid looked, there were beautiful, obviously expensive things. African-looking paintings and sculptures on the wall and, well . . . it was really something. Something to stand in a house like this and know that it belonged to someone black. It's not like he didn't *know* this existed but damn . . . now that he was standing here . . . Damn.

"Rashid, I'm so pleased to meet you."

A voice like music cut into his silence. Rashid turned around and there was the most beautiful black woman he'd ever seen smiling at him. She was older, a mom's age, like forty or something, but her skin was smooth, like chocolate cream, and she had the warmest brown eyes and a short haircut that made her look like she'd stepped out of one of his mother's issues of *Essence*. A girl of about ten, still just a kid but with promise of being just as beautiful, stood next to her, staring at him. "I'm Gerald's mother. And this is his sister, Kim."

"Nice to meet you, Mrs. Davis. Hi, Kim."

He hoped he didn't look too thunderstruck. He'd never met anyone's mother who looked like her.

"Gerald, why don't you show Rashid your room?"

Gerald picked up his bag and said, "Come on, man," and they went upstairs, their feet hushed by the carpet.

"Well, here it is, man. My domain—when I'm home anyway. You can have that bed." He tossed his bags down wearily and flopped onto the bed after them. "It's nice to be home."

"Yeah. It must be." He paused. "This is a nice room, man."

Gerald sat up and fixed him with a penetrating look. Rashid gazed back, unconsciously smoothing the soft mudcloth printed quilt on his bed with his hand. After a moment or two, Gerald spoke, a bit uncertainly. "It's all right, I guess. Beats the dorm, anyway." He jumped up. "You wanna shoot some hoops before dinner?"

The weekend went by. They went to a ball game with Gerald's dad. They hung out and played Dreamcast with some of Gerald's old friends from home. They watched television—no cable in the dorms at school, so MTV seemed like a joyous, raunchy missive from some forgotten civilization. Gerald teased his sister about her newly gangling arms and legs. Gerald's mom asked Rashid a lot of polite questions about where in Brooklyn he was from and did he like school and what did his parents do? (She did look a little surprised when he said they worked for the MTA.)

The weekend passed in an increasingly pleasant daze. On the last night, they all sat down to dinner together—Gerald's mother bringing the food to the table with a look of shy pleasure, Gerald's dad smiling proudly, occasionally interjecting a comment. They were really nice people. Rashid had finally relaxed. He felt more at ease than he had in weeks. They were having chicken with some kind of sauce. It looked good. Rashid picked it up with his hands, just the way that he had every single time he'd eaten chicken his entire life. As he brought it to his mouth and took the first bite, he realized that everyone else at the table was using a knife and fork. Even Kim. He put his food down quietly. His hands and mouth felt oily, and his face was hot. Gerald caught his eye briefly, but his expression was unreadable. There was a minute—it felt like an hour—when it seemed that everyone was looking at him. Then Gerald made a joke about something, and the moment passed. But the heat in Rashid's face remained for the rest of the evening.

Now, lying awake in this strange, prosperous bed, he remembered an incident from earlier in the school year. After English class one day, Rashid had said that he'd never heard of this Hemingway guy. "You didn't read any of his stories in eighth grade or anything?" Gerald said.

"No," said Rashid, suddenly embarrassed.

"Wow. I thought everybody had to read *The Old Man and the Sea*." A pause as the two regarded each other. Then Gerald spoke, grinning. "Well, it don't matter, cuz. Book ain't that good anyway. And you know who he is now, right?"

"Right."

Gerald never said "ain't" around his parents. And his parents spoke as clearly and precisely as any white people. Rashid rolled over, wanting to groan. His face was pressed into the pillow, his hands between his legs. Was there nowhere he belonged? At least there was one way to get back to sleep. He did it quickly, without a sound, without much pleasure. The night was very quiet as he finished. It was nearly four-thirty A.M.

⌒

Gerald seemed to have forgotten the incident at dinner by the next day, so Rashid said nothing more about it, though he felt a little sick whenever it crossed his mind. Their trip back to school was uneventful, though Rashid found that he couldn't stop thinking about the easy, confident manner of Gerald's parents. As opposed to his, who walked around looking like they expected to be hit any second. He wished he didn't feel that way, too.

Rashid found it harder and harder to be quiet about what was inside him once he got back to school. And stuff kept happening to push him. Like in that class before midterm break where Ms. Hansen read Hendrickson's essay about his grandmother. Rashid felt as though he were going to burst into tears at any moment the whole rest of that day. He'd been in a bad mood even before class started because of that mess with

Washington—and then he'd had to listen to these white-bread punks whine about losing this and that and how sad it was that their hundred-year-old grandmother died. What did they know? What did they know about really losing someone, way before they were supposed to be gone? That's why he finally wrote that thing when Ms. Hansen asked him to. He couldn't carry the weight by himself anymore. He left it in her box on a day when he didn't have her class so he wouldn't have to talk to her about it. He just had to get it out.

Before he'd come up to Chelsea, his parents had called him into the living room, where they were watching *Diagnosis: Murder*, and made him sit down with them. "So, Rashid, you're off to school in just a few days," said his father. His eyes left the screen only briefly to glance into his remaining son's eyes. "Your mother and I, we don't feel . . ." He trailed off.

"What Daddy is trying to say," his mother chimed in, "is that we don't want to tell everyone up at that school about Kofi. It's not a secret exactly but we don't see any reason to walk in there and announce that your brother was killed, either."

Her eyes filled with tears. Rashid looked from one to the other of his parents, then he spoke. "There's nothing to be ashamed of. I'm going to tell if people ask."

His mother turned back to the television. "If they ask. But I don't see any reason to announce it. We've said that to the headmaster and the admissions people."

Rashid turned to the television, his chest tightening. He'd said there was nothing to be ashamed of. But why did he feel guilty? He felt guilty even for drawing breath. And he was ashamed. That's why he told no one.

He supposed he ought to tell them about the essay. But it was easy enough not to. Right after he got back from Gerald's, he talked to his mother on the phone. She asked about his visit. He told her he had had fun, that they'd fed him well, and that Gerald's parents were very nice. He didn't say, You're supposed to eat chicken with a knife and fork. He didn't say, Gerald's mother looks like a model and their house looks like a TV show. He didn't say, Gerald's sister is alive. He didn't say, I wrote about Kofi because my heart is crumbling in my chest. He didn't say, Mama, I miss you. He hung up the phone at the end of the conversation. He was holding the receiver so tightly that his hand hurt.

The day after he'd handed in his paper, he felt every eye in the school on him—though in fact Ms. Hansen hadn't sought him out to speak with him and no one else knew about it. Still, the only place he felt comfortable all day was in the barn.

He hadn't planned on taking this course when he'd come to visit, and he knew that none of his boys back home would even believe it, but the truth was that he had developed a real affection for the big, black cows. This course probably wouldn't do him any good after he left Chelsea. But he was comfortable in the barn. The cows asked nothing of him, nothing but that he bring them hay and feed. That he could do. Today, he didn't have to deal with other boys much because it was his day in the stalls, a duty each boy took alone. The cows mooed noisily as he entered the barn.

"What up, ya'll? It's chow time." He wrestled a large bag of feed off the stack and tore it open with a knife that hung nearby. The lowing grew more excited, and the cows began to shift and shuffle in their pens. Rashid walked slowly among them, pouring feed into troughs. When he got to his favorite one, the cow they called Mr. T because of the protuberant ridge of fur on her back, he stopped and rubbed her there for a minute. The cow was unmoved by this show of affection, but for some reason of her own, she did not bellow like the others for food, just looked at him with large, liquid brown eyes. After he filled her trough, he slid down the wall opposite her, into the coarse, loose hay scattered throughout the barn. The only sounds that could be heard were the noisy exhalations and mastications of the cows and the ragged, tearing sobs of the boy. The sounds went on for a long time.

Rashid was cold and cramped by the time he struggled to his feet. The cows ignored him. His face was lightly dusted with chaff. He brushed the back of his hand roughly across his eyes and sighed. He had never felt so alone in his life. The only thing he could hear was the beginning-to-be-bitter wind sighing through the trees across the road. He looked at his watch. Almost lunchtime. He'd been in the barn for nearly two hours and missed two classes, Latin among them. He started walking back to campus, his mind completely blank.

By the time he got back to the cafeteria, everyone had gone into lunch already. The din hit his ears as soon as he entered and took his place in line. His heart was tight in his chest, and he could hear his breath in his ears. He saw Gerald sitting in the corner where they usually sat, surrounded by the mix of black, Asian, and white guys that they sat with. Rashid could tell from where he was standing that Gerald was telling some long story. Every face was turned to him, expectant and laughing. Rashid carried his tray to the table as though it were laden with crystal. Gerald acknowledge him briefly: "What's up, cuz? Didn't see you after history today."

"I cut, man. Couldn't deal."

Gerald raised his eyebrows slightly and turned back to the others at the table. "So anyway . . ." He continued his story, some long thing about his exploits with a hometown honey. The other boys at the table hung on every word as though they had been in that dark basement themselves, lights down, clothes half off, breath mingling warmly with hers. Rashid only half listened—he'd heard this one before. Gerald was just trying to keep it live at the table. He seemed to feel that was his function at meals. For his part, Rashid responded to comments directed toward him during lunch with the absolute minimum number of words necessary and ate rapidly. The food tasted of ash. He caught Gerald giving him a couple of sidelong looks, but he acted like he didn't see him. Finally lunch was over. He was just about to leave the table when—oh, shit—Mr. Washington approached them. "Mr. Bryson?"

"Yes, sir?"

"We missed you in class this morning." The table had fallen into absolute silence. "I'd like to have a word with you if I may."

Rashid's stomach dropped into his shoes, but what could he do? "Okay, Mr. Washington. Just let me clear up my stuff here."

He could feel the other guys at the table gazing at him nervously as he picked up his tray. Mr. Washington stood without speaking to them, waiting for him. They walked out through the leaded glass doors together and headed down the path that led back to the classroom buildings.

"I suppose you're wondering why I wanted to speak to you."

"I'm really sorry about class this morning, Mr. Washington. I just . . . I had something I had to do with the cows for Animal Husbandry, and it took a lot longer than I thought it would."

"Yes. The cows. Do you enjoy the cows?"

He's lost his mind, thought Rashid, *but I better just play along*. "Yeah . . . I mean, yes. I like them. I'm from the city and didn't ever get to deal with big animals like that. It's . . . well, they're sort of calm. It's nice, I guess."

"I remember feeling that way when I was young. Down south." Mr. Washington seemed to drop into a momentary reverie, then clapped a hand on Rashid's shoulder so firmly that it made him jump, resting it there for a moment. "Mr. Bryson. I learned of your brother's misfortune, and I wanted to caution you not to let your loss interfere with your studies here." He paused for a moment. When he continued, his voice was husky. "I have felt sadness much as yours. But I always remembered that I had been given a rare opportunity, one that very few Negroes are granted. Just as you have been. It is important that you make the most of it. If I am hard on you in class, it is out of my belief that knowledge fought for is knowledge best remembered. I would suggest, as you go through your time here at Chelsea, that you adopt the attitude of the Stoics, maintaining a disciplined mind that nothing can harm. I think that you will find that to be the best course as you pursue your studies here."

Mr. Washington's hand remained on Rashid's shoulder throughout this speech, tightening slightly as he reached points that he wanted to emphasize, but his gaze was focused on the middle distance, as though he couldn't bear to look Rashid in the eye. Rashid didn't know what freaked him out more—having Washington know about Kofi, that hand on his shoulder, or the peculiar way he was talking. He was too stunned to ask a single question—it was crazy to think that no one else would ever find out about Kofi anyway. Mr. Washington seemed to think that he was helping—but his eyes were far away. It was as if he was talking to someone else. "Um . . . okay, Mr. Washington. I know that this is a great chance. I don't intend to blow it."

"One thing more." *What more could there be?* thought Rashid. "You have a great gift, Mr. Bryson. I have never seen a natural runner like you. I think with the proper coaching, you could excel to an extraordinary degree. Even perhaps compete at the highest level. I'd like to work with you a little outside the team practices, if I may."

By now, they had reached the buildings and boys were beginning to surge past them on both sides. They stood, facing each other. "You would?" said Rashid. He heard his voice squeak a little, but he couldn't control it.

"Absolutely. Come by my office so we can discuss some extra workout times." Mr. Washington paused. "I might even run along with you sometimes. That can be a great encouragement."

Rashid stood speechless, which Washington seemed to take as assent. "I'm glad we had this talk," he said, sticking his hand out to shake. It was cold and dry, unexpectedly callused. "I'll see you in class tomorrow. I don't expect this morning's incident to be repeated."

"No, sir."

With that, Washington turned and walked toward his office. There was a roaring inside Rashid's head. He stood there for a long time after the man had gone.

Rashid went through the rest of the day in a kind of fog. He went to classes to avoid the trouble he'd be in if he didn't go, but he was so distracted that he couldn't really hear. A gifted runner? Extra workout times? The highest levels? He liked running: the smoothness of his stride, the way he didn't have to think, the way it felt to have the tape snap across his chest—ping—and everyone cheering. But how could he even consider more running—as hard as his schoolwork was? And if it meant more time with Wooden Washington . . . He couldn't imagine it. His legs turned to stone at the thought, and his eyes filled with tears. He kept feeling Washington's hand on his shoulder, hearing his voice going on, remembering himself crying in the barn. He didn't even go to dinner. He couldn't eat. When Gerald came in about seven, he was sitting on his bed, staring at the gray-green wall opposite him. Gerald threw his backpack on his bed, took a long look at Rashid, and came to a decision. He spoke.

"What is up with you, man? You ain't said two words to me since you got back from wherever it is you went this morning, and you been acting beyond weird for longer than that. Last couple of days, really. Since we got back from my folks' house. And then Washington wants to speak to you. What is going on?"

That did it. More tears came to Rashid's eyes, but this time he let them fall. He felt something shifting inside of him. He sat up and his mouth opened to set free some words. He didn't know what they would be until he spoke them. "My brother is dead. He's been dead for a year. More than a year." He looked steadily at his feet but he could hear the creak as Gerald sat down on his own bed.

"What? You had a brother? What?"

Rashid nodded. His eyes were burning, and he brought his hands up to keep the tears, the very blood, from flowing out of them. His hands were scalded. Gerald didn't move, but Rashid could feel his eyes on him. There was no sound but Rashid's ragged breath. Then Gerald's question: "What happened?"

What happened. It was eight on a sultry July evening, after dinner. Kofi and Rashid were sitting in their airless living room, silent under the fan's useless whir. Neither boy moved more than necessary, just turned the pages of the books they were reading—trying to read. After a while, Kofi spoke. "Man, it's too hot. I'ma run down to the corner and get a Coke or something. You wanna come?"

"No." Rashid didn't feel like moving.

"Well, I can't sit here anymore. You want anything?"

"Naw. I'm all right, I guess."

Kofi yelled to their mother that he was going to run to the corner, that he would be right back. She cautioned him not to stop anywhere and asked him to pick up some milk. He left. That was the end. The next time Rashid saw Kofi, he was on his back in a pool of blood. His mother's screams could be heard for half a block. Rashid hadn't even looked at him as he'd walked out the door. Why should he have? He was coming right back.

Gerald listened as Rashid talked. He didn't interrupt. He asked no questions. He sat without seeming to breathe. When Rashid was done, he did something he'd never done before. He got up and walked over to Rashid's bed, sat on it, and put his arm around his friend. They sat like that for a long time, while tears streamed down Rashid's face. The room was very quiet.

"You could have told me sooner, man," Gerald said after a while.

"No, I couldn't. I couldn't tell anybody."

Gerald nodded. "Well, what happened? Why you telling me now?"

"That thing that we had to write for English class. That essay that Hendrickson wrote. I felt like the top of my head was going to come off. Ms. Hansen asked me to write something and I wrote about Kofi. Now I just wish I could get it back. Fuck. Then somehow Washington found out. I don't know, maybe she told him or something. You know how teachers are. Or maybe Fox told him. Anyway, that's what he wanted to talk to me about." He brushed fiercely at his eyes. "And he was so *weird*, man. Telling me to be like some kind of damn Roman and that I was lucky to have this chance, I shouldn't blow it. And he kept rubbing my shoulder. The guy's a freak, man. You know what I'm sayin'?"

Gerald was silent for a long time before he spoke. "Washington didn't try anything faggy, did he?"

"No, no, not like that. The whole thing was just weird. He was trying to give me some kind of pep talk, and he was just . . . It was like he was mad at me or something. Like he was trying to get me to shape up from something I did to him and he was trying to be sympathetic at the same time. I don't know how to explain it. It was just fucked up."

"Yeah, well, they don't call him Wooden Washington for nothing."
Gerald paused before speaking again. "Listen," he said, his voice a little
ragged. "I know . . . I know that we haven't had the same kind of lives. I
saw you looking around my house, bro. And I know you've been through
some shit I only know about from CDs and TV shows. But I'm glad you
told me about your brother, man. That's a lot to carry by yourself."

Rashid snuffled and wiped his eyes with the back of his hand. He nodded and then, in the silence that had suddenly grown awkward, scooted
off the bed and rummaged in his drawer for something to wipe his face
with. For the first time in a week, his stomach didn't hurt. He could feel
Gerald's steady gaze on him as he pulled out a worn handkerchief.
"Thanks, man, for listening and all," he said without looking up.

"No problem." Gerald climbed off the bed, suddenly brisk, his voice a
little too loud. "Let's go see if it's anything left in the Coke machine.
Those knuckleheads probably drank up everything by now."

The boys left the room together. You would have had to look closely to
see the sorrow in their eyes.

Natasha Tarpley

At the end of my sophomore year in college, I changed my major from German, which I had studied since the second grade, to African American studies. But I quickly became frustrated with the way my "Afro-Am" courses were taught. Everything was objective or politically correct. I was outraged. How could we totally disregard the fact that this history had happened to human beings not so different from ourselves? How could we possibly keep "emotion" out of the discussion? As a way to develop a more intimate relationship with the past, I began to write a series of first-person narrative poems in the voices of Black people who had lived at various points in history.

These narratives laid the groundwork for my family memoir, Girl in the Mirror: Three Generations of Black Women in Motion. *I wrote the book in the voices of my grandmother, my mother, and myself. It traces the steps of each woman's journey from one geographical place to another, to independence, self-love, acceptance, and fulfillment. I wrote* Girl in the Mirror *as a way to explore issues in my own life, such as the search for home and community; to find my place in the line of women before me. I discovered a kind of mirror in the lives of my mother and my grandmother, reflections of similar choices, pains, and joys. In addition, while writing this book, I became obsessed with the idea of migration, especially that of African Americans—now a central theme in my work. I am fascinated by our journeys, how we move from one place to the next—physically, psychologically; how the things that happen to us and the choices we make propel us into motion or keep us anchored.*

From *Girl in the Mirror: Three Generations of
Black Women in Motion,* a memoir

I LOOKED AROUND the terminal at black folks from every corner of the
United States, many already draped in colorful oversized African attire, as
we waited to board our flight to Ghana. I listened to snatches of conversations around me, the stories people told of their coming to this place.
Somehow I thought this day would be more important than any other
day, would be the day that the memories of the past that lived deep within
me, buried beneath forgetful years, would come alive again.

We followed the sound of the drum. And the drum led us to the edge
of the world as we knew it. Here we stood, looking across the ocean to a
world we hoped to discover. Africa. I thought of how much we had
invested in this place, how desperately we wanted it to be the thing that
soothed the ache of not knowing our beginnings, the ache that we carried
like restless spirits seeking resolution, a resting place. Africa was the wish,
our greatest hope for salvation, for certainty that we belonged somewhere.
We had constructed our own Africa as we needed it to be. We braid our
hair and wear the flowing garments. Africa, help us to see you more
clearly, so that we may also see ourselves.

We closed our eyes, as one foot after the other left solid ground. We
spiraled into blackness, traveling backwards to the unknown, to memory,
Africa, will it be your arms that catch our fall?

⌣

As we made our descent into Accra, the concrete and pollution-gray
morning of our departure the day before had become the bronze-tinted

mist of this morning's sunrise over the flat Ghanaian landscape; the crossing of an ocean reduced to the blink of an eye. When we touched down, a faint wave of applause rose up and died before it got to our cabin. More than remembrance, Mom and I felt relief at having reached the ground safely, the anticipation of sleep more than the excitement of discovery.

Outside of the plane there were no welcome signs, no drums beating the news of our arrival, only the disgruntled and sleepy ground crew speaking to one another in harsh sounding whispers, as they ushered us into a shuttle bus waiting to drive us the few steps over to the main terminal where we would collect our luggage and meet our tour guides. I looked around for something to grab hold of that would ground me in this place, some small sign of recognition. I looked into the faces of the people I passed as I walked down the steps from the plane, and as I boarded the bus, but their eyes would not meet mine.

At the baggage terminal, we were met by our Ghanaian tour guides, two tall and slender young men in their mid-twenties, who stood like guard posts alongside us. One smiled all the time, the other barely said a word. I looked to them, grateful for their presence and hopeful that they would provide the anchor, the link to this place for which I was searching. But both seemed equally far away, untouchable. The silent one stared off into the distance, over our heads, perhaps looking to the hour when he would be relieved of his tedious duty.

The smiling one chatted while we waited for our luggage. He welcomed us to Accra, asked the usual questions: how was our flight, what was the weather like in the States, was this our first time in Africa. He has us figured: black tourists, searching for our people, our origins; searching for more than he chose or was able to give. He was not there to offer sympathy or to hold our hands along this preposterous journey, or to point us in the right direction. He was there simply to make sure we got to the hotel on time, to develop an itinerary and to see that we stuck to it with as few glitches as possible.

I couldn't deny the distance I felt from this ambitious young man, a distance in which the lines separating businessman and client were clear and indisputable, as was the barrier he had erected around himself to keep us out. And in this way, we were also held captive in his notions of "us," of what we wanted and why we came. He had seen enough of "us" to know that we too would cage him if he wasn't careful; that we would penetrate the surface of his skin with our keen yearnings, with the unyielding eye of the scientist, until we reached the chapel of bone; that we could unclench his pounding fist of a heart, until the blood flowed freely; that, given the chance, we would drink him dry.

Our bags finally rolled around on the squeaky conveyer belt. The tour guides stacked them one by one onto the cart they had brought along. At the customs checkpoint before the exit, they waved a rumpled piece of paper in front of the officials and we breezed through with only a flash of our passports. Before we left the terminal, our guide warned us to watch our bags and not to give anyone any money. So began my heart's slow descent. I had not come all this way to watch my bag. I had come to feel at home, hoping for an alternative to the home I had left where you always had to be careful, where there was no place safe.

〜

Outside, a throng of people waited. They seemed to spring to life as soon as we appeared. What felt like a million eyes turned to us. We stood at the crowd's edge, suspended in a moment of curiosity and panic, before we too were jolted into action, pulled into its midst. We swam through the bodies in staccato motion, each step a collage of disjointed movements, looking the way my sisters and brother and I used to look dancing in the dark of our basement, one of us waving a flashlight rapidly, watching the flickering light turn our bodies into robots. "Can you feel it?" we always asked the one taking his or her turn in front of the light, for the light made our bodies look so cumbersome, made even the slightest finger snap look as though it required all of our energy and the coordination of our entire body to achieve.

But this time I could really feel it. My body was a weight that I dragged through the blurred motion of the crowd closing in around me. *Hunger.* Our two tour guides made their narrow bodies into walls to shield us as they ushered us through the mob. *Goes both ways.* I don't remember faces, just hands reaching, teeth bared, and wondering what I had that they wanted. Mom's fingers gripped my wrist tightly, planting there the red imprint of her terror. One woman rushed up to us with a bunch of wilted flowers she wanted to pin on our collars in exchange for a small contribution. Another man, begging for change, began to help our guides unload our luggage into the silver VW minivan waiting to take us to the hotel.

Inside the van, we were sealed off from the throbbing crowd outside. The sliding door clicked shut and the only sounds were the soft whir of the motor, the wind of the air conditioning blowing into our faces. Part of me wanted to open the door and fling myself into those arms, just to feel them touching me, me touching them, to inhale the scent of the people, let the dust, which left everything covered in its copper-colored kisses, cake on my skin. Instead I sank deeper into the van's comfortable seats, thankful for the quiet and the cool breeze drying the sweat on my forehead.

Our tour guides had assumed their positions. The quiet one took the wheel. The other, sitting next to him, who introduced himself as Kwame, turned to face us. His wide smile beckoned us like a magnet, drawing our eyes away from the man outside who had begun pounding on our windows begging for money; distracting us from the reawakening realization that we were far from home, and that if we called out there was nobody to claim the sound of our voices. The smile, which was at once friendly and capable of eating us alive, was all we had to rely on. "Akwaaba," Kwame said. "This means welcome. Welcome to Africa."

We stumbled into our hotel thinking only of sleep. As Kwame checked us in, we sank exhausted into the lobby's plush couches and armchairs. Upstairs in our room, Mom and I could finally relax, shedding our luggage and layers of winter clothes. I went to the window and pulled back the heavy curtains, still trying to convince myself that I was really here. Someone could have made it all up, like some huge movie set with thousands of extras hired to fill up the streets and meet us at the airport; a tourist trap, to cash in on our hunger. I let the curtain fall back into place, blocking out the light from outside. Just as Accra was coming awake, I fell into bed, hoping that it would all still be there waiting for me when I got up.

Shortly after four o'clock, Mom and I were awakened by the telephone. It was Mary, a Ghanaian tour guide whom we had not yet met. She wanted to know if we would be interested in taking a trip to a seamstress or to a hair braider. I had planned to get my hair rebraided and have some traditional African clothing made while I was here, but Mom wasn't ready to get up yet. She had already fallen back asleep, having only opened her eyes long enough to find out who was on the phone and to comment, "They sure don't waste any time trying to get you to spend your money." Disappointed, I told Mary that we would wait until another time.

By the time we got up, dressed, and made our way downstairs to meet the rest of our group for dinner, the lobby had been transformed for a cocktail party. There were several tables set up with cool drinks, manned by the waiters I had seen from my window this morning darting around the pool. Mom nudged me towards one of the tables. Neither of us had had anything to eat or drink since breakfast on the plane. I stood before the table surveying my choices and ordered two glasses of fruit punch. The waiter smiled flirtatiously as he ladled the pink liquid into tall frosted glasses.

"For you and your boyfriend?" he asked slyly.

"For me and my mom," I answered, flirting back.

"Where is your boyfriend?"

"At home."

"Where is home?"

"Washington, D.C."

"What about Africa? You don't consider Africa home?" he admonished, handing me the drinks. Our fingers touched as I took them. "Let me tell you," he said, lowering his voice into that sexy register, just above a whisper. "You are home now. And for a new home, you need a new man, mmm?"

"I don't think my boyfriend would appreciate that," I said, turning to walk away. "But thanks for the drinks." He nodded and shifted his attention to the next person in line. I rolled my eyes at the cheap pick-up lines he probably tried on every woman who came to his table.

"What are you grinning about?" my mother asked when I got back to the spot she had staked out by the automatic doors leading out to the courtyard. I shrugged my shoulders. I hadn't realized I was grinning.

~

On the morning of our third day, I woke before sunrise to the bright orange tip of Mom's lighted cigarette, flickering in one spot and then another as she paced around the room.

"What's wrong, Ma?" I asked, sitting up in bed.

"I had this dream," Mom said, turning on the light, "that we were going to be kidnapped." I laughed out loud at how ridiculous this sounded. Mom joined me in my laughter. And for a moment, it was like it always was when we had bad dreams, how once we were awake and could laugh about them, everything was alright, the terror we had felt explained away.

"No, I'm serious," Mom said sitting close to me on the bed, her smile fading. "It was so real. These men were trying to take us away and nobody knew where we were. They wouldn't let us go home."

"Why would anyone want to kidnap us?" I asked, annoyed. Mom always blew everything out of proportion, worried intensely with even the slightest provocation. I didn't want to go through this now, not here. This morning we were leaving Accra for Cape Coast, the site of one of the major holding castles where captured Africans were kept in dungeons before being shipped across the Atlantic Ocean and delivered into slavery. I was especially looking forward to seeing the castles and possibly doing some research on the slave trade from the African perspective.

"Why would anyone want to kidnap us?" I asked again.

"I don't know," Mom sighed. "In my dream, they really only wanted you."

⌒

On the way to Cape Coast, we pulled over onto the gravel shoulder of the highway at the outskirts of a small fishing village, a smattering of thatched-roof huts made of mud, leaves, and straw. This was to be an unscheduled stop, our tour guide announced, even though it had been clearly printed on the itinerary that we received at the beginning of the tour: *Stop At Local Village En Route To Cape Coast.*

"In our culture, it is customary to bring a gift to the chief whenever one visits his village," our guide explained. "Normally, we would present the chief with a gift of Schnapps," she continued, "but since we are arriving unexpectedly, we should give a small monetary offering."

"What kind of culture is that?" someone from our group snorted.

"We call it hustling in the States," someone cracked, and a ripple of laughter spread through the group. Reluctantly, we reached into our pockets and produced a few thousand cedis each (one thousand cedis was roughly equivalent to one American dollar). The tour guide ignored the jokes and the sarcasm as she collected the sweaty, crumpled bills. She counted the money, then walked up to the edge of the village where a lanky teenage boy, dressed in a long-sleeved Western-style button-down shirt and shorts, emerged to meet her. The boy, were were told when our guide rejoined our group, was the nephew of the chief and would present our offering to his uncle. We would know when he returned whether or not the chief had granted us permission to enter the village.

While we waited, I took a few pictures. From where we stood, the village looked like a ghost town. The chief's nephew was the only person we had seen moving throughout the sparse cluster of huts. He reappeared momentarily and began walking toward our group, waving us into the village.

As we entered, we were met by a few of the tribesmen and a small brigade of children, all dressed in dingy Western clothing. Most of the men wore cotton button-down shirts and shorts, like the chief's nephew. The women we passed, most dressed in silk-screened T-shirts and wrap skirts made from African cloth, lingered in the doorways of the huts, or watched from where they sat washing or cooking in their front yards. A girl of about eight and a boy around five or six sidled up to me. The girl, dressed in a faded yellow Sunday dress, casually slipped her hand into mine and asked me where I was from.

"The United States," I answered.

"Oh," she nodded, "I like that place."

"Have you been there?" I asked.

"No, but I've heard of it." She reached into her dress pocket and produced a small square of white paper on which her name and address had been written, I assumed, by a more adult hand than hers. "Will you write me?" she asked. I told her I would and tucked the paper into my notebook.

"Maybe you will bring me there for a visit sometime," she said, letting go of my hand and skipping up to the woman walking ahead of me. I saw her give this woman a square of paper just like the one she had given me.

The little boy stayed behind, his eyes on the camera dangling around my neck.

"What do you call it?" he asked, pointing.

"A camera," I answered.

"May I hold it?" I took the camera off of its strap and placed it cautiously in his tiny hands. He turned it over a few times, looking first through the wide lens in front, and then the small window of the viewfinder. "May I keep it?" he beamed up at me.

"I'm sorry, this is the only camera I have," I said, taking the camera.

"Then maybe you can send me one." He produced a square of paper similar to the girl's and handed it to me. His name, too, had been written by an adult hand.

We were led to the chief's meeting house, a one-room cottage, cool and dark, bare except for two wooden benches running the length of each wall and a smaller bench positioned at the front of the room. The children, who had not entered the house with us, peered at us through the windows, their scrawny arms dangling into the room through the uncovered, paneless openings roughly cut out of the mud walls.

After we were settled on the benches along the wall, the chief and his linguist entered the house. The linguist was the only one who could speak directly to the chief. Our guide introduced us to the linguist, who then addressed the chief. The chief spoke and the linguist translated his greeting. We were told that other groups of black Americans and black British tourists had visited the village. So much for an unscheduled stop.

"The chief would like you to know how happy he is that you have all come home," the linguist said. The chief spoke again, extending his arms and gesturing wildly. Again, the linguist interpreted for us.

"Many years ago, strangers came to our land and took our people. Some of us sold our own people to these strange men. But we didn't know what would happen to those who were sold away. We didn't know. And by the time we had learned the horrors of what our people were experiencing over there, across the water, it was too late. We are so sorry we let you go. But we never gave up hoping that you would come back, that we would see you again. Welcome home, my lost sisters and brothers, Akwaaba."

The linguist then walked around the room and gave each of us a Ghanaian name, speculating on the tribe from which we were descended. When he to got to me, he held my hand in his. I could smell the alcohol on his breath. He had been staring at me the entire time we were there. He gave me the name Aku, which means, "born on a Wednesday," and then said, "Aku is not going back home. She will stay here with me." I stiffened, not wanting to look at Mom.

Mom grabbed my hand from his. "You can't have her," she said hysterically. "This is my daughter!" The rest of the group laughed nervously. The linguist silently locked eyes with Mom.

"Why don't we go outside?" our tour guide suggested, breaking the tension. "The chief will be available for photographs." We lined up to take a picture with the chief. Afterwards, we went on a tour of the village. Mom walked close beside me, the linguist on my other side.

"Hold my hand and walk with me," he said, taking my hand. Mom grabbed me by my free arm. One of the men from our group, seeing how upset Mom was, walked up to the linguist and put his hand on his shoulder to lead him away.

"Come on man, leave her alone. This is a married woman," he lied. The linguist again fixed his red-eyed gaze on Mom before walking ahead to lead the tour.

After leaving the village, we dropped our luggage off at the rooming house where we would be sleeping that night. The hotel where we were supposed to stay had double-booked our rooms and didn't have any others available. We ate a dinner of greasy "Ghanaian style" fried chicken and then came to the evening's event, a march to commemorate slavery.

The minivan dropped us off at the foot of a steep hill. Cape Coast loomed above us. With Mary and Kwame leading the way, we began the climb, winding through the narrow streets. The stench from the open sewage lines dug on either side of the road was unbearable, and it was so dark I could only make out the rough silhouettes of houses and people.

We reached the top of the hill and walked into a wide clearing where a crowd had gathered. Some people were holding torches, others flashlights and candles. A voice speaking in French sounded over a loudspeaker. "They're telling the story of slavery," I heard a nearby tour guide translating for his group. Suddenly the mass of bodies started moving. I allowed myself to be pushed along with it.

There was music now, streaming over our heads. The locals in the crowd began to dance. A dance that was more like running, feet sliding along the pavement. Three steps forward, one back. On the one step back, the entire body would lean backwards, suspended, as though surrendering to a strong wind, then snap upright, curving slightly, head down, fighting this same wind to move forward. Three steps forward, one back. Us, I thought. This is us. History. The body remembers. Though the people dancing seemed to be doing so only for the pleasure of it, perhaps performing for the foreigners in their midst, not grasping or searching for any meaning.

I faced the night and the flickering throng shining against it. I wanted to join them. I wanted to dance. But I could feel Mom behind me, struggling to stay close as she clung to the straps of my backpack. She was still shaken from earlier, the village, the dream, and had stayed close to me all day. She was suffocating me, and I was angry at her for not being able to control her fear.

"Can't you see how ridiculous this is?" I lashed out at her.

"I know, I know, but I can't get rid of this feeling." Over dinner, she had shared her dream with the rest of our group. "You see how nobody questioned the possibility. Nobody ever said that it wouldn't happen," she reminded me.

"I guess they're all in on the plan to kidnap me," I said sarcastically.

⌒

"What are you looking for here? What do you want from this place?" Mom asked me later, once we were alone in our room.

"I don't know," I said. "I'm just sick of always feeling like I'm floating. I want to be settled, happy . . ."

"You think you're going to find that here?"

"I didn't say I was going to find anything here, I just wanted to see what this place has to offer," I said, exasperated.

"The people here don't even know what they have to offer!" Mom railed. "Look at that village. The men were all drunk, the kids were begging. And that crock of bull they fed us about slavery. These people don't care anything about slavery."

The night before we left Accra, our group had attended a lecture given by a Ghanaian scholar on the history of various tribes in Ghana. When I asked how the slave trade had impacted the people of Ghana, the man was evasive. In his tribe, slavery was not something that was discussed, nor was it taught to children in school. Their history courses still focused primarily on Europe, one of the lasting effects of colonization. "We have a saying," he told us. " 'All that you need to know is right in front of you.' There is no need to look back."

Lisa Teasley

Although I usually travel with a beloved, road trips still leave me with an obsessive Thomas Bernhard–esque inner narrative of thought. The northern California coast is particularly inspiring for journeying with dilemmas over joy, pain, eroticism, anger, desolation, and ecstasy. The answers to the questions of existence seem to be carved in the jagged, raw, and gorgeous terrain along the cliffs up the Pacific Coast Highway.

Nepenthe

From *Glow in the Dark,* a short-story collection

I watch the jet trails, hornets' nests under the overpasses, snow on the Grapevine, first time I've ever seen. Nepenthe drives wild, though her temperament never more than 20 mph. I turn to look at her, sometimes snap her picture in between capturing clouds hanging low in the mountains, in the crevices that look like snow-covered vaginas (pussies). We enter a cloud now, a soothing white mist, we are riding it, then just as fast, we are in the clear. Nepenthe steps on the gas, cranks up the music, drives with one hand on the wheel, one hand moving across our space like the boys who use to dance with their own reflection at the Odyssey. She is trying to make me laugh. She keeps it up. I am laughing.

We are in love with the same man. That's how we know each other. But she is so young. She turned 19 yesterday when we were in L.A., now we're going to Berkeley to come to some agreement. No we're not. This isn't planned vacation.

Nepenthe is named for the restaurant—it means "no sorrow" in Greek—her parents conceived her in the women's bathroom. That's what she says anyway, and she's so proud of the story. Her father is black, her mother white, her icy cream coloring is warm. Her hair is dyed black, lots of hair, very big hair, and she wears a tiny gold ring in her nose. There is a tattoo of an ankh on the plush of her arm, just below her shoulder. There is her body, lean but rounded with muscle.

We're coming up on the close dullish pink, blue, and other colorless houses—we must be minutes from Oakland—Nepenthe gets in the lane under the sign, Walnut Creek.

"Hey, and *suss* me out," Nepenthe sings with Marley. She hasn't been saying much of anything, and as we're off the highway it's dark and I'm wondering what I'm doing here. I think of Clive coming out of the water, looking half his size, how he dragged me down in the sand, still wet, the grains sticking to us; when we moved there was that small, sharp pain. I look at Nepenthe as she turns the corner—I hate her beauty. She looks at me and knows it.

Her sister's apartment is so bare I feel suffocated the instant we walk in. Nepenthe is carrying the cooler we brought, so I hold the door open for her. I can tell she is sorry she's with me. It hurts to feel those mutual moments of regret.

"Let me see if I can get this heater to work," she says, rubbing her hands together. I wander off, look into the bedroom of what must be her sister's roommate. The mattress is on the floor, there is a chemical engineering book at the foot of the bed, pictures taped tackily to the closet door, almost everyone in the pictures is Korean. I hear the heat pull in, Nepenthe dragging something from one end of the room to the other. I go to see if I can help her.

"What year is your sister?" I ask her, helping her pull the dresser over a yard. I have no idea why she is rearranging her sister's room like this.

"Fourth. This is her last semester, or so she says." Unsatisfied, Nepenthe is looking at the dresser. She rubs her hands together again.

"What sign is she?"

Nepenthe looks up at the wall near the ceiling.

"Sagittarius." She looks at me with a smile that says, This is irrelevant.

There is a bulletin board over the bed, pictures of her sister, many of Nepenthe and a few of their mother. Her sister is white—their mother's second husband is her father—and she looks nothing whatsoever like Nepenthe. Her name is unexciting, but spelled differently—Sherrel. Their mother has a very tight smile, holding onto the dog as if he might run away.

"Are you hungry, or what?" she asks.

"Sure, I could eat."

"Well, we could go into town, get a bite there, or we could see what they've got in their kitchen."

"Let's go into town." Fresh air would do us good, though I dread getting back in the car.

"Okay. Just let me pee," she says, unzipping her jeans, walking to the bathroom. I hear it come out, a strong, steady stream. She flushes, I figure I should go too. I enter the bathroom, she is standing in front of the mirror and she smiles at me. We look at each other's reflection, I stand behind her. What did he see in me? What doesn't he now see in her? She is too young.

Walking down Telegraph Avenue, Nepenthe stops at a head shop.

"We'd better get some candles and incense if we're going to stand the smell there tonight," she says.

I nod, but take this personally. I know I'm being ridiculous. There have been so many letters between us. Compassion for one another. Nepenthe picks up some exotic oil—I imagine Clive spreading it all over her luscious body and feel as if I might throw up. Out of jealousy for him?

I pull out my wallet, she pushes it away. I don't know where she gets her money from, she doesn't work, her mother is not rich. The cashier admires the charms hanging from Nepenthe's leather jacket, she smiles at her and I want to burn out the cashier's eyes.

We eat at the same Mexican restaurant I've eaten at many times before. Beautiful tiles in the tables, I zone staring at the colors, waiting for our beers. It's chilly outside. Nepenthe pulls out a cigarette, motions to me if I'd like one. I take one even though it's been a year and a half.

"Those mountains looked really incredible, didn't they? On the Grapevine, the snow, I mean. I bet you got some great pictures," she says, so cheerfully, fake.

"Yeah."

"Maybe we should take the 1 back, don't you think?" she asks in the same merry voice, believing it now. She is different, like she has decided something and won't let me in on it.

She blows the smoke up high and to one side, then looks to see that she hasn't bothered anyone. The waiter brings our food, he watches her face as he puts the plates down. When she looks up to thank him, he smiles like he's melting.

"What would you like to do tonight? A club, a movie?" she asks.

"I don't really care if we do anything. I mean, we could just buy some wine and play Scrabble or something. Does your sister have Scrabble?"

"I don't know. We could look," she says smiling. She makes me feel so goddamn inferior. It's almost condescending, the way she talks. Her fucking smile.

I buy the wine—three bottles—I hope it's good, because I plan on drinking it all. Nepenthe opens the door to the apartment, I think I see a rat run down the hall. Nepenthe turns to look at me as if I'd shocked her. She scares me. She is reading my mind, and up until now has expected everything I've been thinking.

She turns on the boom box in the corner, switching the stations quickly until she finds her groove. I'm already on my second glass. She is looking all over for the Scrabble. I look at her ass when she bends over and wonder if this isn't desire.

Nepenthe kneels on the bed next to me, her face so close I can smell her breath. She is showing me a picture of her father.

"I can't believe this is here. Sherrel and I didn't know him really. I mean I was 11 when he left, and she must have been 8, but she wasn't even living with us. She was living with her father."

"He's very handsome," I say awkwardly.

"Yeah."

She gets up, puts the picture away, stands in the corner, stretches, yawns, looks around the room for wings. I feel as if her energy, which seems to have sprung out of a thin weariness, is going to boil up the room. I get tense watching her, until she turns around. Her back to me, I open my mouth to say something, but she cuts me off.

"I brought some hash. Are you into it?"

"Sure," I say.

She lights up quickly. I watch the smoke thick in the air. When I am so high, so drunk I don't know where I am, she turns on the electric blanket, so our butts are hot. She is giggling in beautiful ringing sounds. She starts singing the same line from a song. We're doubling back on the bed, bouncing back up, as she mimics a scratched cd. There are the two small candles with a quiet scent, flickering, the incense I can barely make out. But here she is, so close to me, intoxicating.

We wake up at one in the afternoon—maybe Nepenthe has been up for a while, she is lying with her head propped up, watching some soap. Her eyes tired, her shoulders shine. We are both naked. And I panic as if it were not me last night. How am I supposed to act? She seems bored and cool.

"You hungry?" she asks me, still looking at the TV. I'm fucked up, my head banging inside, but my body so warm in this electric blanket, next to her, I feel I'd die first before I get out of this bed.

"What did you say?"

"Are you hungry?"

"No, not really. My head is killing." I look at the TV, wait to disappear.

"I called Clive this morning," she says suddenly.

"You what?"

"I called Clive. I don't know why really. I guess I wanted to wish him Happy New Year. You know."

"What did he say?" I ask her, sitting up.

"Nothing really. He's used to my confusion. Nothing really shakes him up, you know?" Nepenthe looks down at herself.

I start to hear what they're saying on TV. Absurd words. Nepenthe looks like she might cry and I want to slap her.

"Why can't you leave him alone? He's never known what he wants. He'll never know what he wants."

She leans into me, I hold her anyway. She is incredibly soft, and she smells like the musky oil we must have put on. Nepenthe drives into the city, we go to the Haight. So hungry I can't stand it, we enter the nearest café. There are people here as shiny new as Nepenthe. She keeps looking down at the table, biting her lip. We order hot chocolates, wait for the omelets in silence. It's raining outside, people walking by look wet and beautiful. Today there is something I like about everything.

"Maybe we can look for a bikini after this," Nepenthe says smiling. Her nose is a little red, I wonder if the hole is irritated. I dare not ask her.

"Sure, we can go look for a bikini in this incredibly cold weather. Sounds wonderful," I say laughing.

We buy this little barrette with Coochie dolls on it—something like "coochie," they are Guatemalan—and Nepenthe sticks it in her purse. I've never seen her wear a barrette. But then I haven't seen her very much. Maybe 10 times.

"I like this bar," she says, as we get to the corner.

"This one?"

"Yeah."

It has the most smotheringly pretentious vibe.

Sipping on a gin fizz, she takes the excuse to come alive.

"Why are you always tripping on my age?" she asks me suddenly.

"What do you mean?"

"Everything you say. You looked at the waitress as if she'd card me. You're always saying something about me being so young. I mean how the fuck old are you?"

"Thirty two."

"Yeah. So what's the big deal?"

"I'm a whole *thirteen* years older than you. We don't have the same reference library."

"*Thirteen* years? Who told you that?"

"Those people at your party."

"Well I'm not nineteen. They were kidding. God, just a joke. What the hell difference does it make anyway?"

She is sitting on the edge of her seat, her anger not serious, full of life.

"I'm 25, you twit," she says.

I don't believe her.

"I'm 25."

I start to laugh, she stares at me with the straw between her lips until she is laughing too. A dude walks up to us, asks if he could buy us another drink. She is laughing really hard now, and as I come to the tail end of it, I look up at him, seeing Clive, so I fucking *hate* him.

"Leave us alone."

Nepenthe stops laughing, looks at me deadpan, gets up to walk out.

I follow her at about eight paces behind, she is holding onto her bag tightly, looking down at the sidewalk. Four or five blocks down, I follow her into a pet store. The owner sits above our heads on the steps. She bends down into the aquarium, staring at the reptiles. She wipes her forehead as if sweating. There is a chameleon with eyes like two fists working independently of each other. He looks at me, then back at her, and I'm feeling defeated. That she is not as young as I thought, shouldn't be such a big deal. I just thought she had to have so much more unspoiled than me for him to have left me for her. I don't know what the fucking difference is. I am too jealous, and want to own her.

Driving down the 1 we go through this rain cloud, then sudden bright sun. Nepenthe puts on her shades, contained, shut in. Her skin glows, hot ice cream, milk burning. Clive used to carefully place cookie dough on the sheet, size and order, everything according to plan. Coming up on Big Sur, Nepenthe switches the tape. She hugs the soft shoulder of the road. What would it feel like if she lost control. What will it be like, sober, in daylight, watching her face when she cums.

"We can eat at Nepenthe," I say to her smiling. She looks at me, at first sadly, and then she warms up.

We walk into the restaurant, I give them my name because she is embarrassed. The hostess looks at her with fish eyes bulging out with enthusiasm.

Nepenthe tells me she has to go to the bathroom, and I do too. I follow her, she seems annoyed—I can tell by the tight quickness of her step—but, I'm going anyway. She opens the door to the bright pink, gold, green and blue, flowerchild sort of design of the bathroom. She looks in the mirror, I look at her from behind. I take her in my arms and kiss her.

"We can spend the night in Cambria at the motel with fireplaces you turn on with a switch," she says, her breath in my face.

"That would be good," I say, letting go of her.

She enters the stall, and I listen to the stream of her piss. Strong and steady, I could lie down beneath it.

"Yes, that would be heaven."

Rebecca Walker

I am not one of those writers who loves to write. I dislike sitting alone at the keyboard, wrestling with words and willing elaborate dramas to flow effortlessly from my fingertips. I would much rather be swimming in the ocean or going to see a dance concert by Pina Bausch. Anything but mutely facing the glowing screen, trying to transform people, places, and the love and longing that connects them into art.

Since the sheer pleasure thing isn't happening, for my own sanity I have had to privilege other benefits of writing. More often than not, I write to work through something that haunts me, something that has affected me deeply and will not turn me loose. I reach and reach for what feels like an ever-present but ever-receding thread, knowing that if I can just get ahold of it and discover its source, I will be forever changed.

The section of Black, White, and Jewish *excerpted here is the first of the book that I wrote, and writing it was like catching, finally, the thread that eventually led to the rest of the book. At the time, I knew that the section was the beginning of something important, but I wasn't* sure what, nor was I able to determine whether or not I could pull off what the work seemed to demand: ruthless self-excavation, brutal but well-crafted honesty, and a structure flexible enough to accommodate a narrator with multiple voices who experiences abrupt changes in time and place.

Ultimately, this became only one section of many, but I will always have a singular, humble respect for it. Perhaps this is why I write: because words come and pull me forward, because I feel safe grabbing the rope.

Larchmont

From *Black, White, and Jewish: Autobiography of a Shifting Self,*
a memoir

MY STEPMOTHER wants to live in Larchmont. I don't know at the time
that it is, like, the Jewish dream to live in the suburbs, as close to Scarsdale
as possible; to have a Volvo or two in the garage next to the kids' bikes and
baseball gear; to eat Dannon yogurt and bagels every Sunday and light
Shabbat candles on Friday night; to get a baby-sitter one night a week so
that you and your husband, fresh off the six-forty train from the city, can
go see the romantic comedy playing at the local uniplex. All I know is that
we leave the Bronx. We pack up apartment 18J in The Winston Churchill,
say goodbye to the Liebermans and my piano teacher with her horrible
breath, and drive half an hour up the Cross Bronx Expressway, by way of
the Henry Hudson, to a three-bedroom wooden frame house on half an
acre in Larchmont.

I think that the house is very *Father Knows Best* and the move is some
kind of plot my stepmother has concocted to kill me, to wipe away all
traces of my blackness or to make me so uncomfortable with it that I
myself will it away. I don't know that I am thinking this, but I am. I think
that she and I are doing battle for my father's soul, me with my brown
body pulling him down memory lane to a past more sensual and right-
eous, she scratching the dirt off pale Jewish roots I didn't know he had.

⌒

Everyone in Larchmont is white.

What black kids there are come from the wrong side of the tracks,
Mamaroneck, Larchmont's poor cousin. I don't even see them until I start

school at Hommocks, the middle school at the end of a curvy drive, which on any given morning during the school year is filled with Jaguars, Volvos, and BMWs. It is not a successful integration. We all are there together but are impossibly separate. The black kids are scruffy, unkempt, ashy. They cut school, skulk through the halls, yell to one another loudly, and try in any number of other uncouth ways to assert themselves in the sea of white, rich, Jewish kids who studiously avoid them. After a few weeks at Hommocks I do the same, averting my eyes guiltily when a black kid in patched-up jeans passes me in the lunchroom, in the hallway, in class. Not once does a black student say a word to me while I am at Hommocks, not one time that whole year.

I lie outright that year. To my best friend Lauren in the downstairs bathroom, right down the brown-tiled hallway from the front doors of the school. She has just come out of one of the stalls and I am washing my hands and she asks me what am I, anyhow. She has taken a bathroom break from AP English, where they are reading *A Midsummer Night's Dream*, and I have walked out of Social Studies, where we are learning about the United Nations. I have no idea how to answer her question, though I know what information she is looking for. What am I? The black kids are scruffy, unkempt, ashy. I get really hot. I look at my feet. I wash my hands and begin to hyperventilate.

I'm Spanish, like from Spain, I say, and tear off a paper towel to put a period on it. Really, she says in a way we joke about all year, that way Lauren has of saying *really* that is dorky and weird and sounds like her nose has grown lips. Reelly? And I say yes, and she never asks me about it again, not even when there is a big article in the newspaper about my mother, lauding her as a big African-American writer and mentioning that she has a daughter, this half-Jewish half-black girl living with her father in Larchmont.

⌐

I hate Larchmont. I hate how quaint and provincial it is, that everybody seems to know each other, that there are only two pizza places and one grocery story and one junior high. I hate that everybody is white, that when I walk down the street people look at me funny, as if I don't belong. I hate that Larchmont is not the Bronx, where all my friends are, and I hate that my father is choosing this totally bourgeois lifestyle that makes me puke, and that I'm forced to choose it along with him even though a picket fence is not my idea of happiness.

There is something about the way the houses are, all in a row with their little plots of lawn out front, the way at dusk men and women in black and gray and navy blue suits start filling the streets, walking home from the train station. There's something too predictable about the patterns of life here, as if they're drawn on rather than actually lived. It makes me sick.

⌒

Allison Hoffman's house is smooth gray stone and glass and from the outside looks like it should be in an architectural magazine, all straight lines and flat planes shooting out from each other. I have never seen a house as fancy this close-up, but I pretend not to notice, letting my eyes skip over the manicured lawn out front, the Mercedes and Jaguar in the carport. Allison and I walk up to the house from the direction of our school, which is at the other end of a windy road lined with puffy beige grasses and a little fake lake. The sky is a sparkling blue, and the air is chilly but not quite cold.

When we step inside her house an older Latina woman in a black-and-white maid's uniform comes to the door and takes Allison's book bag and coat. When she does, Allison says to her in this fake nicey nicey voice, "Thank you, Maria," and then smiles that smile that I have seen her smile at people she's not really friends with but who she knows she should be nice to anyway. Then Maria asks if we want anything to eat. Do we want sandwiches, cookies, juice, crackers? Allison answers in the same sing-songy voice, but this time a little too firm and dismissive I think for someone our age to say to a woman so much older, "No thanks, Maria, we can get something ourselves."

I feel embarrassed when Allison talks this way to Maria, and especially when Maria looks at me cautiously before walking away. For a moment I feel closer to Maria than I do to Allison, like I should call her Mrs. Somebody and I should go with her to the kitchen or wherever she's walking to, and not stay back here in the fancy rooms with Allison.

But I do stay in the front rooms with Allison, nodding and trying not to look impressed by everything she's showing me. First it's the sliding glass doors off the living room and the pool they lead to. Then it's the library, with its multiple sets of encyclopedias, big leather chairs, and colorful globe. Then it's her parents' bedroom, where everything is matching gray and beige, with a big television and identical phones on either side of the bed. Then it's her brother's room, with its Lacrosse sticks propped against the wall, and blond women in bathing suits tacked up over his dresser.

As I look around her house and listen to her talk about shopping for her upcoming bat mitzvah, how huge her brother's was a few years before, and how we should watch some videos before her violin teacher comes to give her a lesson, I chatter along with her, keeping it light, trying to match her rich, carefree frequency. I tell her that I'm not having a bat mitzvah because I haven't been to Hebrew school, and when she asks me what San Francisco is like I tell her it's really beautiful, with fog and hills and lots of roller-skating in the park. When she asks me about Riverdale I tell her about how close it is to the city and that my bedroom had like, an amazing view of the Hudson River and the George Washington Bridge.

While I'm talking Allison makes little faces, nodding and squinching up her mouth and her nose until she looks like a mouse. Then she pulls her wavy brown hair in and out of its ponytail holder, fussing with it in a distracted way, like what I'm saying isn't quite capturing her attention. When she does that I try to imagine Allison hanging out with César, Loída, and Sam. I try to imagine her in the Victorian frame house I live in, in my small room with the box fan and slatted wooden floors and flowery sheets my stepmother bought on sale at Bloomingdale's. I feel as if we speak two different languages and I am the only one who can speak both, who even knows that there is more than one to be learned.

⌒

Allison is one of the girls I talk about when Theresa comes to my house to visit, after her new police-officer boyfriend drives up in an old faded blue Plymouth to drop her off. It's late and we've made a pallet on the floor next to my bed out of some old quilts and a comforter. We're both lying down there, fiddling with the knob on my stereo, trying to tune it to WPLJ, and gossiping about who's going out with who back in Riverdale. She tells me that Jesús and Diane are back together, César is going out with this girl who is older than him and really pretty, and Loída finally has a boyfriend but he's a total nerd.

It's strange having Theresa at my house since it's always been the other way around, I'm always the one going into her world, she's never coming into mine. She seems out of place in my room, and even more so sneaking downstairs in the middle of the night to eat the rest of the Entenmann's chocolate chip cookies hidden in the bottom drawer of the refrigerator. It's a bit of a shock to see Theresa in a kitchen that's well lit and full of shiny white Formica. She looks different juxtaposed against it, faded, haggard, and slightly green. I notice the concealer caked under her eyes, her long pink nails, her fake-looking blow-dried hair.

When Theresa asks me about my friends here, when she asks me what the other kids are like, I tell her about Allison, about Allison's house and Allison's maid. I tell her that Allison wouldn't last five minutes at 141 with her uppity attitude. She'd get her ass kicked. I laugh with Theresa as I say this but in the pit of my stomach I feel some guilt, like I am betraying Allison, choosing sides because it's convenient. After Theresa leaves I am exhausted but relieved. I love her but it is too hard to be the translator, the one in between, the one serving as the walkway between two worlds.

⌐

Tina and I are at Dark Star Records, and Shawn is playing the Clash up front while we stack quarters up on the Centipede game in the back. Shawn is from England and he opened Dark Star just a few months before I got to Larchmont. He's got pasty white skin, a pointy nose, and a mass of dark frizzy hair. He always wears the same thing, tight skinny-legged blue jeans with pointy black shoes and a multicolored pullover sweater. When we're in the store, he plays Flock of Seagulls, Modern English, the Clash, and the Who. He plays Duran Duran at our request, turning his back in disgust as we sing along at the top of our lungs to "Rio."

Dark Star is the black sheep of Larchmont, the freaky, out-of-place thing that isn't like all the others on Sesame Street. As it is, it's next to Eggemoggin, the tchotchke store where Tina and I go to buy presents for birthday parties, picking and choosing from teddy bear stickers, edible face paint, and monogrammed pastel stationery. I don't know what possessed Shawn to open Dark Star in Larchmont, but I feel close to him; he, too, is a foreigner.

When Tina and I are out of quarters and our fingers hurt from shooting fluorescent spiders, we hang over the counter and listen to Shawn talk about the punk scene in London. He tells us about Sid Vicious, about all the boys wearing bright orange mohawks and the Union Jack safety-pinned to their black leather jackets. When Tina and I make a music video in Media Arts class, it is Shawn's influence that comes through as we strum on borrowed guitars. In our best British urban ghetto cool, Tina and I prance around the tiny stage in the Media Arts lab, lip-synching the words to our favorite Police tune, "Every Little Thing She Does Is Magic," and flirting with the camera.

⌣

Tina is my best friend here and she's flipping her straight dirty-blond hair over her shoulders in between boards as she plays, but it creeps back and then she has to ask me to hold it for her, to keep it out of her eyes as she clears the hard board of the red Centipede that falls as fast as light from the top of the screen. We're having a tournament with some boys that came with us after school to play: Paul Mangione, Brendan Ryan, Tommy Handler. It's me and her against all of them, and we're winning because we play Centipede after school every day here at Dark Star, and they don't.

We're also waiting for Luca, Tina's brother, to come meet us after hockey practice like he said he would. He said he'd meet us around four-thirty, and it's already five. Even though I'm focused on my game, I can't help but look up at the front of the shop every time the door swings open, half expecting to see Luca walk in wearing his faded army jacket that smells like patchouli, the goofy grin across his angular face that means he got stoned with his friends on the way. The other half of me is expecting to be disappointed.

Luca's being Tina's brother makes making out a lot easier because I am always at Tina's house. Our parents make jokes that I should move in I'm over there so much, that I'm the Nastris' long-lost daughter from Sicily. The truth is I love Tina's roomy house, the way all the kids have floors of their own, the way the parents' room is far enough away from us kids that we can do anything, make any amount of noise without them hearing. At Christmas, the Nastris put up a huge tree and fill the house with Perugina chocolates. At dinner the whole family talks about stuff going on in school, and the kids get to be flip and sarcastic without the world coming to an end.

Luca's room is at the top of a little narrow staircase that's almost secret. His room is small and always smells like a mixture of pot, his dirty hockey uniform, and the patchouli oil he buys in the city. It is always cold in his room, and dark. He has Clash posters on the wall, dirty beat-up Saucony sneakers on the floor, rank and faded jeans in a heap by the bathroom door.

The most exciting thing about Luca Nastri, in addition to the fact that he's cute and a renegade, is that he goes to the *high school*. I'm in eighth grade and I'm going out with a boy from the high school. That means I get to go to high school games and wear his hockey jersey. That means some days I wait for him to come and pick me up at Hommocks when he's done with hockey practice. That means a lot of the girls in my grade look at me different, with a kind of grudging respect. Except for the stuck-up snotty girls who think that the stoner crowd, Luca's crowd, is gross and dirty. But I don't give a shit about them.

⌒

Luca Nastri is the first boy I give a blow job, down under the mussed-up tangled sheets in his bed, after we've taken a few long hits and made sure that Tina and her parents are asleep. We've been making out for a while and Luca has been holding my tiny breasts in his cold hands, kneading them in a way that doesn't feel good but that I tolerate because I don't know yet that I can say, Hey, that doesn't feel good, this would feel better. And we're lying like that, in his bed stoned and giddy and slightly paranoid, when he takes my hand and pulls it down to his penis, which is straining against the white cotton of his Fruit of the Loom briefs.

I'm fascinated. I squeeze it and pull it out from his belly, amazed by the way it snaps back when I let it go. After I press it against my fingers a couple more times and feel it jerk back in response, I reach under the waistband and wrap my palm around his hard, smooth, perfect dick, and then, before I know it, Luca is pushing me down toward it and then he asks me to lick it, and I say, Lick it? And he says, Yeah, and so I do, with little tiny strokes like a lollipop until he pushes the whole thing into my mouth and puts his hand on the back of my neck and then I am sucking and tasting the salty whiteness dribbling out the top and feeling strong and powerful but also nervous and unsure.

After Luca comes, pulling out of my mouth just in time to shoot wildly into a dirty, balled-up tee shirt, he pulls me close to him and tells me that it was great, that he really liked it and did I. I say yes even though part of me wonders, is that it? And another part of me wonders, did I do it right, or is he just saying that? But I don't say anything out loud, I am happy to be lying in his arms where it is warm and I feel for one second like I belong, like Larchmont isn't quite as bad as I thought.

Even after Luca falls asleep and I am lying in his arms, I hold on to that feeling, not wanting to let it go. I am the chosen one, I think. I am in Luca's bed, in his arms, I am inside, not out; I am the one being stayed with, not the one being left. I am not just alone, out in the world, fending for myself.

⌣

I don't tell my father too much about Luca, and he doesn't ask. My father gets up in the morning to 1010 WINS on the radio, showers, shaves, and puts on a suit, blue or brown in the winter, light blue or beige in the summer. My stepmother drives him to the station and me to school, my new baby sister and brother strapped into car seats on my right and left in the backseat as we ride. I don't see my father until dinnertime, or right before I go to bed. When I do see him, Daddy is tired, checked out, sagging. After eating chicken soup or pot roast or broiled chicken, he sits in a chair in the living room, rubbing his temples, his feet and legs heavy on the floor beneath them. Or he stretches out with a book, a biography of Gandhi or Niebuhr's *Moral Man and Immoral Society*, on the big brown sofa. I'm clearing the table or doing homework, loading the dishwasher or reading a story by Flannery O'Connor.

When we do talk for a few minutes before I go to sleep, we talk about his work or about how his back hurts. He asks me cursory questions about school and engages me a little on the one night I tell him I think Larchmont is too white. He asks me to elaborate, and when I do, tells me that some lawyer friend of his, Jim Hargood, who is black and has kids and lives in Larchmont, says he never has any problems and neither do his kids. I nod but can't help wondering what Jim Hargood's experience has to do with me. When I persist, he insists that I am fine, that I have friends and that this school is much better than the one in the Bronx. When I tell him that I'm miserable he tells me I'm exaggerating.

My father and my stepmother know I'm going out with Tina's brother, but they don't ask too many questions about what that means, going out. They don't ask what we do on the nights I spend at Tina's, they don't ask if I'm having sex or giving blow jobs or feeling safe. Back in fourth grade my stepmother told me about how babies were made, what sex is, and what a period is, and I guess she and my father think my mother filled me in on the rest while I was with her in fifth and sixth grades. It suits me fine, I guess, this having a whole life they don't know about, moving around, making decisions without the benefit of their opinion, except that I feel so alone and unsure of myself, like I'm winging every decision, every move, every day, faking like I know what I'm doing all the time rather than being sure.

When my father tells me I'm exaggerating about my feelings about Larchmont, I want to kill him, but more than that I want to kill my white, holier-than-thou, perfect Jewish stepmother, because I'm convinced this whole place is her dream and not his, and because I'm convinced if it wasn't for her my father would still be mine and would listen to me and would tell me to be proud of who I am, that I was born for a reason and that being black and white is better than being just one thing and screw people who can't deal.

⌒

When Luca walks into Dark Star with his Italian army jacket open and the bones of his collarbone sticking out in front of him, my stomach flips and I start to sweat. He says hello to Shawn and the two of them talk about the Clash for a minute, is that new record coming in. I can tell that Luca is high because his eyes have that tight, glossy look they get when he smokes pot, and his smile is sloppy and super wide. He walks to the back of the store where I am standing with his sister and puts his arm around me, right off. I can smell him, and when he turns his lips to me I give him mine and we kiss. Then he is trying to get me to go home with him, devising ways we can convince our parents to let me and Tina have a sleepover on a school night. The last time we did that Luca and I cut school the next day and spent the morning fooling around and the afternoon walking in the woods behind his house. Everything was white and pristine because it had just snowed and the trees were dripping icicles. We rolled around on the powdery mounds, sticking our tongues in each other's mouths, feeling the wet and warm contrast with the bitter dry cold.

With one hand on the rolling ball for direction and the other tapping against the flashing button to fire, Tina asks Luca about something she heard the boys on his hockey team said about me. She heard from Jennie Hauser's brother that the team had some problems with his choice of girlfriend. When she says this Luca's face falls a bit. He reaches up and pulls the hair that has fallen out of his eyes and looks at his sister's back, avoiding my eyes. Fuck them, he says. But Tina doesn't stop. Did you tell *them* that, she wants to know. I don't want to talk about it, he says with a dead calm, and then she lets it go.

I don't hear about this again until the day Luca breaks up with me, abruptly, out of the blue, about a week after Tina told me some of his friends on the hockey team had razzed him for going out with a black girl, or, as they put it, going out with a nigger. I had gone to a hockey game, and when Luca's team won I screamed and screamed and ran up to him, wrapping my arms around his neck and laughing. I felt a few of the stares from the boys and the way Luca's body tensed up a little, but I didn't think about it. I had heard that there was some discussion at the high school about me wearing Luca's jersey around school, but I hadn't paid much attention to that either. I did freak a little when Luca told me that his coach singled him out and told him not to have sex before the game, but I thought that was some strange macho bullshit, a guy thing rather than anything to do with the color of my skin.

After Luca breaks up with me, Tina gets really mad and says that all his so-called friends suck and that her brother is a total coward, but it doesn't help. I don't tell anyone about what happened between Luca and me, not my father or stepmother, not any of the friends from the Bronx that I no longer keep in touch with. I can't imagine calling Melissa or Loída to tell them some hockey-playing boy from northern Italy dumped me because I'm not white. The last time I called Melissa she asked me if my house was big and if all the kids at my school had their own cars. I briefly consider calling Sam, who I know will offer to beat Luca up.

Instead I keep my hurt to myself.

⌣

Ten years later I take the train back to Larchmont from Manhattan to attend a bridal shower for my once best friend Lauren. When I pull up to the house in my father's old Volvo I am thirteen again and coming over to Lauren's to watch U2 videos on MTV, play Phoenix on her Atari, and stay up half the night talking with her sister about boys and how she hates her mother. The house is mostly the same, full of books and art, Lauren's mother's downstairs lair filled with papers and manuscripts, a computer and desk now dominating one whole side of a room. Upstairs in Lauren's room, an amber-colored bottle of Ralph Lauren perfume is still on her old white lacquer dresser, and the single bed is still pressed against the yellow wall.

I haven't seen Lauren in years but when I do see her, after pushing through the throng of chatty mostly middle-aged Jewish women I don't know, she looks exactly the same. Same curly brown hair, same slender fingers and perfectly clean natural-looking nails. Same dewy brown eyes and big open smile. Same slightly awkward posture, same arms around me, same tall white woman looking down at me with love and hope. She's nervous about seeing me, she says, do I hate her because she's getting married? You were so protective of me, she says. I pause for a moment, surprised. I *had* been shocked and a little skeptical when I heard Lauren was engaged, but hating Lauren was never an option. Before I can say that to her, though, another guest pulls at her elbow and then she's off playing princess for somebody else.

It isn't until I watch Lauren opening her presents—a shiny white Cuisinart, some purple-and-black lingerie, a cookbook filled with recipes "to keep your Jewish husband happy and home"—that I begin to remember just how protective of Lauren I was. There was a boyfriend from a mob family I had been extremely concerned about, a girlfriend who had treated Lauren badly and whom I had called one night on Lauren's behalf, there were fights with her sister that I coached her through, and long, emotional phone conversations about her conflicts with her parents.

The next morning as I walk to the station, a well-groomed man in a sweatsuit jogs alongside me, peering into my face as he passes. He goes to the corner, stops, turns around, and comes back to where I am walking. He knows my name. I am surprised. I don't expect anyone in Larchmont to remember me. But it's Chris O'Shea, and he does. He remembers that some girls at the high school were picking on him and I offered to beat them up, standing with him one day after school on the day they were supposed to come. He remembers that I never acted like I was from Larchmont, that I had all this city attitude from living in the Bronx that made me stand out. He says I was real mature, real protective, that he thought of me as a big sister. Chris O'Shea has not crossed my mind once since I left Larchmont, but now, all of a sudden this clean-cut banker is in front of me, a thick gold chain around his neck the only thing left from the days we went to school together, and I see him the way he was, loping down the halls at school with his greasy brown hair and puppy dog eyes, his gloves with the fingers cut out, his tattered winter coat and black boots with the laces spilling out.

Chris was one of those fuck-up kids, the ones who try but never get it quite right, the ones who always seem a little slow, who nod while you talk but can't really repeat back what you just said. He drank in the eighth grade, and carried bottles of alcohol his older friends bought for him in the pockets of his ripped-up trenchcoat. He chain-smoked Marlboros or Camels, they might even have been Newports. His fingers were chewed down below the cuticle and always bleeding. One day at lunchtime Chris told me that his father beat him, and he lifted up his coat and showed me welts. Another day he told me that his father hadn't let him in the house and he spent the night in the tool shed.

I always liked Chris, I would look at his eyes and his fingers and his back and soften, wanting my wing to be bigger and stronger so that he could find some shelter under it. But he was like a security blanket to me too, in all his brokenness, a kindred wandering spirit to keep me warm.

On the train back to the city, it occurs to me that I needed someone to take care of me back in eighth grade, and instead of asking for that I gave it to others, convinced that by protecting them, by wrapping my little arms around them, I could make them mine forever.

Yolanda Young

I had about as much intention of telling my story as a rifle-toting red-neck has of being mistaken for a deer during hunting season. I was in law school in Washington, D.C., at the time, being trained to put other people on the spot. Then my fifteen-year-old cousin, Donna, came to live with me for the summer. In place of the happy and hyper little girl I remembered was a sullen and distant teenager. In addition to dealing with the problems of acne and disastrous hair, which all girls must face down, my cousin's family background had caused her to have low self-esteem. My uncle hadn't married her mother, who at the time was living in the projects and on welfare. I wanted Donna to know that I, too, knew what shame was, and more important, that it is possible to step out of that.

When Donna left Washington, I began to write in earnest, com-pelled to give a commentary just as had Steinbeck, Baldwin, and Heller. While their stories were fiction and raised such weighty issues as labor exploitation, racial injustice, and the insanity of war, I hoped that just as compelling would be the notion that there is a power and redemption in telling a real-life story and that I could convince young girls like my cousin that our experiences should give us perspective, not definition. I wanted Donna to gain from her trials understanding, compassion, and grace.

The first story I put on paper was of my earliest memory—of witnessing, at the age of four, my father shoot my mother six times. Then I began to tell my grandmother's stories—of how as a child during the Depression, she was swamped for a loaf of bread, of how she'd had one son be killed by his wife and another sentenced to prison for raping a child. There were also those of my uncles—how one's dream of playing baseball was cut short by the unfairness of integration and the Vietnam War and how another was suckered out of his college tuition and forced to take a job breaking steel tracks for the railroad. Every new page helped me to uncover how these people churned heartache into gladness. They inspired me, and I hoped they could save Donna, who looked down at her hands every time someone asked about her upbringing. I hoped to show Donna what my mother, grandmother, and great-grandmother had taught me: we can have joy no matter what situation we find ourselves in.

On Our Way to Beautiful

From *On Our Way to Beautiful,* a memoir

When men began to increase in number on the earth and daughters were born to them, the sons of God saw that the daughters of men were beautiful . . . then the Lord said, My spirit shall not always strive with man, for he also is flesh.

—GENESIS 6:1–3

ONCE A YEAR I make the drive back to my hometown of Shreveport, Louisiana. My journey begins as the sun rises over our nation's capital. Before long I'm moving through smaller cities that claim tobacco and the Confederate flag as symbols of pride, wondering how long it will be before the smell of factory smoke is replaced by the fertile aroma of livestock and chicken flocks. Then the narrow roads begin to unwind—hugged on either side by pastures, cows, horses, and shacks—and so too does my mind. As I ramble down bumpy paths, I stumble over the memory of a day spent fishing in a nearby bayou with my uncles, and the familiar smells of rank armpits and beer overwhelm my senses. Later, I see shiny pumps and a black veil waiting on top of an aging quilt and hear children running in bare feet.

A tin of peanut brittle spotted at the counter of a country gas station lands my mind on my great-grandmother because that was her favorite candy. Big Momma was part of a chorus of tabernacle women who mothered me. She always said Shreveport was known as the city of churches because they sprout up on corners like strawberries in July. Word has it that there are more churches in my hometown than in any other city in the country. Hymns flow from their doors on Sunday mornings, while during the week the smiling church ladies greet you with words of encouragement as they skirt around the vestibule like bees on a honeycomb. "Baaaby, that was a fine prayer you did Sunday," Mrs. Davis would say as I walked by. "Whose girl is dat with you? Bring her next Sunday."

But as is the case with all of Louisiana, our little city wobbles between extremes. Our local dishes of gumbo, catfish, and dirty rice must be spicy hot. Juke joints squat next to churches, and betting slips compete with offering envelopes. Fire-and-brimstone ministers point out that we drink and gamble too much. That is, until one in their congregation "hits." Then it's time to bring a tithe of the winnings to the altar. All of this is summed up neatly by the two billboards I notice as I cross the Texas Street Bridge into my city's fold. One beckons you toward the HORSESHOE CASINO STRAIGHT AHEAD. Opposite, another shouts, WANNA WIN THE JACKPOT? COME TO JESUS. There is always the question of which road to take.

To enter Shreveport's downtown, travelers must cross our beloved Red River, which curls like a large garden snake around the city. The river is yet another contradiction. It does not remotely resemble the liquid silver color of the Mississippi. Instead, it pours out a murky clay red and flows as thick as soft mud across Louisiana. The only time it sparkles is at night, when the casino riverboats' carnival lights illuminate the city.

Following the curve of the river, crouched along the road leaving downtown, rests a neighborhood of little shacks that belie a city of over a quarter million. We call the houses shotgun because a bullet fired through the front entrance will pass through every room in the house before exiting the back door. It is a place where the children play dodgeball in the street but know to watch their manners, and every woman worth her salt can make a meal out of meat drippings, flour, eggs, and rice. The unpaved streets are filled with stray dogs, and after a rain the air smells like wet earth. On warm mornings, plump older women wearing blinding white maid uniforms congregate on corners and talk while awaiting the arrival of little blue buses that will take them to the homes where they work.

"Child, Pastor Green liked to got the church on fire Sunday, didn't he?"

"Yeah, girl, and did you hear Mrs. Rogers shouting in the back? You know that boy of hers keeps her on her knees. He ain't got good sense."

"Folks say what they want about her whiskey habit. That woman will give you the shirt off her back. That's how I know she close to God."

That neighborhood was called Stoner Hill. I grew up listening to the women there. Everyone in that phalanx had a family church, and most believed in God and agreed that it was through Jesus Christ that we all gained salvation. Growing up, I don't recall ever meeting someone who didn't have a faith—at least no one who would admit such a thing out loud. It was a place where all doctrine was respected; even door-knocking Jehovah's Witnesses were given the opportunity to speak their piece. Yes, Shreveport was the kind of city where everyone had a church, temple, or chapel they considered theirs, even if they'd only seen it from the inside a dozen times. A child from Stoner Hill seldom made it out of puberty without a distant cousin or a neighbor dragging the youngster off to recite New Testament Scripture in the Easter pageant or sing carols in the Christmas program, blessing the child with at least a C.M.E. membership: attendance at Christmas, Mother's Day, and Easter.

I've been reciting Bible verses since I was old enough to say "Jesus wept." My great-grandmother, Big Momma, used to say about the Bible, "Baby, you can find a word to carry you through anythang." Still, my very religious family managed to pick and choose which Scriptures to live by. The men would pray up a miracle in the deacons' corner and then enjoy a strong glass or two of Jack Daniel's after church. The women sang in the choir but cursed like sailors when their team fumbled on *Monday Night Football.* "I could pull up my skirt and beat that sorry-ass receiver to the ball," Big Momma would shout from the kitchen while stacking freshly washed dishes in cabinets.

I spent most of my childhood summers down the road from home at Big Momma's house. We began each day with the morning ritual she referred to as her labor of love—combing my hair. I would sit on the porch floor with my feet swinging over its edge while my head bobbed back and forth between Big Momma's legs as she tugged, parted, and braided my long, thick, nappy hair. Big Momma always sat perfectly upright, sucking in her breath with each drag of the comb, then releasing the air from her hollow Cherokee cheeks, never once bending her back. After she finished the job, she'd pat me on my head and say, "Now you beautiful." I'd rush to the bathroom, stand on the toilet seat, and peer over the sink into the mirror, eager to view this new and beautiful me. Of course, she never materialized. All I ever saw was my chubby face with a crown of lopsided plaits and a mouth full of what my momma teasingly called "beaver teeth" because they looked large enough to saw wood.

Besides our grooming, Big Momma and her band of swearing sopranos made sure their offspring got a proper Christian upbringing. Every Sunday there was morning church school and Baptist Training Union. And for one week every August the young ones were herded to Grambling, Louisiana, a small college town, for a gigantic statewide revival called Youth-En-Camp. Although the drive took only a few hours, it had the feel of a great adventure. This was due in part to the parcel of sheets, dresses, and fried chicken that always accompanied me but also because the decreased supervision allowed me to experience free will. It was during one of these revivals that I became hopeful that I would one day look into the mirror and see beauty in myself.

I was thirteen at the time—too old to be in one of the crayon classrooms but still too awkward to be cool. Before that summer I'd never thought that I could be beautiful—perhaps cute, on a good day, but never glamorous, radiant, or enchanting. Of course, up to that point, the only form of beauty I knew to desire was physical splendor, in which category I was sorely lacking. I was the tallest girl in my eighth-grade class, and when I tried to walk in dress shoes, my heels would slide out, causing me to trip over myself. Naturally, my only concern was ridding myself of awkwardness. Beauty was something I saw only in others. A woman's even-colored skin and bright white teeth made her beautiful, never the inner peace that sparkled in her eyes. I greatly admired the little girl's sunny Easter dress, adorned with white bows and ribbons, but gave no thought to the mother—needle in one hand, iron in the other, creating this lovely vision. And Big Momma's front lawn with its velvet violets, deep purple grape suckers, and yellow sunflowers floating in the air like balloons was beautiful, but never once did I consider the care they were given even as the flowers' first petals danced indiscriminately in the sunlight. I had always focused on my plainness, and it was this sorry image of myself that I took with me to Youth-En-Camp that summer. Only later would I understand that real beauty emanates from the heart.

At camp that summer, our daily activities started with 5 A.M. prayer and devotion, during which I often volunteered to pray out loud so that everyone could hear my conversation with God. Somewhere along the way I got the notion that you were the biggest coward and hypocrite if you didn't want to pray out loud. That to me suggested you were ashamed of the Lord, and even with all my insecurities and teenage angst, I wanted to be bigger than that. After breakfast, there was Bible-study class, lunch, and midday worship. There teenagers would offer testimonials, and thanks to those I referred to as our "holy staples" (they seemed as necessary to our religious experience as the flour and canned goods that lined the shelves of our neighborhood general store)—the girl who'd been suffering from multiple sclerosis who was walking for the first time in five years and the boys who overnight had been called to preach—the standard for godliness was set high.

Following dinner and church service came the dating game, which commenced on a dusty bridge that stretched a half mile long and linked Grambling to the town of Ruston. As a symbolic gesture, the bridge was closed while the campers lined up at its foot, over a thousand of us girls on the right while the boys, far fewer in number, stood on the left. Once we were all settled down, the boys would cross the street and become like ants sifting through a mound of brown sugar, seeking the perfect young lady to escort to the other side of the bridge for evening service at Rocky Valley Baptist Church. I was always with the leftover girls, and we would trail behind the couples, walking with our heads down, kicking at stones in the street.

Once the service got going, some of the girls would pretend to catch the Holy Spirit, which in our crowd of excitable teenagers was accompanied by a chorus of high-pitched screams, a tossing of hands, body tremors, and an uncontrollable desire to run up and down the aisles. A boy would then come to the rescue of his chosen damsel. In a coy attempt to contain her, the young man would often hold her down while reaching under her dress and squeezing her butt. I couldn't wait to be one of those high school girls who in a frenzy got to kick off my black patent-leather Nina sling-backs and get my butt squished by a handsome preacher boy. This would happen with several couples without fail year after year, and every time, after a few days of camp, our chaperones would realize that what raged within us was induced more by hormones than by the Holy Spirit.

Everyone knew the routine. Within three days of such free-for-all, an announcement would move our 11 P.M. curfew to 9:30. Dorm counselors would distribute leaflets listing the hazards (both spiritual and otherwise) of teen promiscuity. The boys and girls would no longer be allowed to couple but would instead have to sit on separate sides of the auditorium during all services. Then all this would culminate in a stern lecture on the sacredness of our bodies and the proper behavior one should exhibit in an Assembly of God.

That particular summer, however, our new director, Reverend Frank, tried a different approach. The minister was in his twenties and wore his youth on his sleeve. His shoes were always the exact color of his suits, whether burgundy, green, or mustard yellow. His hair was done up in glycerin curls that hung down on the back of his neck. The day he came forward to address our behavior, he knew he didn't need to holler and spit because his carriage and deportment had already captured our attention. That fact was obvious from the way our eyes followed him reverently as he moved to the center of the pulpit. Once in position, he leaned over the podium, pulled up his suit sleeves, and tapped his foot on the floor. His eyes moved about the room dramatically. Then he stood still until the only sound filtering the air was the hum of his breath over the microphone. After clearing his throat, he began to read from Genesis in a deep voice that made every syllable resonate.

When men began to increase in number on the earth and daughters were born to them, the sons of God saw that the daughters of men were beau-ti-full . . .

He snapped his neck up, startling us. Then he rocked his head back and asked in a teasing way, "Y'all having a good time? Y'all having fun yet? Young ladies, y'all looking good in those Calvins, ain't they, boys?"

"Yeah," the boys said, smiling broadly.

"I can't believe they are able to wear them even tighter than they did last summer. I know you fellas can barely keep your eyes in your head. Y'all acting just like the fellas did in Noah's day." Everybody looked around, not quite sure where he was going. "Why y'all looking at me funny? Did you think you invented the super freak? Shoot, women been fine and men been looking since Adam took a bite out of that apple." We fell over ourselves laughing. "Ain't nothin' wrong with that either . . . until you start getting carried away. Then, like God did with the flood, I gotta rein you back in."

Again Reverend Frank took a serious look at the Word.

And the Lord said, My spirit shall not always strive with man, for he also is flesh . . .

"See," he said, playful again, "those men were like you boys. They were like, 'I gotta have me some of that.'" Then, after taking stock of the assemblage, he yelled out, "Hey, which one of you fellas got the most phone numbers? Come on, I know y'all keeping score. Rodney," the reverend shouted out at a tall boy with eyebrows so thick they almost touched, "how many numbers you got?"

"Not too many, Rev," the boy said, looking as though he'd been caught with his hand going up a girl's skirt. A boy sitting next to him chimed in, "He's got over forty last we checked, Rev."

"Now, don't y'all wonder what Rodney or anybody is gon' do with forty phone numbers in one week's time? You know, it's a funny thing about sin and the flesh—they feed off of each other. They're like lined-up dominoes. When one falls, so go the others. That's what happened to Noah's posse." By speaking to us in our own language, Reverend Frank tightened his grip on our consciousness. He stared back at us gravely before continuing to read.

The earth was corrupt before God, and filled with violence; for all flesh had corrupted his way upon earth.

"They weren't just lusting after women either," Reverend Frank said with a finger in the air. "The men competed for the biggest boat to get around in, the flashiest cave to call home. They started lying on each other, being jealous of their fine women, and wanting what the other man had. They forgot all about God and the good that he put us here to do. And what do you think God did? He got mad, just like we did with y'all earlier this week." Back to his Bible he went.

Noah found grace in the yes of the Lord. Noah was just a man and perfect in his generations, and Noah walked with God.

"Now, girls, here's something y'all can shout about. No matter what we've done in the past, God is always looking for the beautiful among us." Leaning closer toward us, he asked, "Why y'all still looking at me funny? Y'all still don't get what I'm trying to say? See, those folk were beautiful on the outside, but on the inside they were busy starting a whole lot of confusion, all but Noah with his old, beat-up, half-blind self. Noah was six hundred years old, so you know he had to be plenty ugly. But Noah was the one in whose eyes God saw beauty. 'Why?' you ask. Because Noah was the one searching himself. Noah was the one listening to the instruction of the spirit of God that dwells within each of us. You see, Noah knew what y'all need to get hip to."

Reverend Frank stooped and fanned his hands from his lavender shoes up to his matching jacket collar. "All of this is going to fade away, and all you'll be left with are the drops of grace you've left in your path. The day you can look in the mirror and say to yourself, 'Yesterday I did the best I could and today I'll do better than that,' is the day that you'll see beauty in your eyes."

Reverend Frank walked to the edge of the stage. With each of his steps, our bodies grew heavier, sinking deeper into the red pew cushions. "You see, young people, we have the power to transform ourselves." He clasped his hands together and pulled them into his chest as though he was pleading with us. "Do this for me," he said slowly, in a somber voice. "Close your eyes and picture the most beautiful thing you've ever seen." I closed my eyes and saw Big Momma's front yard and the wildly sprinkled violets that she nourished with water long before anything pretty ever emerged from the ground. "It may be a pretty face you're seeing, but more than likely it's not. It may be something as small as a ladybug crawing up your arm or as grand as the Christmas lights that hang across Natchitoches during the holidays, but it's something that leaves you filled with a blessedness."

Reverend Frank seemed to shuffle with his thoughts for a moment before continuing. "Let me show it to you another way. Think of a time when you've felt beautiful. Not pretty or admired, but when you were filled with happiness, optimism, and thanksgiving. Picture in your mind's eye the last time you felt safe, at home in yourself."

I didn't have to think back far. I would never have thought to call it such, but this feeling of beauty had come over me just a few months earlier when our family had gathered together for a Sunday celebration. Big Momma had sat in the center of a long banquet table. Flanking her were my sweet-faced grandmother and Momma. Forming an arch around them were my grandfather and many of my aunts and uncles. I sat sprinkled amongst them with all the other children, listening to our parents reflect on the many tragedies they'd endured and the things from which our family had been delivered. As the stories piled up, they all seemed to be saying what I felt at that moment—that every sadness is made bearable and every victory that much sweeter because we shared it all with one another. Among them, I felt loved, complete, and safe.

When I opened my eyes, I saw the church with blurred vision. I didn't look around but knew that everyone around me was crying too. Reverend Frank's sermon had touched us like none we'd heard before. During most scoldings from the pulpit, we'd become disinterested stones listening to lectures that perplexed us as much as the story of Hesiod's *Creation*. But when Reverend Frank sat down, we were silent, still drinking his words. Over the years, their meaning seeped into my heart slowly, like rain into the ground. I have come to understand the many levels of beauty, the core of which for me is home, where my family nurtured the beauty in me the way Big Momma cherished her flowers. Before the spring tickled the buds, Big Momma was filled with anticipation. When her violets blossomed with an intensity that outshone anything her garden had produced the year before, she would clasp her hands together and pull them into her chest much the way Reverend Frank had. "Look a' 'dem, Londa," she would say, gazing out over her flowers. "Lord, they beautiful."

Hers was the beauty in the order of life. The fecund glory of her garden was all the sweeter because of its tenacious place in God's creation. When the days got shorter and the swelling pears and figs thudded to the ground, she knew, as I came to, that they would all rise again come spring like the next generation. It was the inevitability of that return, not the flowers and fruits themselves, that infused Big Momma's faith, and so it was with my gap-toothed beauty. She knew that our family had already planted the seeds—of mistakes, triumphs, and, most important, love. So she could see the hope in a little girl's smile and know that with her wise ministration it would endure through the seasons ahead.

Shay Youngblood

I started writing stories because I wanted to impress the school librarian. I wrote serial drama stories in the style of the soap operas my great-grandmother watched every week, the kind of stories that made my friends who read them ask, "What happens next?" I wanted to write adventure stories that made readers laugh out loud, or made them want to tell somebody, "I love you" the moment the last page was turned. I wanted to write something that would move a reader from dreaming to action.

My life as a writer was rather accidental. I wrote because I had nowhere else to put my emotions. There seemed no other way to express my anger at injustice, my wonder at love, my grief over loss. I grew to love even the physical act of putting pen to paper. I've written poetry, short stories, stage plays, a screenplay, a children's play, articles about food, kissing, and buying a new bed. I enjoy the challenge of writing in different genres, finding new language and ways of expression.

Black Girl in Paris was inspired by a year I spent in Paris—1986. I knew James Baldwin lived in the south of France and so I invented a character, Eden, who takes the kind of journey I did emotionally. In the novel I explored the ways in which an individual could create identity, cross sexual and cultural boundaries. Even the city of Paris becomes a character in the novel. Paris has always been large in my imagination. I knew it was the kind of place that artists went to find the freedom to create and once they were in Paris, well, something happened. In my imagination something was in the air or the water that would transform you. My main character, Eden, found that the writer's life was not so glamorous as she imagined, that freedom had a price and Paris was not without its own variety of racism.

Lover

From *Black Girl in Paris*, a novel

I HEARD HIM FIRST, so I couldn't say that Ving was good-looking to my eyes, but the sound of his horn made him forever handsome to my heart. He was the sound of a slow train leaving, a boat rocking in a stormy port, like something that could take you away or bring you home again. Before my eyes found him, I expected to see an old black man blowing, but Ving was far from that. He was forty then, but he looked to me like an overgrown little boy among the adults.

Do you know what it means to miss New Orleans . . . ?

The music was a strong rope pulling me through the crowded garden, toward him and those dark, blue, familiar notes.

He was pulling me home again with his blues.

His long, dark, curly hair was pulled back into a fluffy ponytail. He wore thick, black-framed glasses on his heart-shaped face. He held his shiny silver trumpet in the air and gestured with it as if blowing holes through the trees. He was tall, flush faced, and lean. He looked like he needed a good meal. His jeans were rumpled and his red wool sweater was unraveling at the wrists. His hiking boots marched softly in time to the music. Eyes closed, head down, then bobbing up again when he blew, he filled his lungs, then his cheeks with wind that he directed through the horn into disturbing sounds. I used to sing the blues like that, at night in smoky places, making old men cry and young women sway and sing along. I could feel his music and it made me miss home. When Ving opened them, his big glossy eyes seemed almost brimming with tears, and his dented lips were pushed out as if he was about to kiss someone.

Indego and Carmen argued all the way to Kenya and back. After a few days of her complaints about money and her endless physical ailments he had returned to Paris until he found another invitation to winter in the sun. When Indego saw me walking past the American Bookstore, he invited me to David's monthly soirée. Artists of all kinds and those who just wanted to be near them came together on the first Sunday of every month in David's atelier near Parc Monceau to eat, drink, and talk politics. By the time we arrived it was just turning dark. Indego pulled a small piece of paper from his breast pocket and squinted at the numbers on its creased surface. He carefully punched in the entrance code on the silver numeric pad bolted inside the arched doorway. The enormous red wooden door was carved with sea creatures. A narrow stone path cut sharply through a wild garden toward a pair of two-story lofts, each with a wall of windows. Our host used one of the upper lofts as a photography studio and lived downstairs, where the soirées were held. The floors were covered with large black futons, where his friends and friends of friends could stay a night or more if they were adventurous and could stand the noise of happiness. The second loft, at the back of the garden, was occupied by an ancient Hungarian count, who according to Indego spent all day sipping cognac in his bathtub. The count no longer paid rent, but David didn't have the heart to throw him out, since he had gambled all his money away.

Indego warned me to be careful of David. "He's kinky," he said with a grin, making an obscene gesture with his hands. It sounded like a challenge. I imagined that having sex with David would be only slightly more daring than having dinner with him. David was a barrel-chested, bearded lumberjack type from Minnesota with a deep, hearty laugh and a philosophical interest in the international politics of sex. He was friendly with everyone and made the sound of a large animal welcoming home its mate whenever he greeted someone he knew. He lived with Basil, a young, frail English poet, and Medea, a voluptuous Greek dancer and performance artist, who was dancing topless against the stone garden wall when we arrived. Indego said he slept with them both and anyone else who'd join them. David was standing at the top of the garden, and when I came near enough he grasped me in an enveloping bear hug that lifted me off my feet and whispered something I couldn't quite understand in my ear. His beard tickled me and I laughed. His smile was warm and wicked. He slapped the leather seat of his pants and winked down at me. Wrapping his thick arm around my waist he moved me though the crowd and Indego followed. I felt light in his arms. He introduced us to a small knot of trendy, well-dressed older women, who smiled politely, acknowledging us with slight nods. When David and Indego stepped away to get drinks, the women turned from me to continue their conversation in French. More than thirty people were gathered in the front garden, snapping their fingers and shaking their bells as accompaniment to Medea's performance. Her long, gray-streaked hennaed hair fanned about her bare shoulders, her strong tanned arms waved in the air like long grass underwater. Her large breasts rolled back and forth across her chest. Her soft round belly trembled. A gold coin belt around her curvy waist jingled, and a long red silk skirt whipped around her thick legs as her bare feet stamped down the damp earth as if it were on fire. David was distracted by the sound of the coins and bells, and I watched him join Medea in the garden. He stripped off his shirt, exposing his huge hairy chest, and moved in circles around her like a big dancing bear.

Indego handed me a drink and gripped me by the elbow, and we walked on toward the house. Inside, a dozen or so young men who all looked like models were sitting, smoking, whispering in small groups along the steps of a wide oak staircase. They were lit by small white votive candles in the curve of each step. Glittering faces. Mascaraed eyes. Tinted lips, wet hair sculpted with styling gel. Their bodies cut sharp profiles in tight T-shirts and tailored pants. The scent of clove cigarettes and perfume overwhelmed me. Their glamour dazzled me. They all were smoking and talking with their hands.

Indego held onto my elbow until we passed the staircase and the main room of the house. Noisy conversation rose and fell all around us. Most of the guests were speaking English, but I could hear French and Spanish mingled with flat American accents too. About twenty people were standing crowded together in a corner of the room, drinking red wine from plastic cups.

Indego tried to keep an eye on me, but he kept getting pulled into conversations and was soon in a heated discussion about the Ethiopian economic situation with a British architect who lived in Nairobi, and I was left alone. I tried to introduce myself to three French women dressed in slim black leather pants and white linen shirts, but they were interested only in the German painter who was trying to describe to them in his limited English how to buy an authentic Turkish carpet. I did meet a carpenter from Oklahoma, Polish refugees, a psychiatrist from Argentina, a painter from Costa Rica.

The sound of the horn stopped suddenly and I missed it. I pressed myself against the wall and made my way into the kitchen area to freshen my glass from an unlabeled gallon jug of wine on a table filled with bottles of alcohol. I heard a voice behind me.

"Ving," he said. As I turned around I almost splashed the front of his sweater with wine. Several drops hit the floor instead. He stretched out his hand for me to shake, and when I took it he held onto mine as if he was falling and needed me to lift him up.

I was staring into bright blue eyes. Something hard pressed into the top of my thigh, and I looked down and saw the silver horn dangling from the fingers of his other hand.

"Eden." I wiggled my fingers in his, but he didn't let go, and because his hand was firm, warm, I relaxed.

"Were you playing before?" I asked.

"You like jazz?" His accent was American, Southern.

"I like to listen to music I can dance to." I pulled my hand away from his and held my plastic cup of wine in both hands between us.

"What kind of music is that?"

"Tina Turner, Aretha, Smoky Robinson, Chaka Khan, you know . . . *soul* music," I said, twisting my hips and shifting my shoulders from side to side as if my body could hear James Brown on his knees singing "Baby Please."

"But jazz is soul music," he said. There was something deep and rich about Ving's music, and the way he said "soul" made me believe he had it. Ving put his dented lips to his horn and blew out something I could dance to.

"That's all right." I danced a few steps, and he waved his trumpet around me like a snake charmer. When I noticed people staring at us I stopped, and he made a romantic flourish with his horn. There was applause from the people behind us in the center of the room. I took a sip of my wine to disguise my nervousness.

"If you heard Sonny Rollins play the sax, he'd change your mind. Have you been to the new dance club at Bastille?" Ving asked, picking at the loose threads at his wrist.

"It costs two hundred francs to get in."

"Two-fifty, but you get a free drink,' he said, as if this was a bargain.

"Any way you look at it, that's a lot of money. I could get a room for the night and a turkey dinner." I took another nervous sip of the tangy red wine and peeked at him over the edge of my cup. Was he asking me out on a date? I wondered if he could dance to soul music. Where I came from, blacks and whites didn't dance together. The white people I had seen dancing on TV seemed to be listening to a different beat, dancing to sounds that didn't have anything to do with the music.

"Don't be afraid of me."

"I'm not afraid," I said, but I was lying. "I don't know enough about you to be afraid."

"I'm forty years old. I was born in New Orleans on Louis Armstrong's birthday. My father was an architect. He died in a car accident when I was three. My mother was a Southern belle. She was crowned Miss French Quarter when she was sixteen and never worked another day in her life. She lives in the south of France with my sister. I don't eat pork, and I laugh in my sleep. I came to Paris to play for a friend's wedding ten years ago and I never left."

"Why did you stay?"

"I went to a gypsy and had my fortune told."

"Serious."

"I guess I was looking for a new note. A different way of being in the music."

"Did you find it?"

"I'm still looking, but I'm enjoying the search. What are you doing here?"

"I'm looking for Langston," I blurted out. I felt dizzy.

"You do know that Langston Hughes is dead."

"I know that," I said. "But James Baldwin isn't." The wine was making me hot. Sweat began forming on my upper lip.

"You know him?" He seemed interested.

"When I finished reading *Giovanni's Room* I felt like I knew him . . . like he knew me. Like he knew everything about loneliness and a lot about pain. His stories make me believe that what I know matters, but what I *do* is more important than anything else. Do you know him?"

"*Another Country, The Fire Next Time, Nobody Knows My Name*. He writes in the language of jazz. He plays the blues on a typewriter. You could say I know him. Jimmy was here in Paris a few months ago."

"You've met him?" Now I was interested.

"He comes to the club where I play sometimes. We had a few drinks, told some lies."

Indego was watching us from where he was holding court on the stairs. He motioned for me to come over, but I ignored him. Ving had hypnotized me.

"I'm writing a novel," I said.

This seemed to intrigue him.

"What's it about?"

"I don't know yet. I guess I'm kind of like you, looking for a new way to be in language, to bring life to words, to make stories real and important like Langston did, like Baldwin does."

I told him about working for the poet Elizabeth, cooking, cleaning, bathing and caring so much it hurt, and he understood why I was so tired. He seemed to understand why being in Paris was so important to me. He promised to help me find Baldwin. His face was incredibly sweet and soft.

"I'm tired, listening to your routine. You don't have much time to write, do you?"

I shook my head as if to clear my mind, took a deep breath, and tried to think of an excuse to leave the party. I was beginning to wonder what sense it had made to leave the comfort of home. Ving seemed to be listening to me, but his eyes roamed around the room. He acted as if he knew everybody, and nodded to people coming and going to the terrace outside, smoking cigarettes.

"Do you want to go listen to jazz sometime?" he asked, looking into the well of his horn.

I was stunned by his question, and it must have shown on my face. I had never been on a date with a white man. I was afraid, but I did want to know this man. I wanted to listen to his private music. I didn't say anything for a minute. I just stared at him as if he had hit me on the head with his horn.

When I was growing up in Georgia, young white boys and men in cars and pickup trucks drove through my neighborhood at night, stopping young black girls to ask if they wanted a ride. My father warned me that those men and boys meant us no good and that all most of the pickup girls had to show for their night rides were light-skinned babies and the distinction of being called niggers when the boys' parents or wives found out. They were raped and left by the side of the road when they were no longer useful. My father called these men white devils, and my mother said trust none but Jesus, and we prayed for the souls of white folks.

And then Ving began to shine, and when he looked at me his face flushed as if he'd been caught. His blue eyes shimmered.

"Yeah, why not," I said, sure my father in heaven would never find out about my betrayal.

Indego reached me, grabbing my arm, pulling me away from the devil.

"You're with me," Indego said, as if I belonged to him. I didn't resist, because I had made up my mind and Ving had offered me something I didn't want to resist.

Later in the evening Ving came up behind me and slipped his phone number into the pocket of my coat and walked away playing a lively New Orleans funeral march, and it was the music that made me decide to call him. I felt that another useless belief had died and that the road ahead of me was paved with new riches. I remembered that I was in Paris and there was no one to judge my actions, no one to remind me of my disloyalty to the race, to accuse me of losing my blackness, no one to remind me of the master-slave relationship. I was a free woman and could choose whom and what I wanted.

"Watch out for them musicians, you can't depend on them. They married to the music," Indego said, watching me watch Ving march out into the garden to serenade the male models, who had stripped down to stark white briefs. They were dancing together under a willow tree decorated with a string of lights that twinkled like real stars. I had never seen men dance together, but there in David's garden it seemed natural. They did not look wicked, they looked happy, and I was happy for them.

I didn't ask what Indego meant about musicians, I just followed him around until it was time to go back to my little room in the house where I was an au pair and sleep in a bed not my own, dreaming of a bed in which I could wake up without my body being on fire.

A few days after David's soirée I had an unexpected holiday. The children's school was closed for the day so that its broken heating system could be repaired. The mother offered to take the children to the zoo. Relieved and elated at my good fortune I took a bus to the Latin Quarter and walked along the quai St-Michel, near the hotel where I stayed my first night in Paris, mingling with the tourists. The Latin Quarter was like a village in many ways. I began to recognize familiar faces. Waiters in the little cafés I had gone to with Delphine remembered me. It was cloudy and raining lightly, but to me it was a beautiful day and all I had to do was daydream and look at the sights. On her days off the Welsh au pair used to follow American tour groups and blend in, making friends with older couples at the back of the group. She would often be asked to join them for meals and invited onto their large buses for tours of the countryside. I could not blend in so well. My skin marked me, set me apart even though I was the American.

I wanted something good to read, and I refused to go to the American Bookstore, where the ugly green suit might be waiting to humiliate me. Indego told me that sometimes the African booksellers had books in English by African Americans. I wondered if there were other books about the black artists' experience in Paris. If there was a guide. An African bookseller wearing a black knit cap pulled over his ears and a short, puffy black parka over a long white caftan shuffled in place, rubbing his hands together as if warming them over a fire. He greeted me with a broad smile, flashing beautiful teeth, one of which was solid gold. His eyes were interested in the more prosperous tourists who passed by his stall to jostle each other at the next stand for postcards of old Paris and French colonial scenes. I looked through the stacks of *Ebony* magazines encased in dusty plastic envelopes. I picked up a magazine with Dorothy Dandridge on the cover. She was so sexy and glamorous and she looked out at me as if offering me something wonderful. Out of the corner of my eye I saw a familiar face. Ving, the horn player, was talking to a tourist in front of the postcard stall. When he saw me he winked and tipped his horn in my direction. He finished his conversation with the tourist and moved toward me.

"Do you think it's raining in Algeria?" he asked, looking up at the sky. My ears were delighted by the sound of his English.

"Is African water wet?" I answered in code as if I were Mata Hari, a spy in the house of a stranger, waiting for a sign.

"Good answer." He smiled, and I bit my suddenly dry lips, aching for a word.

"I didn't get a chance to call you."

"You don't have to now." He walked with me across the bridge to a popular ice cream stand and bought a large cone with three flavors. We took turns eating it, licking the drops off our fingers. He talked jazz like most men I'd known talked sports or cars. Miles Davis, John Coltrane,

Charlie Parker, Lester Young, Coleman Hawkins, King Oliver, and his musical godfather, Louis Armstrong. Most of the names meant nothing to me. He talked about these men as if he knew them, as if they were part of his family. They had taught him about life, he said. He knew things because of them. He knew other important things, like how airplanes stayed in the sky, and he knew philosophy and literature and geography and history. He read Greek plays for fun. He was full of information and kept his heart where I could see it. He wanted to know everything about me, and when I told him, he listened as if my story were the most important in the world. He kept a respectful distance but let me know he would like to come closer when I was ready.

I couldn't turn away from the sound of Ving's voice. When he talked about jazz it sounded as if he was talking about sex. He bought a book of French poetry and we sat on a park bench, where he read to me from Baudelaire's *Les Fleurs du Mal*. I didn't understand the poems in French, but Ving made them sound like romantic love songs. He translated one of the poems for me. "A Une Dame Creole," "To a Creole Woman." Written as a compliment to an exotic island beauty, the poem stated that if she came to Paris, her beauty would inspire sonnets in the hearts of poets, making the French even more submissive than her island blacks.

Later, on the phone, Ving talked to me about sex all night long. His words made me want to come. I whispered with him in the dark after I was done for the day being a poet's helper and an au pair. I sat in the TV room in my nightgown at the card table by the blue light of the mute TV. I was pudding when he softly said words like "pussy" and "fuck." For days all we did was talk. *He tells me what to do to my body in the blue light and I do it.* I slid my body onto the floor under the table and I touched myself. His breathing was deep and steady, soothing. I waited. He was the conductor and my body and entire orchestra.

One finger. Now two.

"What do you smell like? What do you taste like?" he whispered.

I came only when he told me to.

"Are you with me?" he breathed, taking care not to rush the moment.

"Yes." I twisted the phone cord around my wrist, waiting patiently to see how far we would go this time. On Sunday after the family had left for a picnic in the country, I invited Ving to the apartment. He arrived with a bottle of red wine and a small gold box of chocolates. I closed the door to my little room, and we lay on the carpet in front of the tall open window.

The view of the sky was half-obscured by bare-limbed trees. The wine was dry and tasted like cherries. The chocolates were filled with a dark rich mousse. Ving pushed my shirt up over my stomach. He melted one of the little chocolates by rubbing it across my bare belly, then took a sip of wine and licked the chocolate off my skin. He made little sucking noises and tickled me with his breath.

"Let me touch you," he said softly. And he did with good intentions, but his hands were large and clumsy.

"Kiss me there." I pointed to my chest.

I tried to focus on his tongue, soft, wet, and dangerously close to engulfing me. It snaked and glided across the broken places. Suddenly his mouth was full of my breast. I tried to speak, to give him more commands, but I couldn't. There were no words to tell him what I wanted, and even then I wasn't sure he would understand. I wanted tenderness and whispers, rough talk and a little pain. I wanted to feel something deep inside me, pushing to the other side. Shifting my body above his, I slow danced on his lap. I was afraid to need something so much. I was terrified. I pushed against him, slowly guiding him inside me.

"Hold me," he said.

I leaned forward and I took him in my arms and held him. I took a holiday from my body. I became someone else. I watched impassively as the white stream of his cum soaked into the carpet.

When I walked through the park after being with Ving, a new feeling hung in the air around me. On a quiet street under the leaves of a plane tree, love became a possibility. I wanted to tell somebody how new I felt.

Days spent cooking and cleaning for the children and looking after the poet passed in a blur. One Saturday night, after I walked the dog and put the children to bed, I took the metro to Montparnasse to meet Ving at his apartment. We had a date to hear a live jazz concert. Ving told me that he lived down the street from one of Picasso's studios and around the block from the eighteenth-century *maison* where Balzac wrote and hid from his creditors. Ving's place was on the third floor of an old, well-kept building, in a back courtyard. The one-bedroom apartment had a full bath with hot and cold running water. I pushed open the huge door and entered the quiet courtyard. I crossed the clean-swept atrium and entered the hallway of the building. I pressed the light switch, but before I could reach the third floor the light went out and I was surrounded by pitch blackness. I pressed myself against the cracked plaster wall and slowly made my way up the next floor. Food odors were strong. Garlic and onions seemed to sizzle in the air. I walked carefully up the narrow winding staircase.

"Eden?" I heard my name being whispered in the darkness from the floor above. "Follow the sound of my voice. I'm here." Ving was standing in the doorway of his apartment with a big smile on his face.

"I found you," I said, and we hugged each other in the darkness.

Inside Ving's apartment there were books and records everywhere. One entire wall was a floor-to-ceiling built-in bookcase. Framed black-and-white photographs of musicians from Paris in the Fifties lined another of the crisp white walls. The lighting was low, and a lamp shaded by antique lace gave off a yellowish glow. He offered me a drink, but I declined. My hands were shaking. I sat on the sofa and watched him pull his hair back into a ponytail with a rubber band. He wrapped a scarf around his neck and slipped into a navy blue wool peacoat. He took both my hands and pulled me off the sofa and suddenly we were standing so close we could have kissed. I wanted to. My body hesitated. I looked into the flame of his blue eyes and saw something tender there. I slid my arms around his waist and laid my head on his chest. I could feel his heart beating. His arms wrapped around me, and we stood like that, holding each other as if we could delay an important decision.

"Don't you think we should get married?" He sounded serious, but he couldn't be.

"I don't know anything about you," I said into his chest.

"I told you everything about me that was important the first time I met you."

"Not statistics. Tell me a secret," I said. "Something you've never told anyone before."

A quiet mist seemed to settle over the room. Ving pulled me down to the floor, and we sat with our backs against the sofa, our eyes looking at the blank wall in front of us as if the images of his life were rolling against it. I leaned into his side, let him hold me close.

"I used to dress up in my sister's clothes."

I tried to imagine him in a dress, and it wasn't so hard. In some ways he was soft like a woman, gentle, pretty. We blinked and kept looking at the wall, trying to see what was in front of both of us.

"It must've been fun playing dress-up," I said, twisting a lock of his long hair around my finger.

"Yeah, it was fun." He sounded sarcastic. He started picking at the nap in the carpet then crossed his arm over his chest.

"Doesn't sound like fun. Did you get caught?" I giggled, stroking the thick veins on the inside of his wrist.

He hesitated, then curled up beside me. His arm was heavy across my belly. He smelled like smoke, oranges, and wine. I was sorry I laughed. I stroked his hair, kissed the top of his head. He became sober, serious, almost too heavy to hold in my arms. His words were like stones he laid at my feet. *I have become wet earth for stories like these, they take root in me and grow wild, nearly choking me.*

"Every summer my sister went to visit relatives in the south of France. I went to the baby-sitter's house in the mornings, but I spent the afternoons wearing my sister's dresses. Flowered ones with puffed sleeves, simple shifts, and velvet jumpers with bows. My mother caught me after I'd done it only a few times, but she wasn't upset. She said it was our secret. One day she took me shopping for my own dresses. She kept them locked in a suitcase in a corner of the attic. Every summer my mother called me Marie. She plaited ribbons in my hair and bathed me every night in warm milk. She was very affectionate with me and held me like this, but she touched me there. She touched me there."

His tears stained the carpet like blood. I turned to him, attempted to protect him from waves crashing all around us. He crawled inside me, attaching himself to my lungs, my liver, my heart. He was hard, and once he was inside me we rocked back and forth. We made love slowly, tenderly on the floor, in the dim light. My body sucked poison from him and he found relief.

I was not prepared for that kind of secret. My stomach knotted as if I had been the one hurt. I wanted to take it back, make everything all right, but I knew that would be useless.

"I'm sorry," I said, not knowing what else to say.

"You didn't hurt me."

"Do you still see her?" I was hoping his mother was dead. His pain was still visible on his skin.

"I haven't for a long time. Years. I don't want to talk about her anymore."

"Do you want to stay here?" I stroked his back. His fingers traced the outline of my ears, my face and neck.

"I think we'd better go," he said, pulling away.

We dressed in the dim light and moved around the room in silence with the mean secret between us. I kept hold of his right hand, and we walked like that, my brown hand in his pale one, to the boulevard to catch a taxi to the other side of town, and the world did not swallow us up.

The Roxy was packed. A line wrapped around the block. The names of three musicians whom I'd never heard of were emblazoned on the marquee. Sonny Rollins was the headliner. Ving took my arm and led the way to the front door, pushing a path for us. At the front of the line he flashed a press pass one of his journalist friends had loaned him, and suddenly we were inside the glittering lobby and up the red-carpeted stairs and leaning back into the dark plush balcony seats in a theater packed with more than five hundred people. When the house lights dimmed Ving took my hand and put it in his pocket.

The first note startled me. A sharp, long, winding thread of sound that stretched far beyond my notions of the limits of music. The second note danced, the third made me want to stand up and shout. Sonny Rollins played the sax like Mahalia sang gospel like John Lee Hooker sang the blues like a preacher prayed on Sunday, with true devotion. I became a believer. This was soul music. My eyes were wet from crying. I was grateful to the messenger. I turned and kissed Ving on his cheek. I had found a new spice on an undiscovered island in my very own sea.

After the concert we walked along the quai. Moonlight was reflected in the Seine. The water looked like blue ink.

"I feel like I've been to church. I want to write like that," I said.

"You'll do it too. When you get your room to write," he said.

"This is what I feel when I read Baldwin. Like I've found my original language." I could still taste the music.

"When I met Baldwin he said he really dug my music, that it reminded him of the old-school guys he listened to when he was young. 'You got talent,' he said, 'but you sound like too many other people. You've got to make the music yours. Tell your own story with the horn.' "

"What was he like?" I asked.

"Baldwin? The night I met him in the nightclub he drank a lot, laughed and told stories, repeated his favorite ones, but you never got tired of listening. He wasn't as angry as his books. He wasn't angry at me for being white, like I thought he would be. I think he is a king. He lives in the south. In Nice or someplace near Cannes. I can't remember. He said the city had too many distractions. He lives in a little village down there. The guy who owns the club where I met him would know. I'll ask." Even though I had Baldwin's address—I'd earned it working for the poet—I didn't know if I'd have the courage to use it. I wanted him to discover me. What would happen if I burst through the hedges and knocked on his door, interrupting his work or disturbing his sleep? I was so close and so afraid that I would get what I wanted after all. I wanted someone to introduce me to him and I hoped that he would be kind.

Under a streetlight I kissed Ving, spontaneously, just because I could, and he kissed me back. His kisses were eager, passionate. I was drunk with the jazz, the kisses, and the fresh night air, and hope was in me.

One of Ving's best friends was a Haitian drummer named Olu-Christophe, a handsome man in his thirties with velvety brown skin and enormous eyes. His face was a map of Africa. He played the talking drum as if possessed. Sweat streamed down his face in little rivers, his wiry warms flying, his hands moving so fast I could hardly see them. He had been a medical student in Haiti, sent to Paris eight years before to further his studies, but his family told him not to return because the government had been harsh to students returning from abroad. They were said to be agitators and suspected Communists. Many were jailed or killed with little evidence. The nearly thirty-year reign of the self-proclaimed Presidents for Life, François and Jean-Claude Duvalier, had ended earlier in the year, but Olu-Christophe was still afraid to go home. He made money playing with Ving. Sometimes he played the métro, and had been sending money home over the years. More than once he had threatened to kill Jean-Claude Duvalier and burn the bones of his father. We had dinner together one night in a Chinese restaurant near Les Halles. Olu-Christophe told us horror stories about life under a dictatorship. He said he had a plan to raise the quality of life for all Haitians. His eyes turned hard and cold, and he didn't speak again for the rest of the meal.

One night, Ving, Olu-Christophe, and I strolled along arm in arm to a club in the basement of a hotel on a side street in Bastille. Only ten or twelve tables. A five-piece band. When we entered the club, a sweaty Spaniard with jet black hair and black eyes that looked like sparkling jewels and the whitest, most perfect teeth I have ever seen was onstage. King Rain was what Ving's friend called himself, Ving called him Omar the Spaniard. He looked like a poor imitation of an Elvis impersonator in his pale blue leather jumpsuit, twisting and howling Seventies pop tunes into a microphone while two skinny white girls, one of whom was his very pregnant Russian girlfriend, gyrated in the background. The women wore garish glittery makeup, their hair teased high on their heads, their bodies squeezed into short, tight, gold tube dresses and their feet into shiny white patent-leather boots. I was shocked to see Omar's girlfriend do a split—her big belly looked like a golden bubble rising from the floor in front of her. After King Rain and his Golden Girls ended their first set they came over to sit with us. Ving bought drinks for everybody at the table. Olu-Christophe flirted with the women. They all spoke English. Ving toasted his friend's opening-night success. They passed around a cigarette I soon realized was hashish. It smelled sweet and made me a little nauseous. I suddenly thought I could speak French and managed a fractured conversation with an Arab journalist who didn't speak English at all. Perhaps I was hallucinating, but we seemed to be discussing modern-day slavery in Sudan. We talked to each other, absorbed in our tangle of languages, for what seemed like an hour. The DJ played salsa and merengue, reggae and Afro pop. When James Brown started singing "Papa's Got a Brand-New Bag," Ving pulled me up out of my seat and onto the dance floor, where he showed me just how much soul he had. His hips were fluid and his feet knew the rhythms well.

"Surprised?" he asked, shifting his shoulders and swiveling his hips like a son of James Brown.

"Truth?"

"Truth."

"You sure about your grandmother?"

"Sure about what?"

"How you got that dark curly hair in New Orleans. You sure there's no smoke in your fire? You could be my distant cousin. I'm an orphan, you know." He smiled and hugged me to him. Ving asked me if I wanted to go to his apartment. I whispered yes and kissed him softly on the ear. I wanted him to fuck me. This thought surprised me, then made itself at home. I wanted him to bury himself inside me and rock-and-roll and jazz me and moan and turn me blue and aquamarine and sink and sink and light me up from the inside. I wanted to turn him out, ruin him, make him forget all the women he ever knew before me. Forget the pain his mother caused him. My body itched against his like a cat in heat.

It was almost one o'clock in the morning when Ving and I left the club. Olu-Christophe had made friends with the single Golden Girl and left with her around midnight. Ving and I were hot and sweaty from dancing. Ving took his hair down and shook it out around his shoulders. He looked like a handsome girl. I touched his hair, then took his hand. We left our coats open and walked out into the cool night air. We walked hand in hand past several bars, toward the métro. A few blocks from the club it felt colder and I shivered. He slipped his arm around my shoulder and pulled me close. He was warm and I felt safe and new in his arms. For a few moments, the world was all right. Then the piss in the gutter began to stink. My body stiffened against Ving's as we approached a group of four young men drinking beer from bottles in front of a crowded bar. They were arguing loudly in French. The group grew quiet as we passed them. Ving didn't seem to notice, but I started to sweat and walked a little faster.

One of them spoke loud enough for us to hear. I could make out a few French words. *T'as vu, le pédé qui promène son chien noir.* Look at the queer walking his black dog. *Salope. Putain.* Bitch. Whore. They were yelling at our backs. *Salope. Putain.* Bitch. Whore. When we were only a few steps from the métro stairs a beer bottle crashed against the sidewalk a few feet in front of us. Another one flew like a missile past the left side of my face. I didn't look back. We ran down the stairs into subway and jumped the turnstile. My heart was beating like an overworked motor. We stood on the platform shaken and scared, listening for the sound of foot-steps that did not come. When the train arrived we entered the empty car and sat in silence, not touching. I was still frightened. I wanted to erase the past few minutes, but I couldn't. *Salope. Putain. Chien noir.* My libido was gone. I didn't want to have sex at all.

"Are you okay?"

I nodded, but I wasn't.

"Bastards. Stupid kids." He tried to lighten our load, but it was still too heavy to bear. Not far enough away to escape a familiar kind of humilia-tion. No translation was necessary.

"Everybody not free, somebody somewhere is a nigger tonight." My father's words blazed in my memory. Those men hadn't cared that I was American, college-educated, and Christian; all they saw was the color of my skin. Back home, I still wouldn't be able to hold Ving's hand without inviting comment or threat. What made me think I could be free? He was a white man, yet he couldn't protect me here in Paris or any part of the world. What kind of future could we have together? What about our chil-dren, if we had any? If I'd had a gun I would've killed somebody. My sweet high was gone.

We were alone in the métro car for the whole ride. The train passed my stop. We got off at Montparnasse and walked down the long deserted blocks to his building. His apartment was dark and cold inside. He lit a candle and cursed when he bumped into a stack of books. He plugged in a small electric heater, put water on to boil, and poured me a cup of hot green tea. He avoided touching me. I avoided his eyes and the secrets I would never tell. Ving wasn't upset when I asked if he would give me covers so that I could spread out on the couch cushions. He tried once more to kiss me, and I let him, but after pushed him away gently without explanation. He watched me curl up under the covers, then bent over and kissed me on my forehead. He pulled the covers up around my neck and put out the candle.

"Sweet dreams," he said. I turned my back to him and cried myself to sleep in the dark. I tried to remember that Ving was not the one who had hurt me, but all I could do was cry.

When I woke up I was cold and could hear Ving in the kitchen, feet shuffling in Italian leather slippers sent by his mother. I could smell the rich aromas of strong Turkish coffee and day-old bread toasting in the broiler. When he came into the room I reached up and put my arms around his neck and kissed his scratchy cheeks until I smelled the bread burning. We pretended we had forgotten the other pain, the thing that had grown between us the night before.

Contributors

asha bandele is the author of two books, a collection of poems, *Absence in the Palms of My Hands*, and a memoir, *The Prisoner's Wife*. She's just finished a novel about police brutality entitled *Daughter* (forthcoming in 2003). A features editor and writer for *Essence* magazine, asha lives in Brooklyn with her three-year-old, Nisa.

Lorene Cary was graduated from St. Paul's School in 1974 and received B.A. and M.A. degrees from the University of Pennsylvania in 1978. She has received Doctorates in Humane Letters from Colby College in Maine, Keene State College in New Hampshire, and Chestnut Hill College in Philadelphia. Her first book, *Black Ice*, was chosen as a Notable Book for 1992 by the American Library Association. She has also written three novels, *Pride*, *Underground Railroad*, and *The Price of a Child*, which was chosen as a "One Book, One Philadelphia" selection by the city's mayor. In 1998, Lorene Cary founded Art Sanctuary, a non-profit lecture and performance series that brings Black thinkers and artists to speak and perform at the Church of the Advocate, a National Historic Landmark Building in North Philadelphia. Cary, who is currently a Senior Lecturer in Creative Writing at the University of Pennnsylvania, lives in Philadelphia with her husband, the Rev. Robert C. Smith, and their daughters Laura and Zoë.

Veronica Chambers, formerly a culture writer for *Newsweek* and executive editor of *Savoy*, has contributed articles to *Glamour*; *O, The Oprah Magazine*; the *New York Times*; and other publications. She is the author of *Mama's Girl* and several books for children. A 2001–02 recipient of Princeton University's Hodder Fellowship, she is currently working on a novel, *Miss Black America*.

Meri Nana-Ama Danquah is the author of *Willow Weep for Me: A Black Woman's Journey Through Depression* and the editor of *Becoming American: Personal Essays by First Generation Immigrant Women*. Ms. Danquah earned her M.F.A. in creative writing and literature from Bennington College. She held a one-year appointment as Visiting Scholar at the University of Ghana, Legon's School of Communication Studies, and was a recipient of the Pauline and Henry Louis Gates Sr. Fellowship from the Djerassi Resident Artists Program. She was awarded a California Arts Council 2002 Individual Artist Fellowship in creative nonfiction. Ms. Danquah is currently writing a memoir, to be published by Riverhead Books.

Edwidge Danticat is the author of *Breath, Eyes, Memory*; *Krik? Krak!*; *The Farming of Bones*; and *Behind the Mountains*, a young adult novel, as well as a nonfiction book, *After the Dance: A Walk through Carnival in Jacmel*. She is also the editor of *The Butterfly's Way: Voices from the Haitian Dyaspora in the United States* and *The Beacon Best of 2000*.

Debra J. Dickerson is an award-winning essayist and author who writes about race, gender, and poverty in publications such as the *Washington Post*, the *New York Times Magazine*, the *Village Voice*, the *Nation*, the *New Republic*, *Slate*, *Salon*, *Mother Jones*, the *Los Angeles Times*, *Vibe*, *Talk*, and *Essence*. Widely anthologized, her essay "Who Shot Johnny?" was included in the 1997 edition of *Best American Essays* and is a staple of undergraduate composition textbooks; her essay "Digging Ditches" was named a 1996 Best American Essays Notable Essay. In 1999, she won the New York Association of Black Journalists' first-place award for personal commentary. A former *Salon* columnist and former senior editor at *U.S. News and World Report*, Ms. Dickerson offers frequent radio and television commentary in addition to maintaining a nationwide speaking schedule. Her memoir, *An American Story*, was published in September 2000 as Pantheon's lead title; it was a *New York Times* Notable Book and named the Books for a Better Life Best Memoir for 2000; it was also included on all the major publications' Best of 2000 lists. While serving twelve years in the United States Air Force, Ms. Dickerson earned a bachelor's degree from the University of Maryland and a master's degree from St. Mary's University. She earned a J.D. from Harvard Law School in 1995. A former senior fellow at the New America Foundation, she lives in New York, where she is at work on her second book, *The End of Blackness*.

Carolyn Ferrell is the author of the short-story collection *Don't Erase Me*, which was awarded the Art Seidenbaum Award of the *Los Angeles Times* Book Prize, the John C. Zacharis Award given by *Ploughshares*, and the Quality Paperback Book Prize for First Fiction. She has had stories anthologized in *The Best American Short Stories of the Century*; *Giant Steps: The New Generation of African American Writers*; *The Blue Light Corner: Black Women Writing on Passion, Sex, and Romantic Love*; and *Children of the Night: The Best Short Stories by Black Writers, 1967 to the Present*. Her grants and fellowships include those from the Fulbright Association, the German Academic Exchange (D.A.A.D.), and the City University of New York MAGNET Program.

Dana Johnson, a native of Los Angeles, now lives in Bloomington, Indiana, where she teaches creative writing and literature. Her collection of short stories, *Break Any Woman Down*, won the 2000 Flannery O'Connor Award and was a finalist for the 2002 Zora Neale Hurston/Richard Wright Legacy Award for debut fiction.

Lisa Jones lives in New York City. As a screenwriter she has adapted Terry McMillan's *Disappearing Acts* and Dorothy West's *The Wedding* for television. *Bulletproof Diva: Tales of Race, Sex, and Hair* was her first book. She is at work on a new collection of nonfiction.

Helen Elaine Lee was born and raised in Detroit, Michigan. She was educated at Harvard College and Harvard Law School, from which she graduated in 1985. Her short stories have appeared in *Callaloo*, *SAGE*, and several anthologies, including *Children of the Night: The Best Short Stories by Black Writers, 1967 to the Present*, edited by Gloria Naylor, and *Ancestral House: The Black Story in the Americas and Europe*, edited by Charles Rowell. Her first novel, *The Serpent's Gift*, was published by Atheneum Publishers in 1994 and Scribner Paperback Fiction in 1995, and her second novel, entitled *Water Marked*, was published by Scribner in 1999 and appeared in paperback in 2001. She is associate professor in the Program in Writing and Humanistic Studies at the Massachusetts Institute of Technology, and she is working on a novel about the lives of inmates in American prisons.

Catherine E. McKinley is the author of the memoir *The Book of Sarahs* (Counterpoint/Basic Books, 2002), and the co-editor of the anthology *Afrekete* (Anchor Books/Doubleday, 1995). She was a recent Fulbright

Scholar in Ghana, West Africa (1999–2001), and was the recipient of an Audre Lorde Estate Award, a New York Foundation for the Arts Fiction Grant, and a MacDowell Colony for the Arts residency. She lives in New York City.

Itabari Njeri, veteran journalist and author, has been the recipient of several major fellowships and reporting awards and was a Pulitzer Prize finalist for her cultural criticism. She won the American Book Award for her memoir, *Every Good-bye Ain't Gone*. Ms. Njeri, who is also the author of *The Last Plantation: Color, Conflict, and Identity: Reflections of a New World Black,* is a former contributing editor to the *Los Angeles Times Sunday* magazine, as well as a staff writer for that paper and the *Miami Herald*. A graduate of Boston University and Columbia University, Ms. Njeri studied to be an opera singer and was a professional jazz and rhythm and blues backup singer and actress before receiving her master's in journalism. She has taught literature and creative writing at Washington University in St. Louis and is currently pursuing a Ph.D. in the history of American civilization from Harvard University. She is a native of that unique universe known as Brooklyn, New York, the setting of her forthcoming novel, *The Secret Life of Fred Astaire.*

ZZ Packer is the author of a short-story collection, *Drinking Coffee Elsewhere*. Her stories have appeared in *The New Yorker, Harper's*, and *The Best American Short Stories*. She attended Yale, and received an M.A. from Johns Hopkins University and an M.F.A. from the University of Iowa. A former Wallace Stegner Fellow, she is currently a Jones Lecturer at Stanford University.

Phyllis Alesia Perry was born in Atlanta and raised in Tuskegee, Alabama. She earned a degree in journalism from the University of Alabama and spent sixteen years working for newspapers as an editor and reporter. She was part of a writing and editing team at the *Alabama Journal* that won the Pulitzer Prize in 1988. Her first novel, *Stigmata*, was published in 1998. Her second novel, *Second Sunday*, will be published by Hyperion in 2003.

Patricia Powell is the author of *Me Dying Trial, A Small Gathering of Bones, The Pagoda*, and a forthcoming novel called *Revelation*. Born in Jamaica, Powell emigrated to the United States in 1982. She is a graduate of Wellesley College and Brown University and was an associate professor of creative writing at the University of Massachusetts Boston before joining the creative writing faculty at Harvard as a Briggs-Copeland Lecturer in fiction. Powell, who was a finalist for Granta's Best of Young American Novelists, received a Lila Wallace Reader's Digest Writers' Award in 1999.

Nelly Rosario was born in the Dominican Republic and raised in Brooklyn, New York. She earned a bachelor's in engineering from MIT and an M.F.A. in fiction from Columbia University. She has received numerous awards, including a PEN American Open Book Award for her novel, *Song of the Water Saints*. Rosario is also published in the anthology *Becoming American*. The *Village Voice Literary Supplement* chose her as one of seven "Writers on the Verge" for 2001.

Danzy Senna's first novel, *Caucasia*, was the winner of the Book-of-the-Month Club's First Fiction Award; it was listed as a *Los Angeles Times* Best Book of the Year and translated into seven languages. Her short fiction and essays have been widely anthologized. She is a recipient of the 2002 Whiting Writers' Award and currently holds the Jenks Chair of Contemporary American Letters at the College of the Holy Cross in Worcester, Massachusetts.

Martha Southgate was born in Cleveland, Ohio, and attended Hawken School, a prep school there. She wrote about this experience in the essay "Between Two Worlds," which was published in *Essence* magazine in 1987. Her novel *The Fall of Rome* grew in part out of her experience there. She is also the author of the novel *Another Way to Dance*, which won the Coretta Scott King Genesis Award for best first novel. She has written for many publications, among them the *New York Times Magazine*, *Premiere* magazine, and *Essence* magazine. Southgate is a graduate of Smith College and the M.F.A. program at Goddard College. She lives in Brooklyn, New York, with her husband and two children.

Natasha Tarpley is the author of *Girl in the Mirror: Three Generations of Black Women in Motion* (Beacon, 1998) and *Testimony: Young African Americans on Self-Discovery and Black Identity* (Beacon, 1995). She is also the author of the best-selling children's books *I Love My Hair!* (Little, Brown, 1998), and *Bippity-Bob Barbershop!* (Little, Brown, 2002). Ms. Tarpley is the recipient of a National Endowment for the Arts Fellowship and numerous other awards. A graduate of Harvard University and Northwestern University School of Law, she currently lives in Chicago.

Lisa Teasley is the author of *Glow in the Dark* (Cune Press), winner of the 2002 Gold Pen Award for best short-story collection, and the Pacificus Foundation Award for outstanding achievement in short fiction. Teasley's past awards include the May Merrill Miller Award for fiction; the National Society of Arts & Letters Short Story Award, Los Angeles; and the Amaranth Review Award for fiction. Forthcoming is her novel *Dive* (Bloomsbury), which will follow the paperback release of *Glow in the Dark*.

Rebecca Walker was educated at Yale University and was named by *Time* magazine as one of the fifty future leaders under forty. Her articles and essays have appeared in *Harper's*, *Vibe*, *Ms.*, *Spin*, *Essence*, and *Glamour*, as well as in several literary anthologies including *Tales from the Couch: Writers on Therapy*, *How We Want to Live Now: Writers on Progress*, and *Giant Steps: The New Generation of African-American Writers*. Her first book, *To Be Real: Telling the Truth and Changing the Face of Feminism*, explores contradiction and complexity within feminist and other political identities and is required reading in women's studies courses around the country. Her most recent book, a memoir about growing up mixed race in various American cities, called *Black, White, and Jewish: Autobiography of a Shifting Self*, is a national best-seller.

Yolanda Young is a graduate of Howard University and the Georgetown University Law Center. She has written for newspapers across the country and for *Essence* magazine. Her memoir, *On Our Way to Beautiful*, is her first book.

Shay Youngblood is the author of the novels *Black Girl in Paris* and *Soul Kiss* and a collection of short fiction, *The Big Mama Stories*. Her published plays *Amazing Grace*, *Shakin' the Mess Out of Misery*, and *Talking Bones* have been widely produced. Her other plays include *Black Power Barbie* and *Communism Killed My Dog*. Ms. Youngblood has received numerous grants and awards, including a Pushcart Prize for fiction, the Lorraine Hansberry Playwriting Prize, and writing residencies at Yaddo, the MacDowell Colony, and the Karolyi Foundation of France. She has taught in the Graduate Creative Writing Program at New York University and is currently the John and Renee Grisham Writer-in-Residence at the University of Mississippi.

Acknowledgments

One of the most important lessons I have learned, in my professional as well as personal life, is the importance of gratitude. There were so many people who—in ways large and small, direct and indirect—guided me through the process of editing this collection. It is a privilege for me to be able to acknowledge a few of them here, on these pages.

I would like to thank my editor, Jill Bialosky, for her wisdom, patience, and vision; and her assistant, Deirdre O'Dwyer, for helping me with all the small details so that I could meet all the big deadlines (or, at least, try). I am indebted to James Fugate and Torn Hamilton at Eso Won Books for their advice and encouragement, and for creating such a beautiful space for those of us who love Black literature. I can't begin to imagine where this project would be without the care and assistance of Cassandra Lane, who so generously offered to read all the books with me and help type up the selected excerpts; Danzy Senna, my nine-thirteen twin, who graciously allowed me to soak up huge chunks of our weekly Sunday afternoon phone calls filling her in on every new development with the book, from the mundane to the miraculous; Jay Nelson, who supplied whatever I needed—shelter, paper, a printer, a ride to Kinko's, take-out Chinese—to get the job done, and keep the wolf away from my door; Kim Foley, who took the time to help me proof the completed manuscript; Mr. Paul Danquah and Dr. Maya Angelou, for placing me on the path and allowing me to walk at my own pace, always knowing deep down that I would eventually arrive where I was always meant to be. Many thanks, as well, to Rev. Michael Beckwith and the Agape International Center of Truth for guidance, clarity, and inspiration.

This project has traveled with me from Los Angeles, California, to Accra, Ghana, back to Los Angeles, and then on to Washington, D.C. It was while I was in Ghana that I truly began to understand the necessity of this book. and of all the books that celebrate our voices, our stories, our survival. I am most grateful to Atta Akyea, Iris Asamoah, Nana Yaa Ofori-Atta, Kofi and Naana Asante, Prof. Kwame Karikari. Nana Yaw "Joe" Ofori-Atta, Duke Ofori-Atta, Earl Ofori-Atta, Anthony Akoto Osei, George Koomson, Frank Adu, J. B. Danquah-Adu, Hon. Nana Akufo-Addo, Dr. Charles "Tarzan" Wereko-Brobby, Abena Boakye, the Carboos of New Ningo, the Okyenhene Osagyefuo Amoatia Ofori Panin, and the entire Danquah family for helping me see that I am part of something larger, that all was not lost.

Many thanks to my parents, Josephine Danquah and Duke Brobby, for their continued commitment to and confidence in "the wild child"; and thanks also to my stepmother, Anne Brobby, my daughter, Korama, and my siblings—Paula, Alexis, D.J., and Doriane.

I am extremely grateful to Julia Cohen, Laura Schiller, Ami Aronson, Shela Halper, Kojo Nnamdi, Sunanda Holmes, Michael Taylor, and Sheryl Barnes for the warm Washington welcome. Thanks also to Chris Abani and Charles Hayford—homeboys, kindred spirits—for always brightening my day.

Over the years, the following individuals have filled my life with such joy, laughter, good expectations, solid faith, and true-blue friendship; and I love them more than words can express: Collins Allan, Jonetta Barras, Anne Beatts, Lisa Black-Cohen, Jackson Browne, Eric Burns, Annie Schneider Burrows, Kenneth Carroll, Eric Edisi, Anedra Elsesser, David Hatcher, Wendy James, Jamal Kadri, Pamela Kawi, Martha M. Manning, Ph.D., Cathy McKinley, E. Ethelbert Miller, Nnamdi Mowetta, Bee-be Smith, Andrew Solomon, Karin Stanford, Ph.D., Greg Tate, Florence Tate, Belisa Vranich, Ph.D., Rebecca Walker, Lisa Kebreau Washington, and Vanessa Williams.

Finally, I would like to thank all of the authors who are featured in this collection for their brilliant artistry, and for welcoming me into a beautiful community of sisterhood, anchored in the belief that there is more than enough room in this literary universe for all of our efforts, for all of our successes. I am so proud to be your colleague, friend, and fan.

Credits